A Critical History of French Children's
Literature, Vol. 1 & 2
by Penny Brown

Once Upon a Time in a Different World
*Issues and Ideas in African American
Children's Literature*
By Neal A. Lester

The Gothic in Children's Literature
Haunting the Borders
Edited by Anna Jackson, Karen Coats,
and Roderick McGillis

Reading Victorian Schoolrooms
*Childhood and Education in
Nineteenth-Century Fiction*
by Elizabeth Gargano

Soon Come Home to This Island
West Indians in British Children's Literature
by Karen Sands-O'Connor

Boys in Children's Literature and
Popular Culture
*Masculinity, Abjection, and the
Fictional Child*
by Annette Wannamaker

Into the Closet
*Cross-dressing and the Gendered Body
in Children's Literature*
by Victoria Flanagan

Russian Children's Literature and Culture
edited by Marina Balina and
Larissa Rudova

The Outside Child In and Out of the Book
Christine Wilkie-Stibbs

Representing Africa in Children's
Literature
Old and New Ways of Seeing
by Vivian Yenika-Agbaw

The Fantasy of Family
*Nineteenth-Century Children's Literature
and the Myth of the Domestic Ideal*
by Liz Thiel

From Nursery Rhymes to Nationhood
*Children's Literature and the Construction
of Canadian Identity*
By Elizabeth A. Galway

The Family in English Children's Literature
Ann Alston

Enterprising Youth
*Social Values and Acculturation in
Nineteenth-Century American
Children's Literature*
Monika Elbert

Constructing Adolescence in
Fantastic Realism
Alison Waller

Crossover Fiction
Global and Historical Perspectives
Sandra L. Beckett

The Crossover Novel
*Contemporary Children's Fiction and Its
Adult Readership*
Rachel Falconer

Shakespeare in Children's Literature
Gender and Cultural Capital
Erica Hateley

Critical Approaches to Food in
Children's Literature
Edited by Kara K. Keeling and
Scott T. Pollard

Neo-Imperialism in Children's Literature
About Africa
A Study of Contemporary Fiction
by Yulisa Amadu Maddy and Donnarae
MacCann

Death, Gender and Sexuality in
Contemporary Adolescent Literature
Kathryn James

Fundamental Concepts of Children's
Literature Research
Literary and Sociological Approaches
Hans-Heino Ewers

Children's Fiction about 9/11
Ethnic, Heroic and National Identities
Jo Lampert

The Place of Lewis Carroll in Children's
Literature
Jan Susina

Power, Voice and Subjectivity in Literature
for Young Readers
Maria Nikolajeva

POWER, VOICE AND SUBJECTIVITY IN LITERATURE FOR YOUNG READERS

MARIA NIKOLAJEVA

Routledge
Taylor & Francis Group
NEW YORK AND LONDON

First published 2010
by Routledge
270 Madison Ave, New York, NY 10016

Simultaneously published in the UK
by Routledge
2 Park Square, Milton Park, Abingdon, Oxon OX14 4RN

Routledge is an imprint of the Taylor & Francis Group, an informa business

© 2010 Taylor & Francis

Typeset in by Minion by IBT Global.

Library of Congress Cataloging-in-Publication Data
Nikolajeva, Maria.
  Power, voice and subjectivity in literature for young readers / Maria Nikolajeva.
    p. cm. —(Children's literature and culture ; 67)
  Includes bibliographical references and index.
1. Children's literature—History and criticism—Theory, etc.   2. Other (Philosophy) in literature.   3. Power (Philosophy) in literature.   4. Voice in literature.   5. Subjectivity in literature.   6. Children's literature—Psychological aspects.   I. Title.
  PN1009.A1N565 2010
    809'.89282—dc22

ISBN10: 0-415-80215-6 (hbk)
ISBN10: 0-203-86692-4 (ebk)

ISBN13: 978-0-415-80215-4 (hbk)
ISBN13: 978-0-203-86692-4 (ebk)

Contents

Series Editor's Foreword

Dedicated to furthering original research in children's literature and culture, the Children's Literature and Culture series includes monographs on individual authors and illustrators, historical examinations of different periods, literary analyses of genres, and comparative studies on literature and the mass media. The series is international in scope and is intended to encourage innovative research in children's literature with a focus on interdisciplinary methodology.

Children's literature and culture are understood in the broadest sense of the term children to encompass the period of childhood up through adolescence. Owing to the fact that the notion of childhood has changed so much since the origination of children's literature, this Routledge series is particularly concerned with transformations in children's culture and how they have affected the representation and socialization of children. While the emphasis of the series is on children's literature, all types of studies that deal with children's radio, film, television, and art are included in an endeavor to grasp the aesthetics and values of children's culture. Not only have there been momentous changes in children's culture in the last fifty years, but there have been radical shifts in the scholarship that deals with these changes. In this regard, the goal of the Children's Literature and Culture series is to enhance research in this field and, at the same time, point to new directions that bring together the best scholarly work throughout the world.

Jack Zipes

Acknowledgments

The first publication identifiable as the nucleus of the present work appeared in Swedish in *Bonniers litterära magasin* 2003:3 under the title "Why does Pippi sleep with her feet on her pillow? Queer, carnival and children's literature." An extended version "Children's Literature: Art, Pedagogy and Power" was presented at the Third Nordic Workshop in Children's Literature Research, in Reykjavik, Iceland, in October 2004, and subsequently published in Danish as "Børnelitteratur: kunst, pædagogik og magt" in *På opdagelse i børnelitteraturen* (2005). My Grimm Award Acceptance Speech, "Children's literature: Subject, Voice and Power," given in Osaka, Japan, in November 2005, was published in *IICLO Bulletin* 2006: 29.

The argument on the use of theory was developed in "What is Theory, and Why and How We Could, or Should, Use It" in *Canadian Children's Literature* 2006:1, and the concept of aetonormativity was first presented as a conference paper in Saõ Paolo, Brazil, in July 2008, subsequently published as "Theory, Post-Theory, and Aetonormative Theory" in the special issue of *Neohelicon: Acta Comparationis Litterarum Universalum*, 2009:1.

The initial version of Chapter 1 was published in Swedish in *Tidskrift för litteraturvetenskap* 2003:4 and developed into the English version, "Harry Potter and the Secrets of Children's Literature" in *Critical Perspectives on Harry Potter* (2008), reprinted with kind permission by Taylor & Francis.

Chapter 2 is based on the article "When *I* use a word it means just what I choose it to mean": Power and (mis)communication in literature for young readers, in: Jason Finch, et al (eds) *Humane Readings: Essays in Literary Mediation and Communication in Honour of Roger D. Sell* (2009), reprinted with kind permission by John Benjamins Publishing Company, Amsterdam/Philadelphia.

The section in Chapter 3 on Diana Wynne Jones's *The Tale of Time City* is developed from the keynote lecture "Time and Totalitarianism" at the International Conference on the Fantastic in Arts in Orlando, in March 2009. The section on Astrid Lindgren is a part of the presentation at Astrid Lindgren centennial conferences in Zagreb, Croatia, and Ljubljana, Slovenia, in April 2007, under the title "Why does Pippi sleep with her feet on her pillow, or

Subversion of power in Astrid Lindgren's works." The paper was published in Croatian and Slovenian.

Chapter 4 was initially presented at MacDonald Centenary Conference, Worcester, UK, July 2005 and published as "Voice, Gender and Alterity in George MacDonald's Fairy Tales" in *"The Noble Unrest": Contemporary Essays on the Work of George MacDonald* (2007). Reprinted with the permission of Cambridge Scholars Publishing.

Chapter 5 is a substantially revised version of the keynote paper "Stereotypes of Dystopia: *The Denials of Kow-Ten* in International Context" presented at the 3rd conference on South African Children's Literature, Potchefstroom, September 2007.

Chapter 7 grew out of a keynote paper at the conference The Child and the Book in Antwerp, Belgium, in April 2005, published as "New Masculinities, New Femininities: Swedish Young Adult Fiction Towards the Twenty-first Century" in *Changing Concepts of Childhood and Children's Literature* (2006). It was complemented by the Introduction to the special issue of *Swedish Book Review* (Supplement 2006), "Girls Take Over in Swedish Young Adult Fiction."

The crucial ideas on crossvocalization developed in Chapter 8 were presented at a conference at Örebro University, Sweden, in November 2002 and published in two partially overlapping essays in Swedish: "Auktoritära män och otillförlitliga kvinnor: Genus och berättande" (Authoritative men and unreliable women: Gender and narration) in *Berättaren: En gäckande röst i texten* (2003); and "Crossvokalisering och subjektivitet: Den performativa rösten i litteraturen" (Crossvocalization and subjectivity: The performative voice in literature) in *Tidskrift för litteraturvetenskap* (2003:1/2). They were further developed in the paper "Crossvocalization and Performance" at the conference Modern Critical Approaches to Children's Literature in Nashville, USA, in April 2003, and in the article "Stemme, magt og genus i børnelitteraturen" (Voice, power and gender in children's literature) in the Danish journal *Passage* (2005:52).

Substantial part of Chapter 9 was published as "Fairy Tales in Society's Service" in *Marvels & Tales. Journal of Fairy-Tale Studies* 16 (2002) 2 © 2002 Wayne State University Press, reprinted with the permission of Wayne State University Press.

Parts of chapter 10, dealing with literary representations of cats, was presented as Inaugural Professorial Lecture at the University of Worcester in May 2007, and published as "Devils, Demons, Familiars, Friends: Towards a Semiotics of Literary Cats" in *Marvels & Tales* 23 (2009) 2, © 2009 Wayne State University Press, reprinted with the permission of Wayne State University Press.

Chapter 11 is an expanded version of the paper "Power and Subjectivity in Picturebooks" given at the conference New Impulses in Picturebook Research, in Barcelona, Spain, in September 2007.

The main concept of Chapter 12, identification fallacy, was launched in the keynote address "The Identification Fallacy: Perspective and Subjectivity in Children's Literature" at the conference Childhoods 2005 in Oslo, Norway, in June 2005. The concept was also used in a Swedish publication, "Bakom rösten. Den implicita författaren i jagberättelser" (Beyond the voice: the implied author in first-person narratives) in *Barnboken* 2008:2 and in "The Identification Fallacy: Perspective and Subjectivity in Children's Literature" in *Telling Children's Stories: Narrative Theory and Children's Literature* (in print with University of Nebraska Press).

Some specific text analyses have been presented in the keynote lecture "Comparative Children's Literature - What is There to Compare?" at Children's Literature International Summer School, University of Roehampton, UK, in July 2007, and subsequently published in *Papers: Explorations into Children's Literature* 2008:1.

I would like to thank all conference organizers who have invited me to present papers, as well as editors who have commissioned chapters and essays and thus stimulated me to develop new ideas.

I must also acknowledge my six-year work on the jury of the Astrid Lindgren Memorial Award, that gave me a unique opportunity to get acquainted with a wide range of international children's authors that I would not have discovered otherwise.

Many colleagues around the world have given me valuable feedback on my work, and I would especially like to emphasize the importance of the Nordic Network for Children's Literature Research, financed by the Nordic Academy of Advanced Studies, a community of established and early-career scholars that provided an exceptionally favorable intellectual climate. I would further specifically like to thank Jean Webb, Kimberley Reynolds, Rod McGillis, David Rudd, Perry Nodelman, Nina Christensen, Janina Orlov, Elina Druker, Karen Coats, Mike Cadden, and André Moura. As usual, my warmest gratitude to Jack Zipes for his unfailing support.

In the middle of my work on this book, I was honored by the highest award that a scholar in my area can receive, The International Brothers Grimm Award for lifetime achievement in children's literature scholarship, given by the International Institute for Children's Literature in Osaka, Japan. This recognition was of great consequence for my further pursuits.

The initial research for this book was sponsored by an internal research grant from Stockholm University. Its completion would not be possible without a generous allocation of research time from my present affiliation, Faculty of Education at the University of Cambridge, UK. It therefore feels adequate to express my gratitude to Morag Styles who encouraged and supported my decision to move to Cambridge.

Introduction
Why Does Pippi Sleep with Her Feet on the Pillow?

In 1984 Peter Hunt called for a children's literature specific theory (Hunt 1984, 192). The encouragement is still legitimate. During the last twenty to thirty years, international children's literature scholars have been applying various theoretical implements to books written, marketed for and read by young people. Yet, while many marginalized literatures have successfully developed their theoretical fields—feminist theory, postcolonial theory, queer theory—children's literature has so far not elaborated a theory of its own. This may seem a paradox considering the number of children's literature studies having the word "theory" in titles or subtitles: Peter Hunt, *Criticism, Theory and Children's Literature* (1991); Jill May, *Children's Literature and Critical Theory* (1995), Roderick McGillis, *The Nimble Reader: Literary Theory and Children's Literature* (1996), Margery Hourihan, *Deconstructing the Hero: Literary Theory and Children's Literature* (1997); and more. Yet "theory" is almost always accompanied by the conjunction "and," as if theory were juxtaposed to children's literature. However, for a theory to emerge and develop, its specific questions must be delineated and its object of inquiry identified.

I will not reiterate the numerous attempts to define the object of our studies, since this has recently been successfully done in Perry Nodelman's book *The Hidden Adult: Defining Children's Literature* (2008). My endeavor in the present study is not to address the question of what children's literature is and what it does, which I did in several previous works, especially *From Mythic to Linear: Time in Children's Literature* (2000). Instead, I would like to explore possible ways of approaching children's literature from a theoretical perspective, thus responding to the recent tendency to reject theory as such. Nodelman's provocative editorial in *Canadian Children's Literature* (Nodelman 2005) offers an overview of the post-theoretical scholarly space and presents interesting arguments for and against theory. In fact, Nodelman began this debate already ten years earlier at the 1995 conference of the International Research Society for

Children's Literature in Stockholm, in his keynote paper titled "Fear of Children's Literature: What is Left (or Right) After Theory" (1997). There have perhaps not been as heated deliberations in our specific area as those Nodelman outlines in the *CCL* editorial; the scope of opinions, however, has been manifest in many publications and conference presentations.

Nodelman states quite rightly that, considering the wide-range discussions on the demise of theory, "there's surprisingly little agreement about just what theory was before it was over" (Nodelman 2005, 3). Since I do not subscribe to "the consensus that we are after theory" (ibid) and do not share Nodelman's experience of the time when "there was no theory. There was no need for theory" (6), I believe that I have relatively clear-cut ideas of what theory is and what it can be used for, which I have consistently attempted to convey and propagate for in my research (e.g. Nikolajeva 1996, 2000, 2002, 2005).

The subsequent *CCL* controversy is amazing in its self-contradiction. Rod McGillis states categorically that we are "after theory" (McGillis 2006b, 78), as he also does in an earlier article (McGillis 2006a). Peter Hunt on the other hand argues, as he frequently does (cf. Hunt 1995), that theoretical studies are exclusively part of the academia and therefore of little use in discussing children's literature which is part of real life (Hunt 2006a). This staggering statement contradicts Hunt's previous acknowledgment that theory has provided children's literature scholars with adequate analytical tools (Hunt 1984, 1985). Indeed, no theory, no application. Yet theory without application is not much worth either, which is perhaps something that theory adversaries imply.

Possibly, the very word "theory" has been contaminated by undesired connotations, at least in North America, substantially less in Europe. Besides, it has begun to indicate abstract constructions and arguments never meant to be applied to concrete literary texts; or, as Nodelman notes, quoting Frederick Jameson, theory supplants philosophy (Nodelman 2005, 4). This "metatheory and meta-metatheory" that critics fear is perhaps similar to mathematicians' "beautiful equations"; yet, in our area, we have always been slightly more pragmatic. The magnitude of Gérard Genette's influential work *Narrative Discourse* lies in that it presents a solid theoretical ground and at the same time shows how to apply it, which is emphasized by the subtitle, "An Essay in Method" (Genette 1980). A theory that cannot be used in concrete text analysis is like a bicycle with square wheels: radical and daring, but hardly functional.

It is therefore necessary to go back to some basic definitions. In the most fundamental sense, theory, in this case literary theory, is a scope of the scholars' position towards their subject, a general attitude toward and framework for the subject matter they are working with. Unlike natural sciences, where new theoretical paradigms occasionally invalidate previous ones, a theory within humanities cannot be right or wrong, it can neither be verified nor disproved, and no theory is better than any other theory. A theory is a set of crucial questions we pose about what we are doing and why we are doing it. We may not be aware of embracing a theory (although I believe it is an essential requirement for any scholarly work) or for some reason deny it, but we cannot approach a literary work without adopting a certain position toward it, since we cannot read a text critically unless we know what kind of questions we should have in mind while reading.

For instance, mimetic theory—not least Marxism, which Nodelman scrutinizes in his *CCL* essay—claims that literary texts reflect the society in which they have been created. From this, for instance, social models of fairy-tale analysis emerge; Jack Zipes' work is the best example (e.g. Zipes 1983). The thesis that literature reflects reality is also the main premise of, for instance, John Stephens's *Language and Ideology in Children's Fiction* (1992), where the areas of inquiry on which the study is grounded include linguistics, sociolinguistics, and speech act theory. These enable Stephens to pose questions about how texts manipulate their readers' understanding, and the concrete focus of analysis lies on genre, narrative structure and other more or less formal issues. He uses analytical implements from narrative theory to investigate how embedded ideology can be revealed. However, ideology is a dimension of a literary text that lies in the tension between the text itself, the reality behind it, the authors and their intentions or implicit views, and also the readers and their ability to create meaning out of texts. Unless Stephens has positioned himself against the material he works with (=adopted a theoretical stance), he would not know what questions to ask. That would be exactly the kind of "pre-theoretical innocence" (Eagleton in Nodelman 2005, 8) that we can expect in undergraduate students, but not among mature scholars.

Northrop Frye, unjustly neglected today, has a radically different attitude toward literature. He does not see it as a reflection of reality, but as a displacement (or corruption) of myth (Frye 1957). This crucial outlook generates a set of analytical tools that enable Frye to propose an original system of genres, showing how particular genres operate with specific narrative patterns and structures, such as upward or downward plot movement, romantic or mimetic characters, and so on. These tools are highly pertinent to children's literature.

Mikhail Bakhtin, who is sometimes erroneously counted among Marxist critics, has presented perhaps the most comprehensive view on the novel as a literary form reflecting modern man's thinking, which is not always easy to perceive from his seemingly disconnected studies and fragments. In his seminal work "Epic and Novel" (1981a) and several other complementary essays (1981b, 1986), Bakhtin shows the principal difference between the novel as an eclectic, synthetic, multilayered, multivoiced, dialogical literary form and the earlier forms that he calls epic; likewise between the character of a novel and the epic hero. Later works highlight the various aspects of the novel, such as its overall carnivalesque—non-mimetic—nature (1968), polyphony (1984) language and intertextuality (1981d), time and space (1981c), and not least the intricate relationship between the author, the narrator, and the character in "Author and Hero in Aesthetic Activity" (1990); the latter long before the notion of narratology was coined. Dialogics, that interrogates a single, fixed subjectivity, precedes by several decades the poststructuralist views on literature, just as carnival as an interpretation strategy precedes the postmodern ideas on the relationship between art and reality.

Since children's literature emerges and becomes established parallel with the emergence and evolution of the Western novel, Bakhtin's all-embracing theory is highly relevant for our field. Although it offers no easily applicable analytical toolkit, children's literature scholarship has successfully employed and developed Bakhtin's concepts of the carnival and intertextuality (Stephens 1992), heteroglossia and subjectivity (McCallum 1999, Wilkie-Stibbs 2002), passage from epic hero toward modern character (Hourihan 1997), and more.

Among the best recent critical studies of children's literature we find those based on Julia Kristevas's theories of literature (Westwater 2002), on Michel Foucault (Trites 2000) and Jacques Lacan (Coates 2004). Neither Kristeva (1982, 1984) nor Lacan (1977) nor Foucault (2002) offer ready-made implements to deal with literary texts; instead, they suggest a general way of thinking about literary texts which the scholars embrace and from which they mould their own methods and approaches. Similarly, deconstruction as a theory is nothing but bogus unless it can produce efficient working tools to open new dimensions of texts. Most important, deconstruction cannot be opposed to earlier theoretical stances as a simple "affirmation of the multiplicity of meanings" (Payne in Nodelman 2005, 7) and hence legitimacy of arbitrary interpretations. No theory is the ultimate answer. To criticize a specific theory for not offering answers to all questions is ridiculous.

Those children's literature scholars who claim that theory has had its day direct their skepticism primarily against general critical theory, without acknowledging that children's literature theory as such has never emerged yet. Do the charges against theory imply that we have returned— or are encouraged to return—to purely empirical (what children read) and descriptive (what books are about) studies where children's literature research began in earnest some fifty years ago? Or still worse, are we back to the prescriptive stage (what children should read) when children's literature was judged from the point of view of its educational purposefulness? We would then have successfully bridged the notorious literary-didactic split, the clash between book people and child people, but merely by rejecting the former in favor of the latter, somewhat in line with Hunts "childist criticism" (Hunt 2006b).

Drawn to the extreme, the central idea of childist criticism implies that children should write their own literature, or harder still, that only children can create true children's literature, as radical adherents of queer or postcolonial theories maintain about their respective marginalized groups. The consequence is apparently that only children can study and assess their own literature. Here children's literature displays features different from other previously silenced artistic expressions—or does it? Adult authors ostensibly write children's books, and adult critics evaluate them, from wider experience, larger vocabulary, higher cognitive capacity—biological and psychological facts hard to dismiss (cf. Nodelman 2008). Yet maybe the term children's literature will one day be reserved for literature *by* children, just as children's culture today includes children's own stories, drawings, and play. Shall we then make a distinction between "children's literature" and "literature for children"? Indisputably, it would make the study object still more blurred. Should we accept "childist criticism" as our theoretical platform, trying to adopt young readers' perception of books created for them by another societal group? Or should we instead make advantage of our adult position to explore and reveal the thematic, narrative and ideological specifics in books marketed for children? I see no point in limiting our critical position to just one perspective.

In his contribution to *CCL*, McGillis seems to disclaim text-oriented studies not only for himself bur also for the research community at large, which feels a rather ungenerous attitude. He also juxtaposes High theory and (low?) theories such as feminism, ecocriticism and queer (McGillis 2006b). This stance certainly does these fields of inquiry, and by extension children's literature studies, a disfavor, since they are then by definition sorted as inferior: high/low is after all a value-oriented binarity. Like many other scholars, McGillis propagates interdisciplinary approaches. Recently, children's literature scholarship has approached childhood studies, which many critics welcome (e.g. Coats 2006). Literary studies can certainly gain a lot from childhood studies, but it would be a danger to get engulfed by it, or by gender studies, or by culture studies, just as it would be a shame to limit children's literature scholarship to purely pragmatic issues.

To summarize the recent discussion on to be or not to be of theory, most of the world's leading scholars would like to see more contextualization in history, culture, society, ideology and so on, the aspects that text-oriented children's literature studies have promptly tried to keep away from, primarily to legitimize their own work in the eyes of literary studies colleagues. The *CCL* debate was mainly concerned with theory as such, not theory in its relationship to children's literature, and still less, the children's literature specific theory. We are thus back to the initially posed question: Is there such a thing at all? While feminist, postcolonial, queer and ecotheory, that McGillis refers to as "low", have becomes deeply anchored in literary studies, there is no comparable theory grown out of the particular conditions of literature for young readers. Zohar Shavit launched already in the 1980s the concept of *ambivalence*, which she, however, primarily applies to particular texts and their status within the cultural polysystem (Shavit 1980, 1999). David Rudd's idea of *hybrid* follows the same lines, yet broadening it substantially to encompass all texts in some way connected with young readers (Rudd 2006). Jean Perrot proposes to ground our field in ludistics, play theory (Perrot 2006), which again borrows it central notion elsewhere, and indeed playfulness is a decisive sign of all so-called postmodern art, but it is less pertinent to early, instructive children's texts. We have witnessed a number of other critical positions, which, whatever our concrete judgment may be, are all equally legitimate. Children's literature is an educational vehicle, the most common; in general criticism we say that literature is an ideological vehicle. Children's literature is a reflection of the status of childhood in the society that produced it (Zornado 2000, Natov 2003, Clark 2003, Zipes, 2001). Children's literature is adult authors' nostalgic memories of their own childhood (Inglis 1981). Children's literature is adult authors' therapeutic treatment of their childhood traumas (Rose 1984; see further Reynolds 2007). And, not quite unexpectedly: there is no such thing as children's literature.

All our research into children's literature is based on one of these premises (or perhaps yet some other that I have overlooked), whether or not they are explicitly stated in our scholarship. No "close reading" can be done without these basic stances. Unless we position ourselves in a theoretical field, as well as establish ourselves in relationship to previous research, we keep reinventing the wheel. Any literary text, even a very short picturebook text containing a few dozen words, is sufficiently complex to allow a multitude of scholarly positions, and no literary analysis can ever be comprehensive, since new theoretical issues can always be brought forward. From these, we can go further and pose questions concerning ideology, structure, reader appeal, or whatever may be the focus of our interest.

Thus we can never get beyond, or after, or past theory until we have answered the major questions about our subject, such as "What is literature?", "What is a child?", "What is childhood?", "How can a child's experience be conveyed by an adult author?" and so on. Yet I fully agree with Nodelman in his discovery that "we in children's literature studies may know something—or at least be in a position to know something—that other scholars don't" (Nodelman 2005, 17). This makes the effort worthwhile—at least for me.

A recurrent question in children's literature research has been whether children's literature as a field of inquiry belongs within education or art, as reflected in the title of the study by the Danish scholar Torben Weinreich, *Children's Literature: Art or Pedagogy?* (2000). It has perhaps been one of the central questions of all children's literature studies, if not *the* central one: should we consider, and consequently study, literature written and marketed for the young audience, primarily as work of literature or primarily as educational implement? I say "primarily," since it is obvious, and often is argued, that children's literature is, or at least can be, both; yet the two opposed standpoints have always had their passionate advocates, therefore the question is still relevant today. It is frequently referred to in children's literature criticism as "literary-didactic split." As I have pointed out, several scholars have suggested that children's literature reflects the adult authors' nostalgic visions of childhood rather than a faithful depiction of it. In other words, children's authors tell their readers what their childhood should be like, rather than what it is. This does not prevent children's literature from being art, but it presupposes a strong pedagogical thrust.

Obviously, the answer is not "either–or," but "both," a hybrid, as David Rudd proposes to label it (Rudd 2006). Yet I am not prepared to use the literary-didactic blend of children's literature as a criterion for distinguishing it from what we normally simply call "literature," but in the context of children's literature have to specify as "general, or adult literature." In fact, I would venture to state that all literature is "both," that is, both an art form and a didactic, or rather ideological vehicle. For instance, both the Christian church and the totalitarian regimes have acknowledged the ideological power of art and used it for their purposes. In this respect, children's literature is not unique. Perhaps the ideological, or pedagogical intention is often more explicit in children's literature, but it is a matter of grade, not of nature.

There is, however, another aspect in the characteristic of children's literature that, unlike the literary-didactic controversy, has only recently been noticed by some critics. It is power, featured in the subtitle of Roberta Trites' study of young adult fiction (Trites 2000), a study that fully subscribes to Michael Foucault's somewhat overexploited statement: "Power is everywhere." Yet while Trites emphasizes power as a trait and motif inherent in adolescent literature, I would argue that it is in some way or other present in all children's literature, from ABC-books to young adult novels, which, perhaps not unexpectedly, makes it conspicuously similar to other literatures dealing with powerless societal groups: women's literature, indigenous literature, or gay literature (cf. Nodelman 1988). In each case, the main thrust of the literary work is the examination of power positions, the affirmation or interrogation of the existing order of power. The "discovery" of each of these suppressed groups has led to the emergence of a critical theory: feminist theory, postcolonial theory, and queer theory. Specific as they are, these theories have much in common as they interrogate power positions and what especially queer theory calls "norm" and "normativity." Roberta Trites remarks repeatedly that a teenage protagonist has basically two choices when meeting with repression: to perish or to become repressive himself. Indeed, many authors of young adult fiction seem not to know what to do with their rebellious characters and get rid of them by violent death or even suicide. Even an open ending may occasionally suggest death as a possible solution. More usually, the protagonist gradually accepts the adult normativity, and thus, leaving adolescence behind and entering adulthood, becomes ready to exercise the same oppression that he has been subjected to. This reproduction of power is especially tangible in school series, where yesterday's oppressed newcomers all too soon become head boy or girl and channel their revenge toward those younger and weaker.

Searching desperately for answers to the basic questions of my own scholarly pursuits, and moving successively away from traditional structuralism as well as pure narrative theory, I came across the term *heterology* ("discourse on the Other," coined, as far as I know, by Michel de Certeau, 1986), the inquiry into imbalance, inequality, asymmetry between different social groups; an umbrella concept for several critical positions dealing with power and discrimination generated by the difference in gender, class, nationhood, or race. While feminist theory has made us aware of male authors creating women characters as the Other, and while postcolonial theory reveals alterity in the images of ethnicity, a heterological approach to juvenile literature will examine power tension between the adult author and the implied young audience. Thus, we are dealing with the imbalance, inequality, asymmetry between children and adults, the way it is presented and assessed in children's books, books intended for the young audience.

On analogy with the central concept of queer theory, heteronormativity, I propose the concept of *aetonormativity* (Lat. *aeto-*, pertaining to age), adult normativity that governs the way children's literature has been patterned from its emergence until the present day. Queer theory is in fact best suited for analyzing power positions, as long as we apply it with imagination, without reducing it to hetero- and homosexual relationships. The essence of queer theory, in this broad interpretation, is the interrogation of one single condition as a norm. Queer studies test how we can exchange an established pattern, in our case, adult normativity, for another one, and examine what happens if we instead depart from child in power as norm and the powerless child as deviation.

The child/adult imbalance is most tangibly manifested in the relationship between the ostensibly adult narrative voice and the child focalizing character. In other words, the way the adult narrator narrates the child reveals the degree of alterity – yet degree only, since alterity is by definition inevitable in writing for children. At this point I could, of course, argue that all literature reflects power structures, which would bring us back to the definition of children's literature as opposed to something else. However, I will not pursue this idea any further, beyond stating that the particular characteristic of children's literature is its focus on child/adult power hierarchy, just as the specifics of feminist literature is the gender-related power structures, and the specifics of postcolonial literature the ethnic-related power structures. Naturally, there are other factors besides age-related cognitive discrepancy in children's literature, which may both enhance and diminish the effect of power imbalance. Still, nowhere else are power structures as visible as in children's literature, the refined instrument used for centuries to educate, socialize and oppress a particular social group. In this respect, children's literature is a unique art and communication form, deliberately created by those in power for the powerless. Further, unlike other previously mentioned kinds of literature, children's literature demonstrates a constant change of power positions: yesterday's children grow up and become oppressors themselves. Or, as Pippi Longstocking describes it:

> "Of course you have to eat your good cereal. If you don't eat your good cereal, then you won't grow and get big and strong. And if you don't get big and strong, then you won't have the strength to force *your* children, when you have some, to eat *their* good cereal ... "
>
> (*Pippi in the South Seas*: 55f; italics in the original)

Children's literature can, however, subvert its own oppressive function, as it can describe situations in which the established power structures are interrogated without necessarily being overthrown. The adults have unlimited power in our society, as compared to children, who lack economic resources of their own, lack voice in political and social decisions, and are subjected to a large number of laws and rules which the adults expect them to obey without interrogation. This is regarded as norm, in real life as well as in literature. Not least is school depicted in children's books, from Tom Sawyer to Pippi Longstocking and beyond, as a mechanism for oppression. But what happens if the adults are no longer the smartest, the richest and the most powerful in the child/adult relationship? What happens if literary texts substitute child normativity for adult normativity?

Pippi Longstocking, for one example, sleeps with her feet on a pillow. This is norm-breaking, but only if the norm is to sleep with your head on the pillow and your feet under the cover. Pippi questions the established norm, both through her own behavior and when she claims that there exist other norms elsewhere, for instance, that in Egypt all people walk backward, or that in Belgian Congo lying is customary. It can eventually turn out that it is after all more convenient to sleep with your head on the pillow or to walk forwards; but this is not the point. Queer theory tries to demonstrate, firstly, that norms are arbitrary, and secondly, and perhaps more important, that the whole argument about "norms" and "deviations" gives the norm priority over deviation, and thus more authority and power. Queer theory does not strive to replace one norm by another, but claims that all conditions are equally normal. When Astrid Lindgren is ironic in *Pippi Longstocking*, saying that "[a]ll children must have someone to advise them, and all children must go to school to learn the multiplication tables" (*Pippi Longstocking* 38), she applies queer theory long before it came into existence. Pippi's norms turn out to be as valuable as the adults'. Pippi is, however, a unique figure in children's literature. In contrast, most children's utopias that unconditionally replace adult normativity with child normativity have shown the latter's unfeasibility. The wonderful and sad book by the Polish educator Janusz Korczak, *King Matt the First* (1923), portrays children who take over power and fail, mostly due to lack of knowledge and experience. Thus even Korczak, the great pedagogue who whole-heartedly stood on the child's side, had to accept that child normativity is merely a pretty dream.

Yet another theory that focuses on power is carnival theory, elaborated by Bakhtin as a component of his all-inclusive theory of the novel. If queer theory has primarily been utilized to investigate sexual normativity, carnival theory has, in general criticism as well as in children's literature research, primarily been applied to texts that clearly show carnivalesque features: hyperbole, distortion, upside-down-world, grotesque, scatological humor, theater, circus, market place, jester trickery, and so on. Far too seldom do scholars embrace Bakhtin's overall view of literature as carnival, a symbolic representation of a socially liberating process, a subversive, that is, disguised, interrogation of authorities. Since Bakhtin lived and worked within a totalitarian state, the issues of power and repression were of special importance for him, even though he masterly hid his criticism of the regime behind his studies of medieval and classic literature. Especially in his book on François Rabelais—a randomly chosen text that he used primarily as a point of departure for his theoretical argument—Bakhtin presents the essence of the medieval carnival (a short period of grotesque festivities and excesses preceding Lent), that was a temporary reversal of the established order when all societal power structures changed places. The fool was crowned king, while kings and bishops were dethroned and denigrated. Carnival was sanctioned by the authorities who therefore had control over it. Moreover, the temporary nature of carnival presupposed the restoration of the initial order. Yet, as Bakhtin sees it, carnival had a subversive effect, since it showed that social hierarchies were not unquestionable. Bakhtin applies the concept of carnival to literature, viewing it as a narrative device used to describe reality in a distorting mirror, in a state of temporary deviation from the existing order, as well as total freedom from societal restrictions.

Together with the idea of norm, pivotal for queer theory, the concept of carnival is highly relevant for children's literature. In fact, carnival and norm-breaking are within the discussed theories semantically related. Children in our society are oppressed and powerless. Yet, paradoxically enough, children are allowed, in fiction written *by adults* for the enlightenment and enjoyment of children, to become strong, brave, rich, powerful, and independent—*on certain conditions and for a limited time*. The most important condition is the physical dislocation and the removal, temporary or permanent, of parental protection, allowing the child protagonist to have the freedom to explore the world and test the boundaries of independence. The child may be placed in a number of extraordinary situations, such as war or revolution, exotic, faraway settings, temporary isolation on a desert island, extreme danger, and so on. All these conditions empower the fictional child, and even though the protagonist is most frequently brought back to the security of home and parental supervision, the narratives have a subversive effect, showing that the rules imposed on the child by the adults are in fact arbitrary. In terms of queer theory, adult normativity is subjected to scrutiny even if the adult is still presented as norm. Borrowing some basic ideas from queer theory and carnival theory to develop more all-embracing heterological analytical tools proves especially helpful to move towards the quintessence of children's literature.

In her book *Don't Tell the Grownups* (1990), Alison Lurie claims that all children's literature is subversive by definition. This is a dubious stance. Children's literature can indeed be subversive against adult normativity, but considerably more often it is conservative and confirms rather than interrogates it. Starting from age-related power hierarchies and adulthood as norm, we may perhaps define in a more satisfactory way the object and goal of our endeavors, much in the line that Perry Nodelman does in *The Hidden Adult* (2008).

Children's literature has *the potential* to question the adults as a norm. Children's writers have employed a variety of strategies for subversivity. Among such strategies, there is the use of specific genres (fantasy, adventure, dystopia), settings (Robinsonnade, Orientalism), and characters (superheroes, anti-heroes, gender-transgressing characters, animals, monsters), as well as narrative devices such as voice, focalization and subjectivity. However, all these strategies can likewise enhance alterity.

In the following chapters I will discuss some strategies employed by children's writers to confirm or interrogate power structures in their texts.

Chapter One
Harry Potter and the
Secrets of Children's Literature

In this chapter, I will use the Harry Potter novels as a master text of children's literature. Adult normativity—as well as heteronormativity and other conventional values—is tangible in the novels and consistently confirmed and reproduced. The protagonist is exposed to various forms of adult heroism ostensibly intended to serve as a role model, but also to emphasize adult supremacy. The repeated glorious death of Harry's parental figures is the most tangible example. The subsequent exposure of the heroic adults' minor faults does not rob them of their high status. It is intriguing to explore the novels in terms of their compliance with or deviation from the conventions of children's literature; both can, paradoxically, account for their popularity. It is also gratifying to examine them in terms of displacement of myth, in Northrop Frye's sense (Frye 1957), and of genre eclecticism. In contemporary Western children's fiction, most of the child characters seem to appear on low mimetic and ironic levels. The universal appeal of Harry Potter can be ascribed to the fortunate attempt to reintroduce the romantic character into children's fiction. The Harry Potter figure has all the necessary components of the romantic hero. There are mystical circumstances around his birth, he is dislocated and oppressed and suddenly given unlimited power. His innocence and intrinsic benevolence make him superior to the evil—adult—forces. He bears the mark of the chosen on his forehead, and he is worshipped in the wizard community as the future savior. The pattern is easily recognizable from world mythologies, even though Harry is not claimed to be a god or a son of god, which, in Frye's typology, disqualifies him as a genuine mythic hero, displacing him to the level of romance. Yet Harry also demonstrates ambiguity in the concepts of good and evil, gender transgression and other tokens of the postmodern aesthetics. The adult appeal originates from other layers of the books: adult issues, the richness of allusions, elaborate linguistic games, or social satire. Here, the novels illustrate the concept of crossover (Beckett

2008).Yet for most readers, the lure of Harry Potter is his total conformity with the idea of a romantic hero.

Harry Potter provides the sense of security subverted by characters such as other young magicians, for instance Ged in Ursula Le Guin's Earthsea novels (1968–2001), Will in Susan Cooper's *The Dark Is Rising* (1973) or Christopher in Diana Wynne Jones' *The Lives of Christopher Chant* (1988), as well as the sign reader Lyra in Philip Pullman's *His Dark Materials* (1995–2000). In following Harry's (mis)adventures, the issue is not whether he wins, but how he gets there. We know that the hero will be miraculously saved in the last moment, and we keep on reading to learn exactly how this happens. The extra-textual knowledge about the existence of sequels adds to our belief in the positive outcome. The sequels cannot possibly go on without Harry. Neither can he be killed and resurrected in the next volume, since mortality is included as a part of the universe. Harry is not a mythic "returning god."

Both carnival and queer theory offer excellent tools to assess power structures in the Harry Potter novels. Power hierarchies in the series are unequivocal. Wizards are superior to non-wizards. Also other writers, such as Diana Wynne Jones, have created worlds where magic is opposed to non-magic, but she never presents non-magical worlds or people without magical powers as inferior. Jones frequently portrays a higher authority that unscrupulously governs ordinary people, much like the Ministry of Magic in Harry Potter imposes its rules on Muggles. Yet in Jones' worlds, the authority is repeatedly interrogated, both explicitly and through the subject position offered by the text.

In the Harry Potter universe, full-blood wizards are superior to Muggle-born, and the persecution of these in the final volume is reminiscent of the worst genocides in human history. British wizards are superior to foreign wizards, some of which are bestowed by ridiculous Eastern-European names. Within the wizard community, foreign-born are never given prominent roles: the Patil twins loom in the periphery, tokens of Hogwarts' equal opportunity policy, and the object of Harry's infatuation—Cho—fades away as the novels progress. Squibs, wizard-born without magical powers, are the lowest of the wizard world. Translated into reality it may correspond to contempt toward mentally impaired people. Human beings are superior to goblins, elves, centaurs and giants, grotesque bodies, or physically impaired. Men are superior to women. It suffices to compare Professor McGonagall's status with the male teachers or to consider the divination professor Trelawney's constant humiliation. The ambiguous role of Hermione and particularly her restricted agency is unobstructed (especially illuminating in the episode in *The Chamber of Secrets* when she becomes literally petrified). Gryffindor Quidditch team features a couple of girls kept in the background: Luna is looney, and Tonks gender-neutral, which is accentuated by her self-imposed androgynous name.

The rich are not unexpectedly superior to the poor, and here Ron's position becomes blurred, or queered: as a male and full-blood he is superior to Hermione, but since his family's financial circumstances are constrained,

Hermione appears a cut above. Harry is well-provided for and can be generous toward others, and even though he never abuses his power, he is allegedly superior to students with less pecuniary assets. The authorities, represented by the Ministry of Magic, are naturally superior to the rank-and-file, and even the mighty Dumbledore must comply. In the Hogwarts' student hierarchy, ageism is tangible. First- and second-year students are not allowed to go to the village, and older students openly bully younger ones. Racist, sexist, imperialistic and other ideologically dubious aspects of the novels have been thoroughly investigated. Yet all these power structures are employed to support the central one: adults are superior to children.

The protagonist fulfils all power criteria except one and thus is presented as the bearer of normativity. Concerning the adult/child tension, Harry is allowed a temporary, carnivalesque superiority, under absolute adult control, on adult conditions and as long as the adults please to let the child play on his own. The adult world takes over in various ways when it is time to restore order. For Bakhtin, the issue would be whether the hero and thus the reader can make inferences from the carnivalesque experience and view the existing power positions as arbitrary, hence something that can be changed. The Harry Potter books rather endorse the adults as norm.

The books have also been discussed as novels of adolescence (Trites 2001). Paradoxically enough, the adolescent novel denies the protagonists the power that books for younger children allow through carnivalization. In a young adult novel, society catches up with the protagonist, depicted in transition from being oppressed to becoming an oppressor—unless he perishes on the way. In the Harry Potter books power clearly reproduces itself. Harry and his friends are initially scornful about Ron's brother Percy who uses every occasion to emphasize his supremacy. Throughout the books, we watch Percy's progression until he finally leaves childhood and gets an important job at the Ministry of Magic. In *The Order of Phoenix*, Ron and Hermione become prefects, and Percy congratulates his brother on the first step in his bureaucratic career. Harry never makes it to prefect, thus his special position is amplified, his freedom to break school rules is not put to trial, but in the first place the prefect appointment is connected with loyalty toward the adults. Naturally, being prefects does not prevent Ron and Hermione from following Harry on his increasingly dangerous adventures, but both take their responsibility according to adult prescriptions. With Ron's and Hermione's foretaste of power their final incorporation into adult hierarchy is anticipated.

Carnival Commences: The Premises of Children's Literature

Harry is a perfect illustration of the archetypal figure in children's literature. Born into the world of humans, he is dislocated from his rightful environment. A child deprived of his or her birthright is one of the most common mythical and folktale motifs. The romantic convention prompts that the weak and the oppressed will be empowered and returned to their proper position in the social hierarchy. Harry is reintroduced to the community from which he has been temporarily expelled and given seemingly unlimited power, even though, with a marvelous ironic twist, he is yet to learn how to use it. Moreover, although restored in his rightful position, Harry is yet to prove himself worthy of it, and is therefore subjected to a number of trials. Each volume is a duplication of this trial pattern (cf. Zipes 2001, 176f), even though the last one deviates from the rest in that it no longer presents Hogwarts as a secure place. The conventions of the romantic mode dictate that the hero should pass the trial. Harry is equipped with an army of gurus and supporters and an infinitely evil and powerful opponent. However, his innocence and his intrinsic benevolence make him superior to the evil—adult—powers.

The removal of parents is the premise of children's literature. The absence of parental authority allows the space that the fictive child needs for development and maturity, in order to test (and taste) his independence and to discover the world without adult protection. Yet, the child cannot be left completely without adult supervision; therefore substitutes provide security, but also maintain the rules that the adult world has set up. It is less offensive to get rid of *in loco parentis* figures than biological parents, but such surrogates are essential in many senses. Not least as the protagonist approaches adolescence, parental figures are needed so that he can rebel against them. As the novels progress, new father substitutes pop up, positive as well as negative: in addition to the initial uncle Vernon, Voldemort, Dumbledore, Hagrid and Snape, also Sirius, Lupin, Mad-Eye Moody, Lucius Malfoy, and more.

With an orphan hero, the identity search theme is amplified while he is also exposed to more serious trials than would be possible with adult protection. He is, however, never totally on his own, since the adult world must maintain control over the child. As compared to real parents, substitutes decrease adult power without abolishing it. Thus the novels are based on the imperative convention of children's literature. From a psychological point of view it seems unreasonable for Dumbledore to leave infant Harry with his wicked relatives (even though there is an explanation later on). Similarly, it feels irresponsive of the Hogwarts teachers to let Harry and his friends run about at night rather than locking them in the dorm with a magic spell. However this negligence is not only indispensable for the plot (what could possibly happen if Harry slept obediently in his bed?) but also for character constellations. It is quite significant that more and more parent substitutes are gotten rid of, finally even Dumbledore. In the last book, friends and supporters are sacrificed in gross and retail.

The overwhelming majority of fantasy novels feature ordinary children temporarily empowered through a magic agent, and Harry seems to deviate from the pattern. However, like his young wizard predecessors, Ged, Will and Christopher, Harry must learn to use magic, it is not the matter of merely waving a wand. As a wizard, Harry is omnipotent only compared to Muggles, notably his foster family. He is in many ways superior to his peers at Hogwarts: famous since birth, unbeatable in Quidditch, and indisputably more energetic and mischievous—considered a virtue in his classmates' eyes, if not the teachers'. He is braver, but in a typically heroic manner: he acts as a hero because he is a hero. In some respects, Harry is inferior to his schoolmates; for instance, not particularly accomplished in academic achievements. Harry and the other wizards are not omnipotent gods, immune to laws of nature: they can be injured, get sick and die. Some wizards are more powerful than others: Dumbledore is among the most powerful, and as we eventually learn, he is not beneath abusing his power. Harry is born with enormous power as compared to many other fantasy characters, yet his power is subjected to a set of regulations. The child may have an illusion of unlimited power during carnival while it is actually restricted by the adults. Although empowered, the child is not given full control; and even though it is understood that Harry is the only one to match the evil force of Voldemort, until the ultimate battle Harry has to comply with the rules imposed by adults. In the end, Dumbledore, the father substitute, has the final say.

The choice of a male protagonist is not a coincidence. The romantic narrative is by definition masculine (Hourihan 1997), and contemporary attempts to place a female character in a masculine plot merely results in a simple gender permutation, creating a quasi-female, "a hero in drag" (Paul 2006). Our gender awareness notwithstanding, males are still superior to females, and being male puts Harry in a privileged position by definition. Yet, Harry is not a gender stereotype, displaying quite a few traits normally associated with feminine stereotypes. He is non-violent, non-aggressive, emotional, caring and vulnerable, which definitely makes him different from conventional romantic heroes. Still he never reaches the complexity of some other contemporary fantasy protagonists.

Carnival Continues: The Hero on Top

Fantasy mode is a highly efficient strategy of empowering a child. Oppressed and humiliated in the ordinary world, Harry is displaced into a magical world where anything can happen. Harry is transported by means of the magical train (not at any way a new invention; a similar device was employed by Edith Nesbit almost a century before, and by many other fantasy writers). He gets into possession of a large variety of magical agents: his fantastic flying broom, his magic wand—a phallus symbol, as a psychoanalytically oriented critic would not fail to notice; an invisibility cloak, a magical interactive map, and more. These attributes make him better equipped than his classmates and most of his teachers. Ron and Hermione become his helpers, and their specific talents, as well as later Luna's and Neville's, fill in when his own prove insufficient. Harry's triumphant ascent from his oppressed position with the

Dursleys to fame, perpetual riches and privileged existence at Hogwarts, is an easily recognizable fairy-tale pattern.

As in most fantasy novels Harry is the chosen one, the coming messiah. There is a prophecy about his mission, exactly as in other fantasy novels, from *The Lion, the Witch and the Wardrobe* (1950) to *His Dark Materials*. Fantasy heroes, or romantic heroes in Frye's sense, lack complexity; they know no nuances, being one hundred percent heroic; they never doubt, fear or despair. If described at all, they possess a standard set of traits: strong, brave, clever, kind, or beautiful. Their moral qualities are impeccable: they are just, loyal and devoted to the cause they pursue. The premise for the romantic child hero is the idealization of childhood during the Romantic era, based on the belief in the child as innocent and therefore capable of conquering evil. Although this ideal child is interrogated (see essays in McGavran 1999), it affects the ways in which child heroes are still constructed in certain text types. Harry is no exception. His chief strength is the very fact that he is a child, and it is stressed that already as an infant he had the power to protect himself against Voldemort. His intrinsic goodness is his most momentous weapon.

There are further ways of empowering the child without magic, and many of these are present in the novels, due to the remarkable genre eclecticism. High mimetic characters, in Frye's model, are humans superior to other humans, for instance, in terms of bravery, wisdom, or patriotism. Superior to other young people, high mimetic characters serve as role models not only for the other character in the story, but for the readers as well. Adult readers may find Harry quite satisfactory as a model for children: humble, well-mannered, respectful toward his seniors, a perfect English gentleman. Young readers may appreciate other traits in Harry. As pointed out before, Harry is superior to his peers in terms of fame, bravery, and sports achievements. He is favored by his teachers, for instance, selected against the rules for the Quidditch team.

Another genre that allows Harry to be superior in a typically carnivalesque manner is mystery. In each novel, he must solve a mystery, using his wits, courage, defiance, curiosity, deduction ability and physical dexterity. The boarding-school story provides excellent opportunities for empowerment. In boarding-school novels the plot revolves around ordinary adventures: lessons, homework, sports, celebration of the first and last day of school, competition between dormitories, mischief, nightly orgies, forbidden outings to off-bound places, spying for enemies, the arrival of new students and teachers, bullying, revenge and so on. Apart from the ongoing progressive plot featuring the struggle of good and evil, the bulk of the Harry Potter volumes contain a chain of everyday episodes, albeit generously seasoned with magic. In all of these, Harry is allowed to be brilliant, even though the triviality of adventures somewhat dilute the heroic nature of our hero. The ordinariness of Harry is magnificently emphasized by his name, which clearly stands out as plain and unpretentious beside Dumbledore, McGonagall or Draco Malfoy. While these associative names are used to contribute to their bearers' individuality,

Harry's name underscores his Everyman nature. Contemporary characters are not meant as examples for young readers to admire, but as equal subjectivities. While Harry is undoubtedly more lucky than most of us, his exceptionality is balanced by his more down-to-earth qualities, including his poor sight. Yet, with his old-fashioned, broken glasses Harry sees better than any other Hogwarts student, a quality especially appreciated by the members of his Quidditch team. Through Quidditch the novels adhere to the sports novels, another excellent genre to empower the child who is initially inept but eventually wins the competition.

The naughty-boy story is also prominent. The protagonist's strength is his intrinsic goodness which allows him to perform pranks without being punished. Harry repeatedly breaks school rules, but since he does so with the best intentions he is always forgiven. A comic effect is created when teachers draw points from Gryffindor because Harry and his friends have been out after hours, while they award the house tenfold for Harry saving Hogwarts from mortal peril. Similarly, the adventure story places the child in an extraordinary situation, an exotic and dangerous setting in which he can show his courage better than in everyday life: reveal villains, solve mysteries and find treasures. The premise of adventure is chance: the hero happens to overhear a complot or get important intelligence, a carnivalesque, empowering device. Much thanks to the invisibility cloak, Harry can repeatedly get hold of vital information. The conventions of adventure genre dictate that the hero accomplishes his mission. There is even a touch of the Biggles novels when Harry and Ron take the magical flying car to get to school when they miss the train.

All these genres, and several more, are interwoven, and the attraction of the novels lies exactly in the fact that they do not clearly adhere to a particular genre. Yet all the various generic features, and all levels of the narrative, from mythic down to ironic, in Frye's terms, cooperate to elevate the hero offering him a wide scope of opportunities to show himself superior to others—as long as the adults in the background have control over the situation.

Carnival Terminates: The Adults' Triumph

It would seem that, being a wizard, Harry is empowered permanently. However the prerequisite of romantic fiction is the return to the initial order, the disempowerment of the hero, and the reestablishment of adult authority. The classic mythic hero kills his father and usurps the father's place, which would be highly improper in a children's book. Instead, Harry's father is, in accordance with children's literature tradition, conveniently killed off while Harry is still a baby; and in the end, Harry does not even have to kill Voldemort. Within the romantic mode, the child hero is brought back from magical journeys to the ordinary, sometimes being explicitly stripped of the attributes of previous power, most tangibly seen in the transformation of the Kings and

Queens of Narnia back to children at the end of *The Lion, the Witch and the Wardrobe*. The magical object is irretrievably lost or loses its magical power (*The Story of the Amulet*), the magical helper is removed (*Mary Poppins*), and the character stands alone without assistance, no longer a hero.

After each year at Hogwarts, Harry returns to the Dursleys. Apart from being a suitable narrative element, providing a natural frame for each school year, the return is a reminder of Harry's temporary departure from the ordinary and his temporary empowerment through the magical setup. For the sake of the plot his staying with the Dursleys is indispensable. When the family are no longer instrumental for the narrative, they are quietly got rid of, and we never hear about them again.

More important, Harry is not omnipotent in the wizard world either. The only one equal with Voldemort in magic force, he must still obey the adult wizards' commands. School setting emphasizes this power structure, spelled out, for instance, through Mrs. Weasley's utterance: "You are still at school and adults responsible for you should not forget it!" (*The Order of Phoenix* 83). Harry tentatively questions this by exclaiming bitterly to himself: "Just stay out while the grown-ups sort it out, Harry!" (*The Order of Phoenix* 495). Yet his silent rebellion has no effect. Dumbledore pops up like *deus ex machina* and concludes Harry's victory with an appreciative pat on the shoulder. It is especially noticeable in *The Order of Phoenix*: as Harry and his friends fight Voldemort's supporters in the secret rooms of the Ministry of Magic, and as all hope is lost, Dumbledore, who has been waiting backstage, steps forward, and the narrator lets the reader in a most didactic manner share Harry's thoughts: "*They were saved*" (*The Order of Phoenix* 805; emphasis in the original). Here is the essence of aetonormativity in a nutshell: the child hero can be as brave, clever and strong as he pleases, but in the end, an adult will take over. And here is perhaps the secret behind those children's books that we sometimes call masterpieces. In some incredible way they manage to solve the dilemma: both to empower the child and to protect him from the dangers of adulthood, that is, to try, against common sense, to hold the child within the innocence of childhood, since it is part of the adults' power strategy. The Harry Potter novels do not even attempt to combine these endeavors.

Carnival Reiterated: The Purpose of Sequels

The carnival structure is faithfully repeated in the first six volumes, following the master pattern of myth and folktale: home—away—home. Harry starts with his abominable foster family, goes to school where a new adventure awaits, allowing him to confirm his position as a hero, whereupon he is exiled to his humiliating existence with the Dursleys. Just as the readers rejoice that Harry at long last will have a proper family with Sirius, the latter is appropriately removed. There are inventive variations within the volumes, and Harry's tasks become increasingly more dangerous and complicated, but the general plot structure is the same. This repetitiveness, or sameness, which some critics associate with the essence of children's literature (e.g. Nodelman 2006), is prominent in series fiction, in which the order of reading is irrelevant since each of the books is a complete and independent narrative. The protagonist does not change nor grow older. It is claimed that the monotony of series fiction offers readers a sense of security, both concerning the invincibility of the hero, the stability of the plot, and their own reading skills. By contrast, the Harry Potter novels presuppose a chronological order. Even though the summary of the previous events are provided in the beginning of each of the earlier volume, details and characters reappear in later books, and the reader is expected to recognize them. While it is possible to read the books at random, as each plot is neatly rounded up, much of the suspense is lost when, for instance, the true nature of certain characters is already revealed or if circumstances behind key events have already been explained. Plotwise then, the novels are not serial fiction (cf. Watson 2000).

The other essential trait of series is the static character. Harry undeniably becomes a year older in each book; he is neither Nancy Drew who is forever sixteen (or eighteen) nor William, deep-frozen at eleven. However, character development can be of two kinds, chronological and ethical. No matter what some critics say about the increasing scope of Harry's emotions, we are not given Harry's thoughts or feelings, if he is at all bestowed with ability to think and feel. He is not a character encumbered by complex inner life. We are told that he is scared or lonely, but these are frequently narrator's statements, not representations of mental states that demand more sophisticated narrative devices. This mediated narrative technique does not allow penetration into the character's mind; in fact, from the later volumes we know more about Voldemort's state of mind through the glimpses Harry gets due to the supernatural connection between the two: or Snape's state of mind through his memories in the Pensieve. Harry does not develop much as a character, but we cannot demand psychological credibility from a character deliberately constructed as a romantic hero. Heroes are by definition static and flat. Even though Harry acquires a touch of ambiguity through his ties with Voldemort, even if he is allowed some slight imperfection, such as temper outbursts, his development is chronological, not ethical. In the last volume, the seventeen-year-old Harry is not radically different from his eleven-year-old self. He does not encounter any adolescence-related problems, as he is too busy saving the world. Even his ubiquitous Parseltongue ability is not a minor inherent flaw in an otherwise perfect hero, but part of the injury afflicted by Voldemort. Like fairy-tale heroes, Harry hardly ever has any ethical dilemmas or moral choices. He may misjudge people or follow false clues, but this is indispensable in a mystery novel. Contemporary modes of conveying psychological states are demanding, since they are ambivalent in allowing the reader to determine the source of utterance. The Harry Potter novels are unequivocal and straightforward in this respect. Harry does contemplate his identity and his mysterious connection with Voldemort, but mostly his thoughts revolve round what is to be done and how to do it; in other words, they propel the plot, but do not contribute to characterization. The novels are clearly action-oriented rather than character-oriented, which, to some critics, is the intrinsic feature of children's fiction (e.g. Nodelman 1992, 192).

According to the myth scholar Mircea Eliade, three aspects are essential for the rite of passage: the sacred, death and sexuality (Eliade 1961). While Harry is excessively exposed to the sacred in the magic world he inhabits, his initiation into the two other components is more problematic. True, Harry's parents died under horrible circumstances, yet as mentioned before, parents' foremost obligation in children's fiction is to be absent, preferably dead. Death is not a character's existential experience, but a necessary narrative device. When Cedric is killed before Harry's eyes in *The Goblet of Fire* it may seem tragic, but who is Cedric to Harry other than rival? In romantic fiction, rivals are to be disposed of. In *The Order of Phoenix*, Sirius is sacrificed, which could signal a step towards Harry's maturation. However, Harry has hardly developed any serious affection toward his new foster father: Sirius is a promise of family that Harry lacks, so this is what Harry really mourns. Furthermore, Sirius dies in a merciful off-stage manner, rather symbolically than physically, which is another convention of children's literature. The novels are considerably more cautious in the depiction of death as compared to many contemporary works that portray a child's confrontation with death in realistic as well as fantastic modes. The fantasy genre makes is especially easy to dispose of characters. When friends and enemies are killed in the final battle in *Deathly Hallows,* we take it for granted. The only death that really affects Harry is, paradoxically, that of Snape.

Sexually, Harry is eternally pre-pubertal. Hermione is a helper, a squire, a mind trust, a fellow combatant. Harry's infatuation with Cho is just another attribute of the romantic hero: the chivalrous worship of a pretty—and exotic—lady. When Cho does show some interest he hurriedly retires to the safety of Hermione's side. Ginny is another romantic dream that Harry is prepared to sacrifice for the sake of his quest. In a psychological interpretation, Harry is amazingly infantile and immature for his age, both emotionally and physiologically. However, as a literary character he can only be what the text makes him, and the text is extremely prudent in depicting Harry's sexual awakening. As compared to some sexually advanced teenagers in contemporary young adult fiction Harry is ridiculously uninformed. Yet this is also a children's literature convention. Critics who have traced character development in the Harry Potter novels have fallen into the pit of wishful thinking. As adults we want the child to grow up and become one of us, the powerful. At the same time, we want to keep the child innocent and ignorant, since we then have power over him.

In the final volume, all loose ends are tied together; details from the previous volumes turn up and prove highly significant. Yet it is still only on the plot level this conclusiveness is visible. As a character, Harry emerges from his carnival without the wisdom that carnivalesque subversivity usually presupposes.

Carnival Interrogated: The Permanence of Aetonormativity

What has then changed in the power hierarchy of Harry Potter universe as the saga concludes? What is interrogated and what is confirmed?

Wizards are obviously still superior to Muggles, and no questions about possible cooperation are ever raised. Although Muggles have been just as much threatened by dark forces as the wizards, they are not invited to join the battle. Unlike *The Lord of the Rings* or Lloyd Alexander's The Chronicles of Prydain, wizards have no intention of leaving the ordinary world; on the contrary, their control is as strong as ever. Wizard children are still attending elite school, closed to Muggles. Muggle-born are not persecuted as severely as under Voldemort's rule, but the distinction remains. Harry is still wealthy and thus respected. Gryffindor is still considered better than Slytherin. Prefects are still enjoying their privileges riding in a separate carriage on Hogwarts Express and having a separate bathroom at school. Bill Weasley has married a girl from an inferior nation, but she never learns proper English, a true token of condescension. The only free house-elf, Dobby, dies for the good cause, while the other elves presumably return to Hogwarts kitchen, happy as ever to serve their masters. Kreacher, whom Harry has inherited as a bonus to the house from Sirius, apparently cooks, cleans and washes clothes in the large Potter household. Grawp the giant, Hagrid's half-brother, has shown his loyalty to Harry, but the other giants are bad and have presumably been slaughtered or exiled together with other supporters of You-Know-Who. The goblins have once again demonstrated their unreliable nature. There is, in other words, no indication of equal rights.

Hermione, Ginny and other female characters have demonstrated valor in battle, but Neville is given the honor of killing Voldemort's snake, which places him on par with Harry in heroism (it is speculated before whether Neville rather than Harry is "the Chosen One"). The girls find happiness in marriage, and if they are at all like the model wife and mother, Mrs. Weasley, they wait for their husbands with hot dinner as these come home from work, and they see to it that the children pack their trunks properly before leaving for Hogwarts. Apparently neither Hermione nor Ginny has made any academic career in their old school. Instead, Neville replaces the female Professor Sprout in Herbology. And while Ron and Hermione have a boy and a girl, Harry and Ginny are blessed with two sons who are already acting superior toward their little sister. Whatever happens with the Muggles, in the wizard world there is no room for diversity, for single or same-sex parents: traditional family values are permanent.

Generally, the values of the novels are traditional. Their Christian ideas are transparent, alongside its many other levels, and are especially amplified in the last volume. This is not only, and not primarily the fact that wizards celebrate Christmas and Easter, and that at some point the house ghosts burst out in "Come all ye faithful." The Christian holidays are a poor match with the otherwise pagan world of magic; perhaps some official at the Department of Muggle Affairs considered the festivities worth importing from the Muggle world, alongside radio and steam engines. In any case, celebrations are depicted exclusively from a child point of view, focusing on presents and food. Further, snakes are associated with evil in Christianity, and this idea is fully developed in the novels. The Christian allusions, however, lie deeper beyond the surface and can for those who so wish be read as a much stronger Christian allegory than the Narnia chronicles. Although Harry is not born of a virgin, there are miraculous circumstances around his early infancy. There is a prophecy about him, and he is chosen to bear his people's pain and sorrow on his shoulders. He is repeatedly tempted by evil and withstands the temptation; he acquires a group of disciples and is pursued by the infidels. During the hour of respite that Voldemort gives him in one of the final chapters, Harry is, like Christ in Gethsemane, torn between the desire for the cup to pass from him and the sense of duty. He dies a voluntary sacrificial death, and Voldemort presents his limp body with a triumphant "Ecce Potter" to a crowd of mourners. He is resurrected and thus delivers the world from evil (the wizard world only, but that is another matter). He is also spared having murder on his conscience. The force that wins over evil is love. If this is not a Christian message, what is? Moreover, Christianity prescribes forgiving those who trespass on us, and consequently Harry's archenemy, Draco Malfoy, is forgiven. Even Percy, the prodigal son of the Weasleys, returns to the family. Dumbledore promises Harry eternal life in wizard heaven, where the faithful will meet again. In *His Dark Materials*, Pullman interrogates not only the church as institution, but any celestial authority. The Harry Potter books confirm the social order based on conventional Western values, on solid beliefs in indisputable dogmas, and on unquestionable authorities.

Most important, however, in terms of power hierarchies is the adult/child axis. When Dumbledore dies at the end of *The Half-Blood Prince*, it appears that Harry is finally left on his own, with only his many substitute fathers' legacy to fulfill his quest. As it turns out, all his success, not only in the final volume, but throughout the series, has depended wholly on Snape's protection, which in its turn is the sign of Snape's eternal love for Harry's mother, an issue somewhat beyond the scope of a child's priorities. In fact, from what Snape's memories reveal for Harry in the Pensieve, the focus of the whole story may easily shift on to Snape. His devotion to the son of his dead beloved is so immense that he is prepared to bear a mark of the Dark Arts on his body, to live a life as a double spy, a life of lies and pretence, of contempt and hate from fellow teachers as well as students, including the object of his concerns. While Harry's life is full of risk and danger, yet with high stakes to win, Snape's is utter misery and no reward. Thus the seven-volume epic appears in this light not the story of a standard, predictable hero of myth, fairy tale and children's literature, but a complex existential narrative of a life and death of a pathetic man who longs for the son he has never had, and who, through thick and thin, remained true to his one and only love. The most celebrated children's book of the recent years turns out, on closer examination, exactly what some critics, alongside *Alice in Wonderland*, *Peter Pan* and *Winnie-the-Pooh*, judge as "in actual fact not books for children." After years of debates, we are back to the "impossibility of children's fiction."

Dumbledore's irresponsible use of Harry "for the greater good," revealed in the last volume, corroborates that the child is secondary and instrumental to the wishes and purposes of adults. Precisely as in the previous volumes, Dumbledore summons Harry—from beyond the grave, so powerful is his clutch on the poor boy – to explain to him everything Harry has not understood, everything the adults have concealed from him "for his own good," everything he has not been considered mature enough to grasp, everything they have lied about, everything they have abused him to perform for their benefit. The didacticism of this final dialogue with Harry's primary guru echoes and amplifies the ideological charge of the whole saga.

The epilogue shows Harry living happily ever after, married and a father of three children, to whom he now can preach and whose fates he has decided once and for all. The wheel of power has gone full circle. Adult normativity is irreversibly cemented.

Chapter Two
Othering the Sense:
Language and (Mis)communication

In a much-quoted passage from Lewis Carroll's *Through the Looking Glass*, the following dialogue takes place:

> "When *I* use a word," Humpty Dumpty said, in rather a scornful tone, "it means just what I choose it to mean—neither more nor less."
>
> "The question is," said Alice, "whether you can make words mean so many different things."
>
> "The question is," said Humpty Dumpty, "which is to be master—that's all" (196, emphasis in the original).

The conversation has mostly been employed in criticism to illustrate the arbitrary nature of verbal signs in the language of fiction. Like Humpty Dumpty, a writer puts meaning into words, and the reader has to share the code in order to understand them. Alice, however, also learns an important lesson from Humpty Dumpty. Language is a vehicle of power, and whoever possesses this power can also suppress and govern other people.

Let us remember that Humpty Dumpty is himself an empty signifier. The figure appears in a nursery rhyme:

> Humpty Dumpty sat on a wall,
> Humpty Dumpty had a great fall ...

Originally, the words "Humpty Dumpty" did not have a meaning: it is a signifier without the signified. Yet Alice "saw clearly that it was HUMPTY DUMPTY himself" (191). The writer thus supplies a signified to a previously empty verbal sign.

Similarly, in the first *Alice* book, several characters are empty names, such as the Gryphon (where the narrator advises the reader to look at the picture

27

if he doesn't know what a Gryphon is) and the Mock Turtle, the March Hare and even the Hatter, since he is essentially merely a representation of the trope "mad as a hatter." When the Queen wonders whether Alice has yet heard Mock Turtle's story, Alice must admit that she doesn't even know what a Mock Turtle is, whereupon the Queen provides an explanation: "It's the thing Mock Turtle soup is made from" (90). Neither Alice nor the reader becomes wiser.

Yet these empty creatures, devoid of substance—Humpty Dumpy, the Gryphon, the Mock Turtle and other bizarre figures in the *Alice* books, can order Alice about because they have more authority in the strange world in which she involuntarily has found herself. By entering this world she is disempowered, even compared to the relative power she might have had as a child and the youngest sister in her own world (when she returns from Wonderland, or rather wakes from her dream, her sister starts ordering her about). She does not know the rules of the game, she loses control of her body, but much more important, the normal logic of language and communication does not exist any longer.

One of the most prominent representatives of power is, notably, not the Queen of Hearts with her whims and useless orders, but the Cheshire Cat. Much has been written about this character, yet less about its connection with Alice's world outside Wonderland, which sheds at least some light into power hierarchies in the child's fictional reality. Alice has a pet cat, Dinah. We do not know much about this figure apart from her being a good mouser, which leads to a conflict between Alice and the Mouse in Wonderland. As Alice is ordered about by the White Rabbit she wonders whether she will one day be ordered about by Dinah and what the grownups would think about it. She also has a vision of herself and Dinah walking hand in hand, Alice seeking an answer to her absurd question: "Do cats eat bats?" Dinah is Alice's playmate, upon whom the girl bestows intelligence and ability to walk upright. As a human, Alice has power over Dinah, yet in her imagination Dinah is a liminal figure, both cat and human, besides, a most tangible link between the strange Wonderland and the secure home. (Incidentally, in the sequel, one of Dinah's kittens is transformed into a chess queen in the looking-glass world).

If Wonderland, as sometimes suggested, is Alice's mindscape, or, as the more conventional interpretation goes, her dream, it would be natural that the projection of the real, familiar cat into the alternative world should retain its gender. The hypothetical cat of Alice's dreamworld would, in such a construction, turn out to be her Old Wise Woman, the Progenitrix guiding the protagonist through the rite of passage. All other symbols of initiation are present in the story: denigration in the form of a physical fall, dark passages, sinister woods, closed doors to force open, trials by alien food, uncontrolled bodily transformations, meeting with a row of monsters, symbolic dismembering ("Off with her head!"), and final resurrection and emergence from the literal underground, presumably as a whole self. Yet, instead of a Wise Old Woman in feline shape we meet a trickster more suitable for a masculine, patricidal story.

Naturally, *Alice in Wonderland* is in many respects a far from traditional novel, in which the author is free to break conventional patterns. It has been pointed out that Alice can be interpreted as the author's Anima, and thus the whole story is a kind of self-therapeutic confession. It is equally possible to see the Cheshire Cat as a self-portrait, a benevolent companion that acts as Alice's protector in an unfamiliar and bizarre world. The Cheshire Cat does indeed have, similarly to Humpty Dumpty in *Through the Looking-Glass*, the function of the mythical guide, telling Alice at least a few necessary facts about the place she had involuntarily come to:

> " . . . we are all mad here. I'm mad. You are mad."
> "How do you know I'm mad?" said Alice.
> "You must be," said the Cat, "or you wouldn't have come here." (65)

The Cat explains the rules of the game, or rather the absence thereof; yet he also comforts Alice who need not feel she is the only one gone crazy. At the croquet ground, she is genuinely glad to see someone she knows to talk to, as if indeed she and the Cat were the only sane people present.

The Cheshire Cat, as well as Humpty Dumpty, practices verbal equilibristic with Alice, making her—and the reader—contemplate the conventionality of language and the illogical nature of logic:

> "Would you tell me, please, which way I ought to walk from here?"
> "That depends a good deal on where you want to get to," said the Cat.
> "I don't much care where—"said Alice.
> "Then it doesn't matter which way you walk," said the Cat.
> "—so long as I get *somewhere*," Alice added as an explanation.
> "Oh, you're sure to do that," said the Cat," if you only walk long enough." (64f, emphasis in the original)

As road directions, whether literal or metaphorical, this is certainly not much help, and at this point the guru's instructions might seem confusing rather than enlightening. It would almost appear that the Cat mocks and humiliates Alice, just as all the other creatures do. Yet for one thing, the Cat here is testing Alice's logical capacity, strongly impeded by her experience of Wonderland; he is further offering his ward spiritual guidance not to be neglected: you are sure to get somewhere if you walk long enough. Thus among the Cat's endless puns and wordplay, great wisdom is hidden, and he is the only one in Wonderland who is nice to Alice. By the end of the book, Alice has got so much practice and become so bold that she can easily switch in the middle of a sentence from being rude about the Queen to praising her, and she talks back, explaining that a cat may look at a king, a set phrase that she, quite appropriately, interprets literally. In other words, she has learned her lesson from the Cat, at least concerning linguistic skills.

Moreover, the Cheshire Cat, just as Humpty Dumpy, is himself a figure of speech ("to grin like a Cheshire Cat"). Taken out of the set phrase, it becomes a signifier without a signified. Subsequently, the Cheshire Cat lacks a physical body. True, when Alice first meets him in the Duchess's house, he seems an ordinary cat, apart from his grin. He is described as large, but not exceptionally large, and he sits on the hearth, like any cat. But outside the house, he is suddenly rather like an oversized image projected on a screen and still more so as he appears on the sky over the croquet ground, a mirage that fades and reappears at will. If he is Carroll's self-portrait, in these scenes he is an image of an image, as distant and mysterious as dreams themselves. The executioner's argument that you couldn't cut off a head unless there is a body to cut it off from is among the most sensible things anybody ever says in the book, and it shows how well the Cat has adapted to the absurd life in Wonderland. The famous "grin without a Cat" is just one of the many paradoxes, presumably reflecting the mathematician Dodgson's tribute to pure mathematical abstraction.

Interestingly enough, the Cat is removed from the plot and has no role in Alice's final ascension and return home, unlike, for instance, the black kitten in *Through the Looking-Glass*. In Alice's sister's pondering about her little sister's curious dream, when she tries to connect the events of the dream with the movements and sounds around her, the Cheshire Cat is not featured. He dissolves without trace, as a true spiritual guide must do when initiation is over.

Yet there is another aspect, going beyond communication between fictional characters and concerning communication between the implied author and the implied reader. The latter is just as helpless as Alice confronted with the distorted norms of Wonderland; the events are unpredictable, the cause and effect inverted, and Alice's vulnerability is equally shared by the reader, not least the young reader. Thus the author of the *Alice* books exercises just as much power toward his readers as the characters do toward the protagonist. Further, while Humpty Dumpy's declaration is explicit and pertains to both relationships: character/character and author/reader, most (mis)communicative acts in the *Alice* books are implicit and can easily put inexperienced readers in a state of utter confusion.

Falling through the Rabbit hole, Alice wonders

> ' . . . what Latitude or Longtitude I've got to?" (Alice had not the slightest idea what Latitude was, or Longtitude either, but she thought they were grand words to say). (17)

There is nobody around to be impressed by Alice's fake erudition, but she knows that grand words give a person a higher status. Apparently she has learned the words from adults, who did not bother to explain them to her, thus demonstrating their superiority. We may interpret the passage as an intention to arouse the readers' curiosity and enrich their vocabulary, encouraging them to find out the meaning of the words. Yet there is also something arrogant in the author's attitude, as he insinuates that using grand words without knowing what they mean is conceit.

The author's condescension toward the reader becomes all the more tangible as Alice goes on with her soliloquy:

> "I wonder if I shall fall right *through* the earth! How funny it'll seem to come out among the people that walk with their heads downwards! The antipathies, I think—" (she was rather glad there *was* no one listening, this time, as it didn't sound at all the right word).(17, emphasis in the original)

The author does not provide his readers with the correct word, apparently assuming that they, unlike Alice, know it. It is, however, doubtful that the implied readers are familiar with both words and the difference between them, so the author's play on words is more geared towards adults. Language is thus used to disempower and deride the readers. (In some translations of Alice, footnotes or boxed texts are used to explain the words. Here adult translators demonstrate their superiority both against the protagonist and the readers whom they condemn as hopelessly ignorant).

Yet occasionally, the author becomes aware of his linguistic self-importance when he lets one of his characters comment on the use of obscure language:

> "In that case," said the Dodo solemnly, rising to his feet, "I move that the meeting adjourn, for the immediate adoption of more energetic remedies—"
>
> "Speak English!" said the Eaglet. "I don't know the meaning of half those long words, and, what's more, I don't believe you do either!" (33)

All the creatures Alice meets in Wonderland and behind the looking glass exercise their power through language, presenting Alice—and the reader—with verbal puzzles, paradoxes and logical contradictions. The Mouse pretends he does not understand what Alice is saying, thus forcing her to remember her almost non-existent French. He also torments Alice and the other creatures by lecturing on history ("the driest thing I know") and using incomprehensible words and syntax. The Lory solves a dispute by stating: "I'm older than you, and must know better" (31), typical adult reaction to an inquisitive child. The Dodo proposes a Caucus-race without being able to explain what it means. The Mad Hatter offers Alice an absurd riddle: "Why is a raven like a writing-desk?" (68) The Caterpillar talks down to Alice with his firm logic:

> "I can't explain *myself*, I am afraid, Sir," said Alice, "because I'm not myself, you see."
>
> "I don't see," said the Caterpillar.
>
> " . . . being so many different sizes in a day is very confusing."
>
> "It isn't," said the Caterpillar.

"one doesn't like changing so often, you know."

"I *don't* know," said the Caterpillar. (52; emphasis in the original)

Besides absurd logic, figurative language, especially puns and wordplay, is used as a means or oppression. In some cases wordplay occurs when a set phrase is misinterpreted by a character. For instance, in *Through the Looking-glass*, when Alice says: "I beg your pardon," the King replies: "It isn't respectable to beg" (205). Mostly, Alice is the target of the pun:

"Mine is a long and sad tale!" said the Mouse, turning to Alice, and sighing.

"It *is* a long tail, certainly," said Alice, looking down with wonder at the Mouse's tail; "but why do you call it sad?" (34)

In some cases, however, it is not clear whether Alice understands the wordplay, or whether the young reader is assumed to understand it. For instance, the chapter title "The Rabbit Sends in a Little Bill" is based on the homonymics of the word "bill" (invoice, statement, receipt) and the name of a character, Bill. Similarly, both Alice and the reader may be baffled by the Duchess's word of wisdom: "Take care of the sense and the sounds will take care of themselves." In order to appreciate the joke, the reader must recognize the original saying: "Take care of the pence and the pounds will take care of themselves." The Duchess's aphorism, one of her many morals, seems completely out of place in a world where there is no sense, while the sounds have taken over.

The most outrageous episode of verbal abuse occurs in the chapters describing Alice's encounter with the Mock Turtle. The character itself is, as previously stated, a linguistic paradox: a physical representation of a word denoting a fake description of another physical phenomenon. Alice gets completely bewildered by the Mock Turtle's story about his school days, with subjects such as:

Reeling and Writhing ... the different branches of Arithmetic—Ambition, Distraction, Uglification, and Derision ... Mystery, ancient and modern, with Seaography: then Drawling—the Drawling-master was an old conger-eel, that used to come once a week: he taught us Drawling, Stretching, and Fainting in Coils ... Laughing and Grief ... (94)

There is a strong comic effect in distortions of existing words, amplified by the connection of subjects to characters, such as an eel teaching drawling and stretching. But the Mock Turtle and the Gryphon take every opportunity to point out Alice's ignorance:

" ... The Master was an old Turtle—we used to call him Tortoise—"

"Why did you call him Tortoise, if he wasn't one?" Alice asked.

"We called him Tortoise because he taught us," said the Mock Turtle angrily. "Really you are very dull!" (93)

When Alice confesses that she has never heard of Uglification, the Gryphon's bland conclusion is "you *are* a simpleton." (94; emphasis in the original). And, as if anticipating Humpty Dumpty in the sequel, to Alice's timid question whether he means "purpose" rather than "porpoise", the Mock Turtle replies promptly: "I mean what I say." In an earlier chapter, Alice has a dispute with the Hatter and the March Hare:

> "Do you mean that you think you can find out the answer to it?" said the March Hare.
> "Exactly so," said Alice.
> "Then you should say what you mean," the March Hare went on.
> "I do," Alice hastily replied; "at least—at least I mean what I say— that's the same thing, you know."
> "Not the same thing a bit!" said the Hatter. (69)

The discrepancy between word and meaning is emphasized once again, and by turning Alice's words back onto her, the creatures of Wonderland can diminish and humiliate her.

Alice in Wonderland may seem a perfect example of a carnival in Mikhail Bakhtin's sense, an upside-down world full of grotesque bodies. Yet carnival is subversive and cathartic, temporarily empowering the oppressed, even though the existing order is finally restored. In fact, Alice's experience is that of total disempowerment, and verbal maltreatment is a major part of it.

In Western children's literature, *Alice in Wonderland* is one of the rare texts that, instead of empowering the fictional child through displacement in an alternative world, explicitly disempowers and even humiliates her. Alice is hardly a role model, and her adventures are nightmares rather than pleasant dreams. Her constant bodily transformations are not merely disturbing and uncomfortable; they reflect abjection, a young girl's dissatisfaction with and fear of the imminent changes in her body. The subject position offered in the text is highly ambivalent, and the implied readers are free to respond in various manners. They have the option of distancing themselves both from Alice and from Wonderland and perceiving the book as it is, with its lack of proper plot, its bizarre figures, its linguistic brilliance and its disappointing closure. From an external subject position Alice's experience as a poignant depiction of a lonely, confused child in the perplexing and absurd adult world. In this sense, the book is truly subversive. Yet for a less sophisticated reader, it may instead cause a sense of discomfort, frustration and aversion, if the reader feels humiliated alongside the protagonist.

Power and Oppression in the Hundred-Acre Wood

Winnie-the-Pooh is another famous children's book that, together with *Alice*, is frequently classified as nonsense, due to its excessive puns and wordplay.

Yet the superficially nonsensical language in the *Pooh* books is also used to make mock of the child, both within and outside the text. The books further demonstrate that power tends to reproduce itself, that the oppressed easily become oppressors. Christopher Robin feels stupid and uneducated in the fictive reality of the book. It is sufficient to contemplate his posture in the illustration where he is going down the stairs, his head hanging down, his eyes hidden from the viewer, a frightened child subject to rules and regulations, allowed for a short while to visit his omnipotent father in his study and promptly exiled back to the nursery. Compared to this image, the portrait of Christopher Robin in his own realm, the Hundred-Acre Wood, shows him as a king and a god, happy, smiling, confident and dynamic. He is no longer wearing the babyish frock. He is clever and powerful; he appears each time his small, stupid subjects have entangled themselves into unsolvable problems; he knows everything, understands everything, he can—allegedly—read and write, and he is always there for his underprivileged friends. Yet if we read the story carefully, Christopher Robin inside the Hundred-Acre Wood is far from benevolent. On the contrary, the boy humiliates and oppresses his toys just as his father oppresses him, much like Max in Maurice Sendak's *Where the Wild Things Are* transfers his mother's oppressive behavior onto the Wild Things, as he does to them as he is done by, sending them to bed without supper.

In the chapter "In Which Pooh and Piglet go Hunting and Nearly Catch a Woozle," the two characters, one of which is a Bear with a Very Little Brain, follow some tracks in the snow. They think they are hunting first a Woozle, then two Woozles, then "two Woozles and one, as it might be, Wizzle, or two, as it might be, Wizzles and one, if so it is Woozle" (35).

As usual, Christopher Robin the Almighty comes to rescue, saying:

> "Silly old Bear . . . what *were* you doing? First you went round the spinney twice by yourself, and then Piglet ran after you and you went round again together, and then you were just going round a fourth time—"
> "Wait a moment," said Winnie-the-Pooh (37–38).

Here, the ambiguity of the text's subject positions is drawn to the extreme. The implied author allows the child to be superior over the toy, but the reader's expected subjectivity is somewhat blurred. For unsophisticated readers, *Pooh* books are about the teddy bear called Winnie-the-Pooh. As critics, we can come with other sophisticated interpretations, but for the young reader, and decidedly for many adult readers, Pooh is the only option. The world is presented through Pooh's eyes, through a naïve, curious and inquisitive view that all children possess until we adults impose our own clever ideas on them. A young reader will be engaged with Pooh, feel his joys and sorrows, his fear of Heffalumps and his admiration for Christopher Robin. Yet, in the chapter about the Woozle hunt, the readers' subject position definitely presents a problem. If they entirely share Pooh's perception, they will, together with

Pooh and Piglet, believe that the two friends are tracking fierce and dangerous animals. On hearing Christopher Robin's comment, they will feel as "Foolish and Deluded" (38) as Pooh. Naturally, there are illustrations to help; still a reader needs to feel at least slightly superior to Pooh to appreciate the scene, or indeed many other episodes. For instance, when Pooh pretends to be a little cloud, Christopher Robin is again allowed to be wiser, yet he pampers Pooh just as an adult would pamper a silly child.

In the chapter in which the characters go searching for the North Pole, when Christopher Robin announces the trip to Pooh, the latter inquires:

> "What *is* the North Pole?" . . .
> "It's just a thing you discover," said Christopher Robin carelessly, not being quite sure himself. (101; emphasis in the original)

The didactic authorial voice makes mock of the child who uses grand words he does not understand. Yet the child immediately transfers his ignorance onto someone inferior.

Later on Christopher Robin is obliged to consult Rabbit:

> "What does the North Pole *look* like? . . . I suppose it's just a pole stuck in the ground?"
> "Sure to be a pole," said Rabbit, "because of calling it a pole . . . " (110; emphasis in the original)

Rabbit is supposed to be educated, and may even be interpreted as an adult, but he is in fact just as ignorant as the boy, yet in order to retain his power position, he needs to pretend. Typically, a child chooses a more concrete meaning of a homonym. In this episode Christopher Robin is obliged to admit that he has been using a word the meaning of which he does not know. What may seem a purely stylistic device turns out to be a clear-cut case of the author's oppression toward the character, and by extension, the reader. It may be argued that the author expects the reader to know what the North Pole is and therefore feel superior to the characters, which happens recurrently in the *Pooh* books, but it is not likely. Rather, the reader will feel confused and disgraced. Moreover, unless the readers actually know what the North Pole is, they will be quite satisfied with Pooh's discovery, since the mistake is never explained.

According to most critical interpretations of the *Pooh* stories, the characters represent the various inner qualities of the true protagonist, Christopher Robin: Pooh his uncontrolled gluttony, Piglet his fears, Tigger his joyful bounciness that has to be "unbounced." Rabbit and Owl are especially interesting from the point of view of power, since they act as projections of the young boy's needs to oppress others, just as he is oppressed by the adult, his father, the alleged narrator of the stories. Both Owl and Rabbit are repeatedly exposed, for instance when they try to decipher Christopher Robin's misspelled message "Gon out. Backson." Since it is for them inconceivable that their master can make a mistake, they, like Pooh, provide a signified for a word they are disinclined to confess they do not know.

> " . . . Have you seen a Backson anywhere about in the Forest lately?"
> "I don't know," said Rabbit. "That's what I came to ask you. What are they like?"
> "Well," said Owl, "the Spotted and Herbaceous Backson is just a . . . " (78)

Rather than admitting his ignorance, Owl hides it behind yet another set of complex words. In the same episode it finally turns out that Owl is bluffing as, unable to read Christopher Robin's message, he coaxes Rabbit to read it to him.

Owl is throughout the two books portrayed as a true sesquipedalian, characterized by using bizarre words: "Owl was telling Kanga an Interesting Anecdote full of long words like Encyclopaedia and Rhododendron" (110). For adults, the two words are rather incompatible, while for a young reader they probably make no sense at all. Kanga resists Owl's linguistic assaults by ignoring them. Pooh develops a different strategy. When he does not know the meaning of the difficult words Owl is using, such as "Customary Procedure," he tries to find the closest possible signified, making it into "Crustimony Pro-seedcake," which also reflects his fixation on food. Similarly, on hearing the word "ambush," Pooh interprets it as a kind of "bush," like a gorse-bush. It is not accidental that Pooh, who represents a very young child, does not know the meaning of abstract notions and instead chooses a signified he perceives as concrete and tangible, even though the signifier may not exist.

Pooh is a great poet, but his poetry is based on imaginary rather than symbolic language, in Lacanian sense: the sounds, rhymes, and rhythm are more important than the meaning, contrary to the Duchess's maxim in *Alice in Wonderland*. The symbolic, correct, ordered language lies far beyond Pooh's horizon. Christopher Robin, however, is already being exposed to symbolic language, and he uses it skilfully as an instrument of power.

> . . . Christopher Robin . . . said carelessly: "I saw a Heffalump to-day, Piglet."
> . . .
> "I saw one once," said Piglet. "At least, I think I did," he said. "Only perhaps it wasn't."
> "So did I," said Pooh, wondering what a Heffalump was like (51).

Like Humpty Dumpty, Heffalump is a signifier without a signified. Unlike the North Pole, this is not a word that Christopher Robin would have heard from an adult; he invents the word with the single intention of showing his superiority. Both Pooh and Piglet play along, reluctant to admit their ignorance. Both fill the empty signifier with a content corresponding to their worst fears:

Pooh as a monster who will deprive him of food, Piglet as a monster who is "Fierce with Pigs" (61). In both cases, Christopher Robin has effectively amplified his subjects' anxieties.

Pooh successfully transfers this power strategy onto Piglet when he suggests that the creatures they are supposedly hunting are woozles and wizzles, signifiers that in Piglet's mind immediately turn into "Hostile Animals . . . of Hostile Intent" (32, 35). In his turn, Piglet has invented a grandfather for himself, as he explains the broken sign in front of his door: "TRESPASSERS W." This, Piglet claims, is his grandfather's name, "short for Trespassers Will, which was short for Trespassers William" (30). The word "grandfather" is not accidental here. In the woozle-hunt chapter, Pooh is wondering whether he and Piglet are following two Grandfathers, and what a Grandfather might look like. This is a complete reversal of notions where a word that is perfectly normal for the reader is for the character as meaningless as "woozle" is for the reader. The author thus draws the reader's attention to the arbitrary nature of language. "Grandfather" is an empty signifier for Pooh, since there is no referent for it in his world. The readers are on the one hand given superiority over the character since they at least know what a grandfather is; yet confronted with the word "woozle" they will feel disarmed. Thus the oppressor/oppressed hierarchy between the characters is constantly reversed. Further, the power hierarchy in the text itself is extremely intricate, since it also involves several agencies, including the axes of implied author/implied reader, narrator/narratee, and character/character. In this complexity, the reader seems mostly to be left disempowered.

To confirm his authority, Christopher Robin constantly calls Pooh "Silly old bear," both concerning Pooh's behavior and his misunderstanding of words. However, in many cases, the boy obviously reserves to his teddy bear in order to disguise his own ignorance. When the father, the overt narrator in the first chapter, says: "Winnie-the-Pooh lived in a forest all by himself under the name of Sanders," the listening child interrupts the story by inquiring: *What does 'under the name' mean?* receiving the explanation: *It means he had the name over the door in gold letters and lived under it* (2; emphasis in the original). Another example of a character's misinterpretation comes from the final chapter in *The House at Pooh Corner*, when Christopher Robin tells Pooh about all kinds of things he has learned from his lessons, including "when Knights were Knighted." Confused, Pooh asks: "Is it a very Grand thing to be an Afternoon?" (173). Not being literate, Pooh goes after the sound rather than spelling of the word, and chooses the most familiar one to him, "night" rather than "knight," further supplanting it with "afternoon." Most probably, the misreading originates in the boy, but Pooh is once again being maltreated.

In the chapter about the discovery of the North Pole, Christopher Robin harasses his toys in a number of ways. First, he announces that they are going on an Expedition. This is a difficult word for a Bear of a Very Little Brain, and Pooh corrupts it into "Expotition."

"Expedition, silly old Bear. It's got an 'x' in it."
"Oh!" said Pooh. "I know." But he didn't really (101).

Notably, "Expotition" also has an "x" in it, but Pooh lacks the insight to point it out, or else he is simply awed by his master's authority.

Further, Christopher Robin declares that everybody must bring Provisions.

"Bring what?"
"Things to eat."
"Oh!" said Pooh happily. "I thought you said Provisions . . . " (102).

Pooh then immediately transfers the verbal attack onto Piglet.

"To discover what?" said Piglet anxiously . . . "Nothing fierce?"
"Christopher Robin didn't say anything about fierce. He just said it has an 'x'."
"It isn't their necks I mind," said Piglet earnestly. "It's their teeth . . . " (103).

While the passage is yet another example of wordplay abundant in the *Pooh* books, it emphasizes how quickly the characters learn the oppressive use of language. Finding Eeyore's lost tail, Pooh says that Eeyore used to be very fond of it, in fact "attached to it" (47). The literal and the transferred meaning of the word "attached" are combined, yet it is not self-evident that the young readers get the point.

However, the author goes so far as to let Owl pay Christopher Robin back and frequently helps his readers by translating Owl's convoluted speech into a more everyday idiom:

"The atmospheric conditions have been very unfavourable lately," said Owl.
"The what?"
"It has been raining," explained Owl.
"Yes," said Christopher Robin. "It has."
"The flood-level has reached an unprecedented height."
"The who?"
"There is a lot of water around," explained Owl (127).

Owl treats Christopher Robin exactly in the same manner the boy has earlier treated Pooh by using the word "provisions" instead of the familiar "things to eat."

Yet *Pooh* books also reflect the young child's resistance towards language oppression, through testing rules by breaking them, and through exploration of the boundaries and possibilities of language. Pooh represents oral culture in which language is not restricted by rules, in which grammar can be incorrect, spelling does not matter (Pooh writes HUNNY on his jars and knows exactly what it means), and new words can be easily invented. By contrast, the education that Christopher Robin receives in the outside (read: adult) world is written, ordered, and strictly regulated; it does not have room for Spotted and Herbaceous Backsons. At the beginning of the sequel, *The House at Pooh Corner*, the boy asks the father:

> "What about that story you were going to tell me about what happened to Pooh when"— I happened to say very quickly, "What about nine times a hundred and seven?" And when we had done that one, we had one about cows going through a gate at two a minute, and there are three hundred in the field, so how many are left after an hour and a half? (ix).

This is a magnificent example of how an adult authority suppresses a child's imagination.

The supremacy of the written language over the oral is promptly demonstrated in the *Pooh* books. Both Christopher Robin and his toys are in the pre-verbal stage as the book opens, but throughout the story we repeatedly witness how Christopher Robin is trained in symbolic, verbal language. Several of the chapters revolve around the toys' inability to read and write. If the inhabitants of the Hundred-Acre Woods are, as the psychoanalytical interpretation suggests, the projections of the boy's inner traits, then the Owl's spelling difficulties as he is asked to write "Happy birthday" or his inability to read Christopher Robin's message is merely transference of the boy's own problems. Obviously, Christopher Robin has cheated his surroundings in that he can indeed read and write, but this aptitude resembles Pooh's naïve confession: "Christopher Robin told me what [the sign] said, and then I could" (74). It is clear from the signs that the boy is fairly poor in spelling, and we can extrapolate that, outside the secondary world, he is nagged by his father for this deficiency. Writing the signs, he still makes a direct connection between the name of letters and their pronunciation, thus spelling "please" as "PLES" and "answer" as "RNSER;" yet he is recognized as "the only one on the forest who could spell" (43).

Similarly, Owl has the reputation of being literate, albeit with some limitations: he is "able to read and write and spell his own name WOL, yet somehow went all to pieces over delicate words like MEASLES and BUTTEREDTOAST" (43). The readers are expected to understand that the name is misspelled, but the irony may easily escape them. Thus the author again cleverly shifts the boy's ineptitude onto his animal friends, which is especially tangible in the chapter about Eeyore's birthday. Quite apparently, Owl cannot read and write, but is reluctant to admit it. He asks Pooh whether he can read the signs on his door, and Pooh explains that he can if he is told what they mean. Relieved, Owl says that he will tell Pooh what he has written, and then Pooh will be able to read it. So he writes: "HIPY PAPY BTHUTHDTH THUTHDA BTHYTHDY"

(74). From the point of view of the Symbolic Order, this is gibberish. Within the Imaginary, it can just as well mean "Happy birthday," if this is what it is intended to mean. If the signifier "HIPY PAPY . . . " has been connected by the sender with the signified "Happy birthday," the addressee merely needs a code to understand it properly. However, to return to Humpty Dumpy, a word means just what the sender chooses it to mean. Through literacy, the sender has unlimited power over the addressee.

The most lucid illustration of the discrepancy between the Imaginary and the Symbolic is, however, to be found in Chapter Five in *The House at Pooh Corner* "What Christopher Robin Does in the Mornings." Piglet comes to visit Eeyore who is fully engrossed in contemplating three sticks on the ground in front of him. "Two of the sticks were touching at one end, but not at the other, and the third was laid across them" (84). Piglet, who is illiterate without being concerned about it, "thought that perhaps it was a Trap of some kind" (84). That is, Piglet sees the Imaginary, iconic value of the sign rather than its symbolic value. Eeyore enlightens Piglet, acting as a mouthpiece for a wise adult: "Do you know what A means, little Piglet? . . . It means Learning, it means Education, it means all the things that you and Pooh haven't got" (85). Eeyore is here given the role of the authoritative adult who can debase the child entirely in his capacity of being literate, but the initial knowledge, and thus power, comes, not surprisingly, from Christopher Robin: "Christopher Robin said it was an A, and an A it is . . . " (85). Ironically, Eeyore's literacy has not gone beyond the first letter of the alphabet, and he, like the other characters, uses words he does not understand: "Christopher Robin . . . instigorates— I *think* this is the word he mentioned . . . he instigorates Knowledge" (87; emphasis in the original). In this chapter, Christopher Robin writes his first correct note, thus taking a definite step away from the innocence of childhood, from the Imaginary into the Symbolic. The author's message seems to be that however pleasurable, the Imaginary has to be left behind. The adult power from the "real" world finally catches up with the escapist child, in the image of spelling and multiplication tables, and the imminent departure to a boarding school. Unlike, for instance, Pippi Longstocking, Christopher Robin has nothing to defend himself against the attacks of the adult world. In the end, adult normativity wins.

Chapter Three
Othering the Genre:
Fantasy and Realism

Throughout my discussion of the *Harry Potter* books as a model text for children's literature I've pointed out that the fantastic mode in itself is a perfect alterity device. Within the non-mimetic modes, all other power hierarchies become less conspicuous because of the generic conventions. Yet unlike many other scholars I do not view fantasy as opposed to realism. Realism is an extraordinarily complex concept, as shown clearly in Erich Auerbach's *Mimesis* (1974); and although in the context of children's literature studies realism frequently equals a narrative devoid of supernatural elements, there is a broad variety of mimetic modes within children's literature that all have their specific othering strategies. Yet, also non-mimetic modes are of different kinds, and the degree and nature of the fantastic elements present a wide continuum. The term "magical realism" is a good illustration of the complexity of the concepts.

John Stephens, who identifies the distinction between fantasy and realism as "the most important generic distinction in children's fiction" (Stephens 1992, 7), describes fantasy in terms of metaphor and realism in terms of metonymy. While I can admit the legitimacy of this statement, I would claim that in many cases it is a matter of interpretation. All genres can be perceived as metaphorical or metonymical, depending on the level of the reader's sophistication. I therefore see no point in ascribing fantasy an a priori stronger potential for subversivity, but rather would like to consider the various genres as strategies for alterity.

Fantasy as Carnival

It is true that fantasy is the most common carnivalesque device in children's literature, as an ordinary child is empowered through transportation to a magical realm, through the possession of a magical agent (object or helper), and through the acquisition of a set of heroic traits or magical force, impossible or at least improbable within the existing order of things (what we normally call the "real world"). Carnival, reversing the existing order, elevates the fictional child to a position superior to adults. This view of a child as omnipotent is based on the Romantic idea of childhood as a time of innocence, before the evil of society exercises its influence. In most fantasy novels for young readers, there is a prophecy about a child who will overthrow the established order of an evil ruler. Yet, the inevitable reestablishment of order in the end of a carnivalesque children's story brings the characters down to levels at which they are only slightly more powerful than their environment, equal to—or inferior to it.

Notably, fantasy for children has always enjoyed a higher status within children's literature than fantasy in general literature where it is normally treated as formulaic fiction. Apparently, fantasy is considered suitable for children on the same premises as folk- and fairy tales, mostly as a socialization vehicle. The characters are supposed to learn something, to mature and in some cases come of age. Yet, paradoxically, the best examples of children's fantasy have always been questioned as books for children, such as *Alice in Wonderland* and *Winnie-the-Pooh*. This trend has culminated in the contemporary phenomenon of crossover, best illustrated by Phillip Pullman and J. K. Rowling.

Considering some principal differences between fantasy for children and fantasy for adults, it is not sufficient to state that the former has a child as protagonist. At its best, fantasy for children provides moral and spiritual guidance for young people, addressing an audience that has not yet discovered any firm distinction between reality and imagination; that does not dismiss magical worlds and events as implausible; that has stronger potential for secondary belief. While much of fantasy can be viewed as mere entertainment, the best examples of fantasy for children use the fantastic form as a narrative device, as a metaphor for reality. The fantastic mode allows children's writers to deal with important psychological, ethical, and existential questions in a slightly detached manner, which frequently proves more effective with young readers than straightforward realism. For instance, the battle of good and evil may be less disturbing, yet more persuasive when described within an imaginary world than in the reader's immediate surroundings. The spiritual growth of the protagonist can be presented more tangibly when depicted in terms of struggle with external magic forces than in terms of inner tension. In particular, fantasy can empower a child protagonist in a way that so called realistic prose is incapable of doing. In this respect fantasy has indeed a huge subversive potential as it can interrogate the existing power relationships, including those between child and adult, without necessarily shattering the real order of the world.

If we take a brief look back in history, fantasy for children, similar to children's literature at large, could not emerge until childhood was acknowledged as a separate and especially formative period in human life. However, while

Enlightenment primarily resulted in instructive works for young readers, Romanticism, with its interest for, on the one hand, folklore, and on the other, the child as primitive and untouched by civilization, provided rich soil for the first fantasy stories specifically published for children, even though marginal cases, such as George MacDonald's works, continued to appear.

E. T. A. Hoffmann's *The Nutcracker and the Mouse King* (1816) is internationally acknowledged as the first fantasy explicitly addressed to children, since the protagonist is a little girl, the point of departure is the nursery, and many characters are toys. The child is, however, instrumental in the story, which rather involves the animated toy, the Nutcracker, and his quest for the princess in the fairy land. The connection between the Nutcracker, an enchanted prince, and the enigmatic old man in the real world, is hinted at. Yet play and playfulness, associated with childhood, make this story different from Hoffmann's other fantastic novels, even though it carries many philosophical and ethical aspects far beyond a child's comprehension. Similarly, Carlo Collodi's *The Adventures of Pinocchio* (1881) with its puppet as the central character, has always been considered a story for children, despite its narrative and moral complexity. Its main thrust, however, lies fully along the lines of the primary purpose of early children's literature: to educate and socialize the child.

Edith Nesbit is frequently given credit as the creator of modern fantasy for children. Rather than sending her child characters into magical realms, Nesbit introduced magic into the everyday. She certainly brought enjoyment and comic into the genre; yet her main purpose remains educational and power-related. *Five Children and It* (1901), *The Phoenix and the Carpet* (1904), *The Story of the Amulet* (1906), *The Enchanted Castle* (1907), and *The House of Arden* (1908) feature magical agents (objects or creatures) that make mock of the children and demonstrate their inferiority as they prove incapable of controlling magic. Learning bitter lessons from their adventures, the children voluntarily give up their empowering implements. While this certainly provides a necessary closure of the plot, the message is a child's incompetence when encountering limitations and consistency of magic. In Pamela Travers's *Mary Poppins* (1934) and sequels, too, the magical agent (a true heir of Nesbit's Psammead, although superficially human) is arrogant and conceited, repeatedly reminding the children of her own superiority, not merely because of the magical abilities but in the first place as an adult. This power hierarchy between the adult author and the child protagonist and reader, is the foremost token of early twentieth-century children's fantasy. Empowered temporarily, the child protagonists are inevitably brought back into dependency upon the adults.

A different strategy for power negotiations is maintained in L. Frank Baum's *The Wizard of Oz* (1900), a typical secondary-world fantasy. Dorothy finds herself in a foreign country where she performs deeds impossible in her everyday life in Kansas. Characteristically, she considers herself weak and powerless, as well as dependent on someone else's help. Her three companions, who can be interpreted psychoanalytically as three projections of her inner self, seek the three different qualities: brain, heart, and courage, which are exactly what Dorothy repeatedly reveals during the journey: she is clever, caring and brave, yet she believes that only an adult can send her back home, and as a very young child, she longs back home to the protection of her foster parents. What neither Dorothy nor the reader knows is that she from the first day in the land of Oz has the power to go back home unassisted: the silver shoes. It is hinted that the shoes have many wonderful qualities, and as the Wicked Witch of the West tries to get them from Dorothy, it should be obvious that they are an instrument of power, yet the secret of this power is promptly kept from Dorothy. She is further empowered by the Golden Cap that governs the Winged Monkeys, but she has to submit it to the Witch of the South in exchange for the secret of the silver shoes. Finally, as Dorothy is sent back to Kansas, she is stripped of her power (she loses her silver shoes during the flight), and we never learn whether she can use her newly gained insights. While in the land of Oz she was respected and even feared by adults, including Oz the Great and Terrible himself, as a powerful witch, in Kansas she returns to the position of a child and female, doubly oppressed.

C. S. Lewis's *The Lion, the Witch and the Wardrobe* (1950) presents a still stronger empowerment of ordinary children, literally transforming them into heroes. While Dorothy's victories over the two wicked witches are accidental, making her conscience free from the burdens of murder, Peter is supposed to participate in a real battle, including intentional killing. Further, Peter and his siblings are literally crowned in the end, thus occupying the highest possible position in the medieval world of Narnia. Yet their enthronement is tempo-rary: after many happy years of rule in Narnia, they are brought back to their own world, regress into their child shapes, and are apparently stripped not only of the power, but also of the wisdom they gained during their time-out in Narnia. From the sequels, it becomes clear that also Narnia goes back to normal order where rulers are adults (and without exception male). In fact, the very first king in Narnia, crowned by Aslan, was an adult, Frank the cabby in *The Magician's Nephew* (1955).

One of the recent examples of a fantasy story where adult normativity is endorsed in every detail, without ever questioning it, is the post-Harry Pot-ter novel that for a short time threatened to acquire the Potter-size hysteria worldwide: *Shadowmancer* (2004) by G. P. Taylor. In this so-called Christian fantasy the two child protagonists blindly obey the adults telling them what to do; by the author's will they get into contact with the good forces first; otherwise they probably would as blindly follow the orders of the dark side. The adults come to rescue whenever the situation seems hopeless; and when the male protagonist hears the true voice of God, he responds by promising to always follow and obey. Thus the highest authority—adult and male—not only deprives the child of free will, independence of mind, and the ability to distinguish between good and evil, but demands total obedience and faith. The Christian church has always been aware of the power of literature, and in this case, the promoters of the novel have used the label of "a Christian reply to Harry Potter" to manipulate the readers.

The Power of Time

Time-shift fantasy would seem to have strong potential for subverting aetonormativity. Time travelers, endowed by historical knowledge, gain supremacy over adults, yet frequently, for instance in Nesbit's *The Story of the Amulet*, lack power to make use of their knowledge. Moreover, the narrator repeatedly ridicules her protagonists' inadequate education, thus exercising adult power over the young characters. Adults are also used, in Nesbit's works as well as in her successors', to explain the nature of time to ignorant children.

In many later time-shift novels, the device empowers the protagonists allowing them to explore their identities through time displacement. On the other hand, time dislocation can disempower the protagonists and become highly traumatic, as they are lost in the past, uncertain whether they will be able to return to their own time, and as their own time seldom holds the promise of anything enjoyable, they often consider staying in the past. The strong involvement in the past and the emotional bands with people in the distant epoch produce a disturbing effect. For instance, the young protagonist of Philippa Pearce's *Tom's Midnight Garden* (1958) discovers that his nightly excursions into the past are caused by an old woman's nostalgic memories. The focus is thus transferred from a child's experience of a remote epoch to an adult's fear of ageing and death.

Time displacement can be directly connected with power, when history, rather than a personal experience, becomes the authorities' way of manipulating the masses. In Diana Wynne Jones' *A Tale of Time City* (1987), a totalitarian regime is described, represented by a structure outside of history where a chosen minority has not only the material privileges, including slaves, but also the knowledge and experience of all human history, from Stone Age to Depopulation, the latter implying humanity leaving the unsustainable Earth for other planets and stars. The citizens of Time City import everything to satisfy their needs from history, in exchange for intellectual property. They benefit from extensive time tourism and collect every rarity in human civilization. They are contemptuous toward the inhabitants of history, and the worst punishment in their society is to be exiled into history. At the same time, the best minds and talents are recruited from various historical periods, occasionally to be planted back and introduce ideas far ahead of the time, "to make sure Science goes the right way" (132). The language of Time City is Universal. The rulers hide behind roles and titles such as Sempitern, and streets and buildings have intimidating names such as Chronologue, Annuate Palace, Continuum, Perpetuum, Aeon Square and Pendulum Gardens. The highest authority is Time Council. Time Patrol monitors all movement in time. Observers are planted in history to report back to Time City.

The sovereigns of Time City do not perform reality changes, as, for instance, is the case in Isaac Asimov's science fiction novel *The End of Eternity* (1955), but on the contrary, strive to maintain history as stable as possible. They have succeeded in most centuries and millennia, called Fixed Eras, but there are still Unstable Eras, not only the uncivilized pre-twenty-fourth century, but several other periods of decline of civilization, referred to as Dark Ages. Time City has no control over Unstable Eras, but aspires strongly to gain such control: " . . . we need the Unstable Eras to stay just as they are in order to keep the Fixed Eras steady" (172). On closer consideration, the policy adds up to the well-being of the ruling elite. Vivian, the protagonist, contemplates: " . . . learned people in Time City kept watch on the rest of history and tried to push it into behaving the way Time City wanted" (79). Yet the text lets one of the rulers state: "We will not sacrifice the art of the seventies nor deprive the Hundreds of their expansion to the stars" (84). When the seventies are referred to here it does not mean the 1970s, but the span of time between the years 7000 and 8000, merely a passing moment to Time City dwellers.

To indicate the instability of the multiverse, the text signals from the very first page that Vivian's history is different from the one we readers know, since World War II begins on Christmas 1938. The distorted and de-familiarized reality is clarified later in the novel, as the start of the war rolls back, causing upheaval in the rest of the temporal continuum. For instance, World War I has merged with the Boer War. Not unexpectedly, the authorities of Time City are most concerned that "several major inventions" (presumably nuclear fission) are made in the 1940s rather than in the twenty-third century. In passing, an unexpected volcano eruption in 79 AD near Pompeii is mentioned as a backwards effect.

Time City is not permanent, but has its own temporal existence, moving in a giant circle from creation to destruction. This view of universe reflects contemporary scholarly concepts of time, especially the ongoing controversy on finite versus infinite universe. At the moment of Vivian's accidental arrival, Time City is on the verge of destruction, and it would seem that the rulers are at any price trying to preserve the order. As it turns out, the fall of Time City is predicted and inevitable, but it is supposed to be resurrected so that a new Grand Circle, or Platonic Year, can commence. The task of the protagonist thus becomes ambivalent: her attempts to save Time City in order to be able to return to her own history in fact lead to its end. Vivian's involuntary support of the dictatorship follows naturally from her involvement in time.

Thus the novel probes into some fundamental ethical issues. The protagonist has a special mission; she is chosen, unique, and holds the very existence of repressive time structures in her hands. Vivian is actually the factor that has set history unstable; although it is never explained exactly why and how. Vivian is further highly dedicated to her family. Busy as she is with saving Time City, her thoughts keep going back to her parents: " . . . of Mum sitting in Lewisham with bombs dropping and history going wronger and wronger around her" (143). As she learns that the temporal disruptions can radically change the course of history, her worries are different from those of the rulers of Time City, concerned about the consequences somewhere in the thirty-fifth century and later. "If Time City broke down entirely, it could damage the rest of history horribly. In which case, what would become of Mum and Dad?" (251). Vivian is thinking about her parents and ultimately about herself. Her deepest fears are never uttered, but the line of argument prompted to the reader is something like: what if history changes so that my parents never meet, what happens to me, maybe I will never be born at all. The continuity and interconnectedness of history and the fortuity of our own existence is a disturbing thought. Thus the protagonist has private interests in resisting the regime, and her issues are connected with human condition, growing up. Death, the natural part of this cycle, although never spelled out, is hovering between lines.

Apart from the personal level, there is a societal and a moral one. Vivian's experience of history is close at hand, dramatic and engaging. She becomes displaced in time just as she is being dislocated in space, evacuated from air raids over London. War is a traumatic experience for a young child, since it shatters the customary order. Life becomes unstable, routines constantly change, every day brings new rules, future is uncertain and menacing, ordinary values such as human life are questioned, good and evil may trade places quickly as yesterday's allies become the enemy. The fantasy mode adds to the depiction of trauma, suggesting that Otherworld is a projection—in the Jungian sense, that is, externalization—of the protagonist's fears and anxieties in the shadow of war. The distortion going on in the continuum of time reflects the chaos in the young person's mind. Her internal images become concrete settings and people of Otherworld. The idea of time being non-linear and malleable—clearly a postmodern element—adds to the overall sense of insecurity.

It is not only the question of Vivian being physically dislocated, separated from her parents, sent to a relative she has never met, to the countryside that feels as strange to a London girl as the futuristic Time City. In Duration, which is the ingenious label for elementary school in Time City, Vivian's classmates, who have never been "in history," are curious to hear about war. To them, war is exotic and exciting. They envision battles and invasions, apparently prompted by costume movies. To Vivian, war is food rations, blackout curtains, anxiety and uncertainty. The authorities have thus withheld essential historical knowledge from their citizens, making them unaware of other people's concerns.

In her passionate accusation of Time City, Vivian bursts out:

> They are *not* history! They're real people! You people in Time City make me *sick* the way you sit here studying things. You never raise a finger to *help* anyone. This is all Time City's fault anyway! It was you that tinkered with history . . . (308; author's emphasis)

Behind this overt declaration lies the implied author's didactic project, following from conventions of children's literature; however, a child rather than a judicious adult is allowed to verbalize the judgment.

Moreover, the messiah in this novel is, again according to conventions, an ignorant and innocent child, and Faber John, the father figure, remarks in a rather self-assured manner: " . . . I had an idea that some children would arrive somehow in time for the renewal" (352). The superficial villains of the story are, not unexpectedly, two adults, plotting to usurp the rule over Time City. Their objectives are to multiply material wealth, which the regime has been doing all along, so it is merely a matter of redistribution. On closer look, the adult saviours, Faber John and Time Lady, the creators of Time City, turn out to be the true villains, cold, indifferent and cruel. The connection between the creator of Time City and Vivian is subtly emphasized by their names: Faber and Smith (which is explained in plain words for the benefit of young readers). The connection between Time Lady and Vivian is supplied by the confusion in the beginning of the novel, when Vivian is believed to be Time Lady, who can save Time City (Vivian is also one of the names of Merlin's treacherous beloved in the Arthurian cycle, an underlying layer of the novel). Yet Faber John's only concern is to build up Time City from its ruins and set up the order of the universe again. The restoration of Time City implies the restoration of the existing order. Faber is not the redeemer, but a returning tyrant, taking over from his provisional envoys. Although it is never said explicitly, Faber John and Time Lady are not much different from the evil couple, who intend to seize power in Time City for their own purposes.

The celebration scene in the final chapters is revolting in its depiction of victorious dictatorship, and here the author perhaps trusts her readers too much to assess the irony of the closure. Yet Vivian's fate prompts the reader's critical evaluation. Vivian cannot be reintroduced into her own history without disturbing it, since she was the source of disturbance in the first place. Faber John's wise decision is to banish her to an era sufficiently remote not to affect the subsequent flow of human history. Stone Age appears to be a suitable place of deportation. Vivian's parent substitutes in Time City, as well as her biological parents in the twentieth century, are allowed to accompany her.

In most of her works, Diana Wynne Jones accentuates an individual's inevitable surrender to the higher authorities, most prominently perhaps in *The Homeward Bounders* (1981). In this context, the ending of *A Tale of Time City* is discouraging, yet in a manner subversive. Vivian is a victim of totalitarian rule. She thus has strong incentive to resist oppression. Her emotional bonds with her own time are essential. As existing in time and history, we as readers can relate to her predicament.

Yet if dictatorship can be destroyed, it presumably can be restored, and Time City actually is. The seemingly satisfactory closure of the novel, the fall of totalitarian hierarchies, firmly tied to the protagonist's personal interests, serves, as in many literary works, as a warning. History can repeat itself, in or out of time.

Vivian has been manipulated in her protest against authority, yet the purpose of her revolt appears to be to secure the restoration of dictatorship.

Taking the Child's Side

Pippi Longstocking (1945) is one of the most convincing examples of unconditional child empowerment in children's literature. However, Pippi does not have to long or fight for power. From the start she is equipped with everything a child normally does not possess: strength, wealth, self-assurance, and independence, which enable her to challenge the social institutions and the individuals who cannot accept her status.

In *Pippi* books, adults are presented as ridiculous and hypocritical, including Tommy and Annika's parents and relatives, such as Aunt Laura, the ladies who come to the infamous coffee party, the schoolteacher, the police, the firemen, the circus and theater people, the fine gentleman who wants to buy Pippi's house and not least the notorious Miss Rosenblom. The author criticizes indiscriminately; respectable citizens and criminals, men and women fall under her ruthless judgment. The message seems to be that adults are inferior to children in intelligence and in every other respect, and therefore adulthood is nothing for children to look forward to. This is what many critics find offensive in the Pippi stories, failing to see the complexity of the issue.

It has been repeatedly pointed out that in *Pippi Longstocking* Astrid Lindgren takes the child's side. In fact, taking the child's side, lending out her voice to the silenced child and similar metaphors of power have been used to emphasize the author's unique position in writing for children. However, an adult author can no better wholly "take the child's side" than a white author can wholly take a black character's side or a male author wholly take a female character's side, and so on, as heterological studies make us aware of.

Pippi interrogates adult power and adult normativity in everything she does. Yet she does not in any way strive to overthrow the adult power, she merely mocks and ridicules it. In the end, the people of the little town are prepared to give Pippi the power, saying that they do not need police or fireman when they have Pippi. Pippi happily participates in the celebration of her courage and wit, but as to seizing power, she is the eternal child, who, like Peter Pan, prefers to play.

There are plenty of superficially carnivalesque elements in Pippi, including the circus, the theater, the time-out on the cannibal island, and the truly Rabelaisian gluttony. Yet, as a carnival figure, Pippi seems at first sight to be an exception. She is neither bestowed with power in the beginning nor stripped of it in the end. She is rich beyond the imagination of an ordinary child; she has no parents to obey, and she does not obey any other adult who tries to get control over her. Does then Pippi represent carnival made permanent?

The peculiarity of the carnivalesque nature of Pippi Longstocking is that Pippi herself is not affected by the carnival, but is herself the carnival factor that affects the lives and attitudes of two ordinary children, Tommy and Annika, and through them, the reader. Tommy and Annika, as well as the reader, know that Pippi is one-of-a-kind and that they can never be like her. They are not the strongest in the world, they are not rich, and they are not powerful. The temporality of their carnival implies that they are for a couple of years, supposedly the most formative years of their lives, exposed to the carnival factor represented by Pippi. But, then again, isn't Pippi a permanent carnival? I am inclined to interpret the ending of the novel as the affirmation of the necessity of growing up rather than the nostalgic longing back to the eternal childhood.

Unlike Pippi, Tommy and Annika will have to grow up. So will the young readers—and so they have, several generations of readers all over the world, inspired and enthused by Pippi, but not to misbehave, as many educators have feared, but to be critical, inquisitive and imaginative. Growing up is the central theme of children's literature, so also of all Astrid Lindgren's books. On different levels and to different degrees all her books reflect the traumatic passage from childhood to adulthood. The protagonists have everything in front of them, they have not yet matured, their trials are so far only play, make-believe, a test of bravery, honor, and kindness. They are still in the making. Probably this is the secret of Astrid Lindgren. Probably this is also the attraction of her books which we re-read as adults, since in them we find the promise of unrealized possibilities, if not for ourselves then at least for our children.

Together with Pippi, *Karlsson on the Roof* (1955) is perhaps Lindgren's most derisive book toward adults. Superficially, Midge has a happy, idyllic childhood. He knows neither hunger nor misery. He has both parents close at hand and two older siblings, who may tease him, but show support when necessary. His mother is just as perfect as a mother in an idyllic world should be: she comforts him with warm chocolate and fresh cinnamon rolls after he has been in a fight; she constantly has a cake in the oven. Midge perceives this as absolutely natural: mothers' task is to see to it that the child never lacks cake and cinnamon rolls. One could regard this as an obsolete gender stereotype; yet rather it is the child's view of his mother's function in his life.

Yet something is apparently missing from Midge's secure existence. He dreams of a dog—a recurrent motif in Astrid Lindgren's works. The dog, for instance, in a short story 'Best-Beloved Sister,' becomes a compensation for the adults' lack of attention. Waiting for a dog, the lonely and self-centered Midge consoles himself with a different kind of companion. Midge is a nice, well-behaved, submissive child, not in any way a naughty boy. He is fully socialized, that is, adapted to the norms that adult design for children. Among other things, these norms involve food and behavior toward food: what is to be eaten, when and how much. In order to compensate for his suppressed desires Midge invents a fantasy figure and transposes his own insatiable hunger for sweets onto this "reasonably stout man in his prime." The portrait of Karlsson matches exactly Bakhtin's concept of the grotesque body.

Karlsson thus represents a very young child who cannot control his nutrition needs. Although Karlsson superficially looks grown-up (he is created according to a child's image of the adults' superior power position), he lacks age and basically lacks gender, or at least sexuality connected with adulthood. Instead, his only satisfaction is, as for a very young child, the oral one. Food is an important power engine for Karlsson. For instance, he repeatedly cheats on Midge to get sweets, rolls and meatballs. His table manners are nonexistent. Instead, he accuses others for gluttony. In a central episode Karlsson pretends to be sick and orders Midge to cure him with cakes, cookies, chocolate and lollypops. Midge empties his piggybank to comply with his friend. The fact that Midge abides by all Karlsson's injustice supports the interpretation of the figure being a projection of the boy's own problems with adult rules. Midge spoils Karlsson exactly the way he wishes to be spoilt by his mother.

Karlsson is in other words Midge's reflection, and the mirror that the author holds in front of her character is Bakhtin's carnivalesque mirror that amplifies and distorts human traits to make them more tangible, while it also becomes liberating since it can be met with laughter. Midge soon learns to see through Karlsson—a projection of his own shortcomings—and feel ironic toward his desires, which means that Midge eventually has overcome his own problems and thus also his dependence on his mother's cakes and buns. When, in the end of the first volume, the parents are forced to admit that Karlsson is real, Midge has won his first battle against adult hegemony: they must acknowledge the child's equal rights to exist.

In one obvious way Karlsson is directly opposed to Pippi: Pippi prefers to give, Karlsson prefers to take. Yet there is another essential difference between the relationship of the children with their supernatural companions in these books. Pippi is not an imaginary friend; she is not created by a child's compensatory needs. Karlsson is an inferior child pretending to be an adult. Pippi is a superior adult pretending to be a child. Yet friendship with Karlsson both creates a sense of security in Midge and pushes boundaries for his submissiveness. Watching Karlsson playfully terrorizing Miss Bock, Midge tests the horrifying idea that he himself might be equally disrespectful toward an adult. Miss Bock is the evil (step)mother of the story, the mother who not merely neglects, but maltreats the child. Rather than providing Midge with cinnamon rolls, she prefers to eat them herself, locking Midge in his room. She openly admits that she loathes children. Karlsson, however, will not be intimidated, and his victory over the belligerent woman also becomes Midge's victory over the adult rule.

Everyday Carnival

John Stephens chooses to illustrate the idea of carnival, or time-out as he prefers to call it, exclusively by fantasy novels (Stephens 1992, 120–157). Yet obviously carnival is as much pertinent to the so-called realistic stories as it is to fantasy, even though the fictive child is empowered in a different manner. Like many children's literature heroes, Tom Sawyer in Mark Twain's *The Adventures of Tom Sawyer* (1876), is incredibly lucky to be an orphan (almost a sacrilege to state from a mimetic point of view, but a necessary condition for carnival) and to have an almost unrestricted freedom of movement. The two characters, Tom and Huck, are empowered by finding a treasure that immediately gives them a considerably higher social status. That Huck voluntarily rejects this elevation is another question.

Louis Sachar's *Holes* (1998) is a modern and original version of treasure-seeker theme, considerably harsher in its portrayal of society as well as more ambivalent in reflecting power structures. Twelve-year-old Stanley Yelnats is sent to a labor camp for a crime he has not committed; he is literally deprived of freedom and elementary human rights. He comes from an underprivileged environment: his father is a failed inventor, his mother a weak and confused homemaker. Stanley is obese, bullied in school and has no friends. In other words, he is from the start disempowered beyond measure. The narrator is quite ironical toward the practice of forced labor: "If you take a bad boy and make him dig a hole every day in the hot sun, it will turn him into a good boy. That was what some people thought" (5). Yet in Stanley's case he really benefits from being exposed to hard labor. He becomes better physically fit, he gets some friends, which he lacked in his previous life. To use a cliché, Stanley finds his identity through manual work. Ruthless as it is described, his imprisonment makes his situation more tolerable.

The camp itself presents a convincing and scornful miniature of power hierarchies in society. The Warden has absolute power; she forces the boys to do meaningless work, as it eventually turns out, for her own purposes. The counselors are a step beneath the Warden, but they in their turn have unlimited power over the boys; they can reward and punish as they please, and deny the young inmates food, drink, and other basic necessities. Among the boys, power relations of their own are created and fluctuate, as the humiliated and exploited become themselves exploiters. Stanley, for one thing, teaches another boy to read. Literacy is thus a power factor that Stanley has retained in his otherwise total denigration. In exchange, Stanley makes Zero dig his holes for him, exercising whatever power he has. On the other hand, X-Ray, the leading boy, can make other boys work for him by the mere power of his authority. The Warden encourages this reproduction of power and oppression since it suits her aims and creates animosity and competition between the inmates.

In a parallel plot, we are allowed to follow the fate of Stanley's great-grandfather, a poor Jewish boy who comes to the country of his dreams, the USA, seeking his fortune. Stanley happens to be exactly in the same place where his forefather once was robbed by a female robber. He finally finds the treasure chest which once belonged to his great-grandfather, with all the necessary documents, so that the family can engage a good lawyer, buy a luxury home in California and live happily ever after. This elevation of the protagonist feels quite implausible if we read the novel mimetically, but on a symbolic, carnivalesque level it shows the supremacy of adult values, such as wealth and respectable societal status. Rather than showing the empowerment of the child in his own right, the novel incorporates him in the existing order of adult norms.

Running away from home is another carnivalesque strategy applicable in non-fantastic narratives. It is tentative and an innocent prank in *The Adventures of Tom Sawyer*, but fully developed and a matter of life and death in *The Adventures of Huckleberry Finn* (1884). Tom is thus, with this particular motif, empowered temporarily, and indeed his carnival fails as he feels homesick and miserable on the island. As a young child, Tom is not yet ready to challenge the power of family, school and society at large. Huck, on the contrary, not only interrogates society by voluntarily abstaining from his sudden wealth, but also promptly rebels against parental authority. In its central conflict, the novel plays out a significant question of power. Jim is inferior to Huck as a runaway slave, and Huck is very much aware of it, preparing to exercise his power to turn Jim in. At the same time, Jim is superior to Huck in terms of age, experience and also meekness and conciliation, which Huck acknowledges and makes his moral choice. Unlike Tom, Huck does not return to the security of home, and his carnival turns into a true rite of passage. His newly won insight will never again allow him to see slavery as a normal condition, which makes him at least ethically superior to the adults around him. This is obviously a more subtle way of empowerment than finding a treasure.

In children's mystery books, the young heroes are smarter than the adults and are allowed by the authors to be in the right place at the right time, several steps ahead of the adults. Mystery novels for children empower the protagonists by letting them succeed where real detectives fail. Although devoid of supernatural features, mystery novels are no more realistic than the most incredible fairy tales, and the young heroes are far from ordinary. Indeed, they excel in everything: the ability to drive cars and fly airplanes, have quick brains, intuition and observation aptitude; can perform chemical analyses, operate obscure machinery, and find their way around without maps or compass; they come out safe from the most dangerous situations.

Perhaps unexpectedly, the somewhat despised genre of horse and pony stories carries enormous subversive potentials. The stable creates a perfect carnivalesque situation in which girls are allowed to be everything that normally contradicts female stereotypes: strong, enterprising, independent, competitive, while at the same time retaining their traditionally feminine traits as caring and emotional. The carnival nature of pony books explains their popularity among young female readers. The question is, however, whether readers of mystery novels and pony books are empowered along with protagonists. Nancy Drew is a supergirl, and most readers will presumably realize that she is not a credible character if we apply criteria of realism. The heroine of a pony book is closer to the recognizable everyday world, but why does she always win competitions, tame the wildest beast and is allowed to keep her favorite by receiving an unexpected gift from a rich relative? Narratives based on serendipity are seldom fully plausible; yet more importantly, serendipity as such is or at least can be, an empowering device.

Also in contemporary psychological novels children and young people are allowed to be cleverer, more sensible and more empathic than many adults. Yet the adult rules are valid even when the child is superior to adults, and the adult world takes ruthless revenge on the child. In book after book we see the authors' tribute to adult normativity. There are, however, exceptions, many of them in recent texts that are also, strictly speaking, not fully realistic. For instance, *Aldabra, or the Tortoise Who Loved Shakespeare* (2001), by the Italian writer Silvana Gandolfi, lies close to the tradition of Latin American magical realism in its subtle borderlines between the everyday and the fantastic—or perhaps simply the imagined. The novel has a literary allusion in the title, and it is used in the novel as a means of characterization. The title creates ambivalent expectations in the reader, since we do not normally associate tortoises with sophisticated reading tastes. At the least, the title sounds comical. More important, however, is how the plot connects to the archetypal pattern of shape-shifting, and further to the literary intertext of Kafka's *Metamorphosis*. Elisa, the protagonist and narrator of *Aldabra*, yet one more of those emotionally abandoned children of contemporary children's literature, gradually discovers that her grandmother is changing. First her daily habits are affected; then her body starts transforming, she goes on all fours, eats raw cabbage, grows a shell on her back; finally she loses the ability of speech. One day Elisa realizes that Granny is turning into a giant tortoise. The transformation is treated in a matter-of-fact manner, but for Eliza it means not only overcoming her own anxiety, but feeling superior to the adult world. Not surprisingly, the girl's mother does not believe her accounts of Granny's transformation, but sharing the secret and taking care of Granny gives Eliza's life a meaning. Granny is the wise old woman of the myth, and such women were often known to have the skills of shape-shifting and transgressing the limits of human existence. The figure of Granny acquires much grander proportions and offers interpretations that would perhaps escape us at a more superficial reading. Trying to collect as much information about the species Eliza learns that tortoises live for many hundred years. Metaphorically, then, Granny's transformation can be interpreted as the girl's reconciliation with Granny's imminent death.

In Guus Kuijer's *The Book of Everything* (2005) the protagonist's father is a horrible tyrant who not only imposes strict rules on his wife and children, but does not stop at hitting them. The nine-year-old Thomas is mortally scared of his father, but gradually learns to interrogate his authority, and with some help from both adults and other children finally causes his total defeat. Significantly enough, there is a figure in the novel similar to Granny in *Aldabra* in her role of the wise woman. She is in fact believed to be a witch, but both the character and the reader are left to make their own inferences whether the seven plagues she sends on the Thomas's father are real witchcraft, a coincidence, or the product of wishful thinking. Thomas is, unlike Pippi Longstocking, not the strongest boy in the world, but his special gift is seeing things that aren't there, that is, having powerful imagination. He also finds strength and inspiration in reading. Three other children's books are mentioned in *The Book of Everything*—and one non-children's book. The latter is the Bible, which the father states is the only true book, while all other books, including those children are assigned to read at school, are false. The children's books, that the witch neighbor gives Thomas to read, are *Emil and the Detectives*, by Erich Kästner, and *Sans Famille*, or *The Foundling*, by Hector Malot. Neither the author nor the adult character comment on the choice, but the protagonist contemplates why he has been given the books. He realizes that both books are about lonely children, children that have to cope on their own; books that encourage him not to be afraid. The third book is a collection of nonsense verses by the Grand Old Lady of Dutch children's literature, Annie M. G. Schmidt, that apart from their role in the narrative itself, also demonstrates the liberating effect of reading for pleasure as compared to the boring Bible recitations by the father. Kuijer thus depicts a competent child, whose moral and intellectual strength wins over the adult's physical superiority. When asked what he wants to be when he grows up, Thomas says that he wants to be happy. In some way, this is a proper dialogical reply to the affirmative ending of *Pippi Longstocking*.

Chapter Four
Othering the Child:
George MacDonald's Fairy Tales

In my introductory remarks and in the previous chapters, I have discussed how writers can empower and disempower fictive children through the use of the fantastic mode. As I have shown, *Alice in Wonderland* is one of the texts in which the child is threatened and humiliated. George MacDonald was one of Lewis Carroll's contemporaries and personal friends, and their works which ostensibly address young readers have many traits in common, not least in their treatment of power positions. In this chapter, I aim to look into some strategies of alterity in MacDonald's texts and consider the synergy of their impact on our perception.

In his statement about the use of fantastic mode MacDonald's foremost thesis was that fairy tales and fantasy are like music in which form is more important than meaning (MacDonald 1984). His choice of mode and genre was thus conscious and deliberate, a strategy aimed at the utmost estrangement of the experience of the fictive characters from that of the narratee and the implied reader, may it be adult or young.

In MacDonald's adult fantasy novels, *Phantastes* (1858) and *Lilith* (1895), there are two worlds, the "real" fictional world of the protagonists/narrators and the dreamworld, or Faerie world, which they enter in a variety of ways. In Tzvetan Todorov's classification of non-mimetic writing (Todorov 1973), MacDonald's adult fantasies would fall within the category of the pure fantastic, since neither the characters nor the readers can ever be certain whether the events described are actually happening or are the products of the characters' imagination, dreams, hallucinations or nightmares. The fantasies have often been called "dream romances," and their events and images have been treated either allegorically (Prickett 1979) or psychoanalytically (Jackson 1981).

Most of the fairy tales, ostensibly addressed to children, are less ambiguous; marvelous in Todorov's sense. As soon as the central characters are princesses, the detached fairy-tale chronotope is evoked. 'The Light Princess' opens in the

conventional fairy-tale topos "Once upon a time"[1] and an imaginary kingdom, a convention that the narratee is supposed to share. The original context
of this particular story, the adult novel *Adela Cathcart* (1862), allows the narrator and the narratees to interact, and at one point the narratee comments on
the credibility of the story. The setting is thus firmly removed from the narratee's experience. Similarly, 'The Giant's Heart' begins: "There was once a giant
who lived on the borders of Giantland ..." (81). Time, place and the supernatural character create a sense of detachment, similar to Mikhail Bakhtin's
description of the folktale chronotope (Bakhtin 1981c, 149ff). In 'Cross Purposes,' there is a borderline between the real and the magic world, that can be
traversed; yet the setting is again disconnected from the narratee:

> Once upon a time, the Queen of Fairyland, finding her own subjects far
> too well-behaved to be amusing, took a sudden longing to have a mortal
> or two at her court. (103)

In both cases, the story opens within the magic world, whereupon ordinary
children are brought into it. In 'The Giant's Heart' Tricksey-Wee merely walks
into Giantland, looking for her lost brother, a well-known folktale motif. The
crossing of the border is only marked by the change in size of the man-made
objects: the giantess's thimble is as big as a bucket for Tricksey—an echo from
Gulliver's Travels and anticipating *Alice in Wonderland*.

In 'Cross Purposes' the narrator states that "[n]o mortal, or fairy either,
can tell where Fairyland begins and where it ends. But somewhere on the borders of Fairyland there was a nice country village" (104). To bring mortals
into Fairyland, messengers, or magic agents, are necessary, and the passage for
both main characters is through water—perhaps an allusion to Charles Kingsley's *Water Babies* (1863); more likely an archetypal image. In this fairy tale,
the temporal principle is introduced which many twentieth-century fantasy
writers, beginning with Edith Nesbit, adopted: the principle that the adventure in Fairyland does not take any of the primary time: " ... Alice ran in the
back way, and reached her own room before any one had missed her" (119).
This is not really consistent with the earlier statement that she and Richard
have grown up in Fairyland; but this can be interpreted metaphorically, as
spiritual and mental growth. The temporal pattern is otherwise the reverse of
that in folktales, in which the hero spends three, alternatively seven days with
the fairies, only to discover on return that thousands of years have passed in
his own world. When Diamond in *At the Back of the North Wind* (1871) feels
that he has been at the back of the North Wind " ... years and years ... a
hundred years ... " (104), only seven days have passed in his real world. By
suggesting that Fairyland has its own temporal as well as spatial dimension,
the text enhances the sense of estrangement.

'The Golden Key' is slightly different from the other short fairy tales since
it does not as explicitly place the narrative at a distance, but on the contrary,

makes it sound commonplace: "There was a boy who used to sit in the twilight and listen to his great-aunt's stories" (120). The twilight, however, suggests the liminal state, just as other similar topoi such as solstice, midsummer or midwinter. The liminality is immediately confirmed by the precision of the setting, which we recognize from MacDonald's other fairy tales: " . . . their little house stood on the borders of Fairyland" (120). There seems to be no marker between the worlds, yet Fairyland is distinct from the boy's real world since things work differently in it, such as the rainbow is clearly more solid. Unlike 'Cross Purposes,' this fairy tale does adhere to the traditional temporal pattern: while Tangle feels she has only been away from home a short time, three years pass in her own time; and while wandering through Fairyland, both Tangle and Mossy grow up and age, only to be rejuvenated in the bath offered by the Old Man of the Sea. Growing up and growing old is presented as a reversible process; or the magical bath can be viewed as a ritual death and rebirth. At the same time, this is the only fairy tale with a linear plot: rather than returning to their own world, the characters go further on to the country whence the shadows fall, and, the narrator adds, "by this time I think they must have got there" (144).

At the Back of the North Wind is obviously the most reality-based of MacDonald's fairy tales. Except for the episodes with North Wind, it is a realistic story much in Dickens' style, full of misery and social injustice. With its supernatural elements, it could be perceived as genuinely fantastic in Todorov's sense, since the young protagonist truly feels hesitation as to the nature of his experience:

> . . . he could hardly believe it himself when he thought about it in the middle of the day, although when the twilight was once half-way on to night he had no doubt about it, at least for the first few days after he had been with [North Wind]. (47)

Here again twilight is the liminal topos in which the fantastic becomes believable. The narrator never expresses any doubt, explicitly or implicitly, that Diamond's experience is real; yet nobody except Diamond can see North Wind or hear her voice, thus the experience seems to have no objective truth to it—within the frames of the fictive topos of course, and the narrative rather falls into the category of uncanny. Diamond's initial flights over London and to the sea with North Wind are, from the objective, outside viewpoint, his dreams or perhaps daydreams, which is amplified by North Wind's words: "you must go to bed first. I can't take you till you're in bed. That's the law about the children" (53). Diamond's journey to the country behind the North Wind can be interpreted as his feverish hallucinations. The narrator states that "he could not quite satisfy himself whether the whole affair was not a dream which he had dreamed when he was a very little boy" (151). The hesitation sustains almost to the end of the story; after a long time has passed since Diamond has seen North Wind, he begins to mistrust once again: "So strong did this feeling become, that at last he began to doubt whether he was not in one of those precious dreams" (316). The inserted fairy tales are explicitly presented either as the characters' actual dreams ('Diamond's Dream,' 'Nanny's Dream') or as a hyponarrative ('Little Daylight').

Princess Irene in *The Princess and the Goblin* (1872) also feels recurrent doubts about the nature of her encounters with her great-great-grandmother: "Sometimes she came almost to the nurse's opinion that she had dreamed" (32); "'Then it must all be a dream,' said Irene. 'I half thought it was; but I couldn't be sure. Now I am sure of it'" (76); " 'Please, I thought you were a dream'" (81); "even now she could not feel quite sure that she had not been dreaming" (95); "She grew frightened once more, thinking, that . . . the old lady might be a dream after all" (100). Since nobody can see the grandmother except Irene, just as nobody can see North Wind, it is natural to interpret the beautiful spinning-lady as a product of Irene's imagination and thus classify the story as uncanny. (We can also perceive her as an allegory, which in Todorov's view totally disqualifies the text as fantastic). However, in the sequel, *The Princess and Curdie* (1883), the young miner is also given the privilege of meeting the grand Progenitrix, the subjective experience thus giving way for a more objective one, and the narrative leaning toward marvelous rather than uncanny.

In any case, the choice of mode is the foremost way of estrangement, since the characters are always honored in being able to transcend the border of Otherworld.

Child in the Focus

The second strategy I would like to explore is the choice of child protagonists. The fairy tales have been generally classified as addressed to children, most likely since the fairy-tale genre was (as it still is) erroneously connected with children's literature, and no controversy similar to the status of *Alice in Wonderland* has occurred around them. In the adult fantasies, adult protagonists are employed, while the fairy tales portray children. In this, MacDonald is not different from many other Romantic fantasy writers; for instance, his German model E. T. A. Hoffmann, whose *Nutcracker* is considered as written explicitly for children, while all his other works are addressed to adults; or the numerous Russian Romantic writers, who wrote for both audiences. In all these cases, the plots are somewhat similar, preferably featuring a quest, often combined with mysterious, weird experience. The difference lies not so much in the complexity, but in the adult issues, not least the erotic ones. It is sufficient to compare the innocent world of toys in *Nutcracker* and the eerie world of automatons in *The Sandman*.

Among MacDonald's works, especially *Lilith* has distinct erotic subtones. It is, however, problematic, as always, to decide whether certain stories have been perceived and thus marketed as children's stories because they have young protagonists, or whether the author consciously addressed the young audience and therefore chose protagonists of suitable age ("my child readers"). Using a child protagonist as a symbol of innocence is the very essence of Romantic tradition, as is the close association of childhood and imagination. Yet can it also be that MacDonald, after the experience of writing *Phantastes*, chose child protagonists to avoid or circumvent the inevitable erotic aspects of dream narratives? In fact, in 'The Light Princess' the protagonist is seventeen, of marriageable age, and indeed the story has quite explicit erotic scenes. On the other hand, Anodos in *Phantastes* is twenty-one, and Mr. Vane in *Lilith* has "just finished [his] studies at Oxford"; thus the difference is not that great.

The age of the children in 'Cross Purposes' is not stated, but as they fall in love with each other, the sexual aspect is immediately added. It is then explicitly stated they "seemed to have grown quite man and woman in Fairy-land" (119), which is reminiscent of the ending of Hans Christian Andersen's *The Snow Queen*. Also Tangle and Mossy in 'The Golden Key' are children at the beginning of the story; Tangle is ten years old as she starts from home and age thirteen as she arrives at the fairy's cottage: the change is significant since she is then a young woman rather than a little girl. At the end of the story, after having grown old and then young again, the characters are definitely adults. Princess Irene is eight "at the time my story begins" (*The Princess and the Goblin* 11), says the narrator, and continues: "but she got older very fast" (12). Curdie is twelve and, and as a working-class boy, he almost counts as an adult. It is never mentioned explicitly how old Diamond is, but the narrator points out that Nanny, who earns her living by sweeping crossings, "was not really a month older than he was; only she had to work for her bread, and that so soon makes people older" (*North Wind* 45). In a coachman's family, a boy would likely be sent to earn his living by the age of seven, although probably not to drive a coach on his own, as Diamond eventually does. Everybody seems to think that he is too young to work.

Since the narrator lets several characters repeatedly, in a variety of ways, suggest that Diamond is a halfwit, and also demonstrates the boy's naïve way of reasoning, the character is created as superficially inferior to his surrounding, what Northrop Frye calls ironic (Frye 1957). At the same time, Diamond's extreme goodness, kindness, intrinsic wisdom and impeccable morals give him almost mythic dimensions, and the privilege of having been at the back of the North Wind, whatever meaning we may put into this assertion, makes him indeed exceptional. He is repeatedly referred to as a "God's baby," which, even stripped of its direct Christian meaning, suggests a common belief in the parity of madness and sanctity. Dostoyevsky's Prince Myshkin is a good example; yet in Diamond's case, his being a child adds an overall sense of innocence to the image. No matter how the readers perceive and interpret the protagonist, the subjectivity offered by the text is indisputably displaced from Diamond.

The author here uses the child as a symbol, or archetype, in the Jungian sense; as a bearer of ideology and ethics rather than a human character. Not surprisingly, then, he eventually gives Diamond a slightly more earthbound adult double, Mr. Raymond, who is a poet, even though he has not been at the back of the North Wind. Here, Diamond's sacrosanct insanity is equalled with the adult's creativity. Mr. Raymond recognizes this, saying: "'I suspect the child's a genius . . . and that's what makes people think him silly'" (186). In 'Diamond's Dream,' his celestial origin is hinted at, which puts him in the long row of "alien children," once again going back to E. T. A. Hoffmann and his second children's book, *Das fremde Kind* (1818). In other words, Diamond is a magic agent in a plot that, paradoxically, lacks a hero, unless we can count the little sweeping-girl Nancy, whom he helps, as a hero. Alternatively, Mr. Raymond or indeed the anonymous narrator can be interpreted as the true protagonists of the novel, while Diamond is their "inner child."

It has been repeatedly pointed out that MacDonald claimed to have a special power of addressing children, the notorious "for the childlike" (McGillis 1992); however, we need yet to take a closer look at the texts to decide whether there is indeed a single child address in them. Rather they offer, as most contemporary works, double address in which adult co-readers can find levels of meaning to their own satisfaction, whether allegorical or psychological. The texts definitely do not employ the dual address, or "the twentieth-century voice," characteristic of MacDonald's close successor Edith Nesbit (Wall 1991). The texts never descend to the child's level of perception, never take the child's side. The child in the fairy tales is and remains "the other," the perfect image of lost and irretrievable purity. We can of course maintain that some stories, not least 'The Light Princess,' do involve the dilemma of growing up and acquiring gravity in more than one sense, thus prefiguring *Peter Pan*. Yet the adult experience is treated in a casual fairy-tale manner similar to "happily ever after," in 'The Light Princess' somewhat more elaborate: "the prince and princess lived and were happy, and had crowns of gold, and clothes of cloth, and shoes of leather, and children of boys and girls" (53).

Whatever the reason for choosing child characters, they are narrated from an unequal power balance, whether the opposition is simply: adult–child, or the more intricate and psychologically complex: experience–innocence. While the literal point of view in, for instance, *The Princess and the Goblin*, might be that of Irene, the narrator persistently refers to her as "the little princess" and mentions her "little head" (19), or "little feet" (80), a typical example of talking down to children, which immediately creates a discrepancy between the "childlike" point of view and the adult, detached voice (similarly to the use of the word "child" about Tangle as well as Diamond and Nanny). In this, MacDonald is no different from any other writer for children. What can differ is the degree in which the adult writers manage to subvert their own power position and empower the fictive child. It seems that MacDonald has no intention whatsoever of being subversive in this respect. The subjectivity of his texts lies firmly with the adult narrator, and child characters are merely instrumental to his purposes.

The Narrator and the Character

This leads to the next aspect, that of narrative perspective. In adult fantasies MacDonald chooses personal narration, which brings their experience as close to the reader as can be. In the fairy tales, by contrast, the narration is, like in most nineteenth-century children's books, what normally is called impersonal, or third person. I say "normally," since the narrator frequently makes himself explicitly present in the text as a voice, and, in *At the Back of the North Wind*, even makes the child protagonist's acquaintance. Yet, this apparent metafictional trait rather enhances the distance between the narrator and the narratee. Although appearing in flesh and blood in Chapter 35 of the story, the anonymous "I" has otherwise all the features ascribed to the omniscient narrator of the traditional fairy tales. Let us consider the famous beginning of the book:

> I have been asked to tell you about the back of the North Wind. An old Greek writer mentions a people who lived there . . . My story is not the same as his. I do not think Herodotus had got the right account of the place. I am going to tell you how it fared with a boy who went there. (7)

First of all, the narrator has a clear and self-confident voice, and he claims to have knowledge and authority beyond the ordinary. The source of his information is Diamond, who by all means should be perceived as unreliable. When Diamond eventually gets to the country at the back of the North Wind, the narrator admits his incapacity to deal with it:

> I have now come to the most difficult part of my story. And why? Because I do not know enough about it. And why should I not know as much about this part as about any other part? for of course I could know nothing about the story except Diamond had told it; and why should not Diamond tell about the country at the back of the North Wind, as well as about his adventures in getting there? Because, when he came back, he had forgotten a great deal. And what he did remember was very hard to tell. (96)

At this point, in Chapter 10, the narrator has yet not disclosed how he has gained access to Diamond's story, saying that "Diamond never told these things to anyone but—no, I had better not say who it was, but whoever it was told me" (99). As it turns out, the mysterious person is the narrator himself, which, however, is not revealed until almost the very end of the story. Seeing Diamond's lifeless body, the narrator concludes: "They thought he was dead. I knew he had gone to the back of the North Wind" (332). As the narrator by this time has established himself as homodiegetic, that is, a material part of his own fictive world, we can only perceive this statement as his belief, not as an ultimate truth. However, also the less perceptible narrator of 'The Golden Key' concludes his story by a supposition about the fate of his characters. This ambivalent position of the narrator contributes to the complexity of some of the stories.

In most of the fairy tales the narrator is straightforwardly omniscient and shifts easily between the characters, including the evil ones, for instance, the bad fairy in 'The Light Princess,' revealing her wicked plans of draining the lake. The narrator emphasizes his exclusive omnipresence by saying: "If any one had followed the witch-princess, he would have heard her unlock exactly one hundred doors" (41). He can enter people's minds: "I cannot tell whether Diamond knew what she was thinking, but I think I know (*North Wind* 116); or "[Mr. Raymond] had meant to test Joseph when he made the bargain about Ruby" (291). As omniscient, the narrator can see into the future, in form of prolepses, for instance, the explanation why princess Irene is not allowed to go out after dark: "they had good reasons, as we shall see by and by" (*The Princess and the Goblin* 14); or "when I have informed [my readers] concerning what Curdie learned the very next night, they will be able to understand" (50).

Omniscience also includes omnipresence and effortless switching between different places of action: "And now I will go back to the borders of the forest" (123); "Meanwhile Mossy had got out of the lake . . . " (141); "Now while [Diamond] is lying there, getting strong again with chicken broth and other nice things, I will tell my readers what had been taking place at his home, for they ought to be told it" (*North Wind* 109); "Diamond set off, never suspecting that the policeman, who was a kind-hearted man, with children of his own, was following him close . . . " (178).

The narrator repeatedly underscores his authority that enables him to have access to knowledge unattainable to other mortals: "nobody even knew she was a fairy, except the other fairies" (*North Wind* 227). While this is the common convention of fictionality, the narrator accentuates his special knowledge of events, such as: "Once upon a time, so long ago that *I have quite forgotten the date*" (15; emphasis added); as well as characters, as in the description of the evil fairy: "What [her eyes] looked like when she loved anybody, I do not know; for I never heard of her loving anybody, but herself" (16). On the other hand, the statement "I may here remark that it was very amusing to see [the princess] run" (24) creates a sense that the narrator is corporeally present at the events described, which contradicts the setting of the story as "once upon a time". Similarly, when in *At the Back of the North Wind*, the narrator says: "It was great fun *to see* Diamond teaching [Nanny] how to hold the baby" (271; emphasis added), we may wonder whose literal point of view we are invited to share. It is exactly such tiny details that shatter the character-tied subjectivity.

In particular, the narrator almost boasts of his familiarity with the Fairyland and its ways. "I have seen this world—only sometimes, just now and then . . . —look as strange as ever I saw Fairyland. But I confess that I have not seen Fairyland at its best" (20). We may assume that the narrator has a first-hand experience of the Fairyland, similar to that of Anodos and Mr. Vane.

Occasionally the narrator accounts for this authority: "I refer any one who doubts this part of my story to certain chronicles of Giantland preserved among the Celtic nations" (85). The motif of a giant or ogre whose heart is preserved outside his body is common in folktales all over the world, so to an informed reader this statement may sound ironic.

There are quite a few typical features that the intrusive narrator shows. He is free to pass judgments on the character, such as: "She was, *indeed*, a very nice queen ... (15; emphasis added); "it was *no wonder* that her brother forgot her" (16); "[The princess] never could be brought to see the serious side of anything" (23); "She was perfectly obstinate" (29); "The *poor* princess nearly went out of *the little mind she had*" (39); "[Diamond] was not frightened, for he had not yet learned how to be" (*North Wind* 10); "[Diamond] thought he had been of no use to her. He was mistaken there" (44); "Mr. Raymond was one of the kindest men in London" (182); "she was as brave as could be expected of a princess her age" (*The Princess and the Goblin* 17), and so on.

Further, the narrator shows metafictional awareness of the genre, as he says: "Of course somebody was forgotten" for the christening in 'The Light Princess' (16). Interestingly enough, in 'Little Daylight' the narrator is just as conscious of the genre, as he comments: "I never knew of any interference on the part of a wicked fairy that did not turn out a good thing in the end" (228). Taken separately, the story may then seem to have exactly the same intrusive narrator as the other fairy tale; in its original context, Chapter 28 of *At the Back of the North Wind*, it is told by Mr. Raymond to the children at the hospital, so that the comment on genre has its very concrete narratees.

The narrator repeatedly employs direct address (or perhaps rhetorical questions): "poor relations don't do anything to keep you in mind of them. Why don't they? The king could not see into the garret [his sister] lived in, could he?" (16); or "What do you think she saw? A very old lady who sat spinning" (*The Princess and the Goblin* 19). Many of the similar remarks have the function of creating an intimate, conversational tone, quite common in nineteenth-century children's literature: "Now, as I have already said" (*North Wind* 9). Besides, the readers are invoked in phrases such as: "It is plain enough to every one of my readers" (*The Princess and the Goblin* 97); "lest my reader should have his qualms ... I venture to remind him" (*North Wind* 177); "My readers will not wonder that ... I did my very best to gain the friendship of Diamond" (312). One comment in *At the Back of the North Wind* is of a special significance for my purpose: "Now if any of my child readers want to know what a genius is—shall I try to tell them, or shall I not?" (186). The statement shows the narrator's distrust in—if not contempt toward a young audience, amplified on the following page: "And if you do not understand that, I am afraid you must be content to wait till you grow older and know more" (187).

Irony is yet another means of displacing the narrator's subject position toward the character's, and thus the reader's:

> Whether the prince was so near perfection that he has a right to demand perfection itself, I cannot pretend to say. All I know is, that he was a fine, handsome, brave, generous, well-bred, and well-behaved youth, as all princes are. (31).

Also the following comment on narration is obviously meant to be ironic: "I won't vouch for what the old horse was thinking, for it is very difficult to find out what any old horse is thinking" (*North Wind* 147). Here the omniscient narrator suddenly admits his limit, although, within genre conventions, it would not be more remarkable for him to enter the mind of a horse than to enter the mind of a fairy. In fact, Diamond is later allowed to overhear the two horses' conversation.

Every now and then the narrator takes pain to account for the events he is describing: "Her atrocious aunt had deprived the child of all her gravity. If you ask me how this was effected, I answer, 'In the easiest way in the world. She had only to destroy gravitation'" (17). This explanation would probably leave a child reader puzzled, but gives the narrative voice a quasi-authority. On the other hand, the narrator can state that he cannot explain how gravity worked for the princess: "The exact preposition expressing this relation I do not happen to know" (25); or "Whether this was owing to the fact that water had been employed as the means of conveying the injury, I do not know" (29).

The fairy tales are not free from didacticism common for the nineteenth-century children's literature (totally absent from MacDonald's adult fantasies). It may be a question of a single sentence, such as: " . . . the wearer of Grandmother's clothes never thinks how he or she looks, but thinks always how handsome other people are" (130) or "I have observed that the most wonderful thing in the world is how people come to understand anything" (*North Wind* 21); but also the whole account of Mr. Coleman's misfortunes in Chapter 12 of *At the Back of the North Wind* is a didactic sermon on virtue, as are reflections on self-praise in Chapter 16 and the story of the drunken cabman in Chapter 18.

Significant for the understanding of the narrator's function are his metafictional comments on the narrative process: "in her laugh there was something missing. What is was, I find myself unable to describe" (24); "How long they were in crossing this plain I cannot tell" (133); "It is quite impossible for me to describe what he saw" (*North Wind* 63); "I must not go on describing what cannot be described" (65); "What Mr. Raymond thought, I dare hardly attempt to put down here" (296); "I will not describe the varied feelings of the party" (296). Notably, the hypodiegetic narrator of 'Little Daylight' repeatedly uses the same formula as the main narrator: "I will not attempt to describe what they had to go through" (*North Wind* 230); "I shall not attempt to describe his misery" (239). Such statements may be used to inspire the reader's imagination, but they also remind us of the narrator's constant presence. On a deeper level, they convey a writer's frustration, which is more evident in the fantasies.

The most tangible illustrations of the narrator's awareness of his own narrative status are his repeated excuses for the liberties he takes with putting correct words to his young characters' experiences. Pondering on Diamond's memories of the country at the back of the North Wind, he says: "I do not

mean that he thought these very words. They are perhaps too grown-up for
him to have thought, but they represent the kind of thing that was in his heart
and his head" (*North Wind* 130). It is still more explicit in his dealing with
Nanny's hyponarrative:

> My readers must not suppose that poor Nanny was able to say what she
> meant so well as I put it down here. She had never been to school, and had
> heard very little else than vulgar speech . . . But I have been to school, and . . .
> it has made me able to tell her dream better than she could herself. (253)

This, if anything, reveals the narrator's superior position toward the
characters—as well as the readers, who ostensibly need an explanation of the
conventions of fictive discourse. On a more sophisticated level, the narrator
appeals to the child or the "childlike," who may not yet have mastered the language to perfection, and lends out his voice to those who lack a voice of their
own. Stephen Prickett calls MacDonald's struggle with language "a theologi-
cal activity" (Prickett 1979, 176) and concludes that for MacDonald the inadequacy of language to convey a metaphysical experience is the very essence
of fantasy. Jacques Lacan would refer to this dilemma as the tension between
the imaginary and the symbolic. MacDonald's endeavor is thus to translate
the imaginary into the symbolic, and as the imaginary is that of the child, the
mission implies estranging the child from its natural way of experience.

Yet it should be quite obvious from my discussion that the authoritative
adult voice has a significantly stronger effect than the child characters' point
of view. I do not see any invitation to child readers to participate in a dialogue
on equal rights (cf. Thacker and Webb 2002, 44). Instead, the texts are mono-
logically transmitted from the adult narrator to child narratees, whether overt
or covert.

Besides, it is far from always that child characters are used as focalizers,
and when they are, primarily external focalization is employed. Here it is
tempting to test my ideas about gender and alterity. One might expect that
the male author would be likely to reflect male protagonist's experiences more
profoundly.

Gender

The intriguing feature of the fairy tales is the alternative uses of male and
female protagonists, which is not as common as it may seem; in fact, statisti-
cally, male authors tend to choose male protagonists and female authors choose
female protagonists. If we consider some of MacDonald's contemporaries,
Charles Kingsley has a male protagonist in *Water Babies*, Mrs. Molesworth
has a female protagonist in *The Cuckoo Clock* (1877), while Lewis Carroll has a
female protagonist in the two *Alice* books. MacDonald's immediate successor,

Edith Nesbit, introduced the multiple protagonist, a group of girls and boys, a device successfully circumventing the issue of gender. In approaching Mac-Donald, I assumed that heterofocalization, the use of a focalizer of the opposite gender, would involve different narrative devices than homofocalization; that is, the female children would be narrated in a different manner than male. My hypothesis was thus that MacDonald chose female characters in order to still further distance the narrating agency from the experiencing one (once again, contrary to the established views).

In a psychoanalytical interpretation of heterofocalization (Veglahn 1987), evil figures in fiction are based on the author's subconscious perception of evil as being of the opposite gender, a clear case of gender-related othering. MacDonald is one of Veglahn's examples, alongside *Alice* books, *The Wizard of Oz* and the *Narnia* stories. She demonstrates further that to counterbalance the female monsters, male authors employ strong female characters, typically ascribed the Jungian function as the author's Anima. Far from subscribing to the psychoanalytical theory of literature, I nevertheless find Veglahn's patterns fascinating. Yet she has obviously neglected the fact that MacDonald employs both genders in his fairy tales (while deviating from Veglahn's model in the fantasies, at least as far as the protagonist is concerned). Veglahn's paradigm of male author—female monster—female protagonist fits, besides her own examples, the princess books, also 'The Light Princess' and 'Little Daylight.'

The North Wind is a monster in the Jungian sense, as a mysterious and ambivalent Other; however, she is at the same time the positive female principle, combining the Jungian archetypes of Anima and the Wise Old Woman. As to protagonist, Diamond is, at least superficially, male. This may seem a strange statement, as the character is definitely referred to as "a boy" and with the masculine personal pronoun; however, gender is a social construction, while fictive children are literary constructions; gender in fiction is part of characterization and can be constructed unrestricted by the limitations of biological sex. The gendered features ascribed to characters and their gendered behavior, or performance, are more important than their formal description as male or female.

Changing, by way of mental exercise or narratological commutative test, the protagonist's gender in *At the Back of the North Wind*, will clearly demonstrate that no other major changes would be required. Some subtle erotic hints might be lost; yet the magnitude of the North Wind as the image of death surpasses her possible erotic attraction (unlike the figure of Lilith). The story would be viable with a female protagonist. In fact, Diamond is an androgynous figure, described as possessing many feminine traits and performing in a feminine manner. The text supports the general perception of Diamond as effeminate by several direct statements:

> He never touched any of the flowers or blossoms, for he was not like some boys who cannot enjoy a thing without pulling it to pieces, and so preventing everyone from enjoying it after them. (50)

Also his surroundings perceive him as feminine, as the cabmen say: "You're a plucky one, for all your girl's looks!" (195).

The Princess and the Goblin can be viewed as a feminine version of *At the Back of the North Wind*, with Irene meeting the monster who is at the same time a mentor. Likewise, a boy can be substituted for Irene without the story needing other substantial revisions. One could possibly argue that the spinning symbolism, connected to the feminine, would be lost; however, since it works just as well with Curdie, it still would be valid. The children in MacDonald's fairy tales are more or less gender-neutral, generic "children" rather than boys and girls.

In the chapters in 'The Light Princess' where the princess acts as a focalizer, her experience is based on the external senses: sight, sound, and in the first place, touch. She is depicted by the narrator as enjoying her weightlessness or the touch of the water; however, her inner emotions are never portrayed. One might argue that external focalization is normal in the 19th-century children's literature, yet it would seem that the author of *Phantastes* should not have problems with entering a character's mind. The choice of external focalization must then be deliberate and serve an artistic purpose. I see the purpose as contributing to othering. Moreover, rather than looking, the princess is looked at—by the prince, and not least by the narrator, with the notorious male gaze as well as the Victorian child-eroticizing gaze. Objectification is one of the foremost indications of alterity. When the prince first meets the princess, the scene is explicitly voyeuristic:

> Looking over the lake, he saw something white in the water ... There was not light enough to show that she was a princess, but quite enough to show that she was a lady, for it does not want much light to see that. (32)

As the story progresses, the male rescuer—much like in traditional folktales—supersedes the female protagonist, sacrificing his life and becoming the hero. The Christian connotations of the sacrifice are obvious and have been repeatedly observed; and while some elements of parody are evident as well, the story turns out as a conventional female coming-of-age narrative in which the bewitched female waits for the right male to save her. In fact, the prince's emotions, presented through simple quoted monologue (44), at least allow a glimpse of his inner life, views and morals. The princess, even though she gains gravity, remains completely flat as a character. Much the same happens in 'Little Daylight.'

However, we may detect a similar strategy in the description of Diamond. On his journeys with North Wind, he is an observer: he looks, sees, or espies, but very seldom reflects on what he sees. When he is traveling north, the landscape is described in figural discourse, especially emphasized by the statement: "How long this lasted Diamond had no idea" (*North Wind* 89). But generally, Diamond is, as earlier proposed, an archetype rather than a real character.

The Princess and the Goblin suggests by its title that princess Irene is the protagonist, while the goblin is the antagonist (here I could argue with Nancy Veglahn whether the goblin queen is the main villain and the image of MacDonald's perverted perception of the opposite sex). Irene is focalized externally in slightly more than half of the chapters; the rest, with just a few exceptions, take on Curdie's point of view. Curdie has the helper function in the plot, but through focalization becomes almost as important as Irene. In the description of Irene's and Curdie's escape through the underground tunnels, the most dramatic episode of the story, the point of view is switched back and forth between them. In the sequel, Curdie overrules Irene and becomes the hero. Thus *The Princess and the Goblin* in practice features a multiple protagonist, that also appears in 'The Giant's Heart,' 'Cross Purposes,' and 'The Golden Key,' anticipating Edith Nesbit. However, while Nesbit most often has a group of children in the center (emphasized by such titles as *Five Children and It* or *The Railway Children*), MacDonald presents a cross-gender *actant* consisting of a boy and a girl.

'The Giant's Heart' features the sister and brother, with the significant names of Tricksey-Wee and Buffy-Bob, who largely perform as a single *actant* in the story. Tricksey has a more substantial and active role; yet in the many versions of the folktale, on which 'The Giant's Heart' is modelled, the trickster part can be played by a male as well as a female actor. In 'Cross Purposes' class opposition is added to the gender one, as Alice is the daughter of a squire, and Richard the son of a poor widow, a heterological conflict fully developed in *The Princess and the Goblin*. The pattern is common in folktales as well as popular romances of the time; class difference is emphasized by giving the children appropriate messengers who bring them to Fairyland: a pretty fairy for the girl and an ugly goblin for the boy. Although they initially get a chapter each, describing their separate passages into Fairyland, and although Alice is introduced first, she is in this fairy tale given the traditional role of the "princess" in Proppian sense, the object of the quest, devoid of agency, which is repeatedly emphasized as Alice bursts into tears while Richard comes with solutions, as well as statements such as: "he caught up Alice in his *strong arms*" (115; emphasis added). Richard also looks at Alice with "male gaze" as he discovers that he is in love. Prior to that, Alice has been presented, through the narrator's view, as spoilt and disagreeable. However, we get a glimpse of Alice's thoughts: "Can it be that I love the poor widow's son?" (115), and the two characters more or less amalgamate into one single actant with the common goal of getting back home.

The two children are equally objectified, presented as toys at the Fairy Queen's will. Their successful rite of passage notwithstanding, they are not united, but have to part, since class borders seem, unlike the borders of Fairyland, to be impenetrable. Instead, "[i]n reward of their courage, the Fairy Queen sent them permission to visit Fairy-land as often as they pleased" (119). This is an equivocal ending; as Fairy-land may stand for dreamland as well as the realm of the dead, the young lovers are promised that they can only be together in their imagination or in death. By adding two short paragraphs about the fate of the fairy Peaseblossom and the goblin Toadstool, the text definitely detaches its subject position from the young protagonists. In other words, the implied author feels quite indifferent about them and does not invite the reader's empathy either.

In 'The Golden Key,' contrary to 'Cross Purposes,' the male character is introduced first. As he finds the golden key, the reader is encouraged to perceive him as the hero of the story and share his subjectivity. Interestingly enough, this strategy is partially undermined as he initially does not have a name and thus has a very vague identity. At the same time, 'The Golden Key' comes conspicuously close to figural discourse, such as free indirect speech conveying the boy's ponderings upon the golden key: "Where was the lock to which the key belonged? It must be somewhere, for how could anybody be so silly as make a key for which there was no lock? Where should he go to look for it?" (122). Figural discourse creates a sense of intimacy and proximity to the character.

The female protagonist, who also initially has no name, is introduced as lacking agency, neglected and almost unpleasant, although the narrator stresses that it is not her fault. She is thus immediately put into an objectified position, and even though she is focalized externally, the omniscience of the narrator is constantly manifested: " . . . although she did not know it, this was the very best way she could have gone" (124). When the characters part on the quest, Tangle is given more room, but on the other hand, she has to go through more trials than Mossy, which not only shows that male and female initiation takes different forms, but also gives preference to the male as "the chosen" and leaves the passive role to the female: "Seven years had she sat there waiting" (143). While the story in many details shows striking similarities to Andersen's *The Snow Queen*, the gender performance of MacDonald's characters is the opposite of Andersen's.

My argument is supposed to show that in MacDonald's fairy tales, the child characters are exchangeable as far as gender is concerned, and when multiple protagonists are used, gender permutation is effective. The choice of the protagonists' gender seems arbitrary, at least from the narratological point of view, and no significant difference between homofocalization and heterofocalization can be detected. Among many other details, the word "child," with the ambivalent undertones of admiration and condescension, is used about boys and girls indiscriminately. The overall perception of power balance in any given text depends on a synergetic effect of the various aspects of alterity. In Kristevian/Lacanian readings of MacDonald (Gray 1996; Jenkins 2004) the idea of "the precariousness of subject position" is developed. It seems that the adult/child axis of the power tension is so significantly stronger than the gender axis that the latter is practically negligible. Adult normativity is the primary, albeit unconscious, starting point. It has been suggested that MacDonald is "queering" gender in his works, putting into the concept the original significance of "strange," "peculiar," "different" (McGillis 2003), by extension, Other. I would pursue the argument saying that MacDonald queers his protagonists, in the same sense, irrespective of gender; that a child in itself is strange, odd and different.

Note

1. Unless otherwise indicated, all quotes are from *Complete Fairy Tales*.

Chapter Five
Othering the Future: Stereotypes of Dystopia

During the 1990s and well into the twenty-first century, we have witnessed a flourishing of dystopian trends in children's and juvenile literature all over the world. Yet dystopia is, or should be, by definition an impossible genre in children's fiction. As many critics have repeatedly pointed out, children's literature is utopian by nature. As a consequence, children's fiction maintains a myth of a happy and innocent childhood, apparently based on adult writers' nostalgic memories and bitter insights about the impossibility of returning to the childhood idyll. With a prominent new trend in children's fiction showing tangible traits of dystopia, children's literature seems to have come to its antithesis. As critics and mediators of children's literature, we are still trying to view it as optimistic, with a strong faith in the future. But we hardly find any of these features in contemporary children's novels set in the near or distant future. Instead, we find ruthless depictions of the destruction of humankind and the end of the Earth, of moral decay and increasing societal divergence.

In dystopian novels for children, the adult world is interrogated, as it is presumably the adults who have created the highly ordered, hierarchical, but dull society that serves as a backdrop for a dystopian plot. In fact, such an interrogation is one of the many stereotypes of the dystopian novel for young readers. Further, in accordance with the conventions of children's literature, a child or a young person questions the society and reaches the insight about its injustice, but it is the adult society that suppresses the revolt. In this chapter I have chosen to illustrate recurrent dystopian features by a number of recent novels such as *The Giver* (1993), by Lois Lowry, *The Denials of Kow-Ten* (1998), by Jenny Robson, *Noughts and Crosses* (2001), by Malorie Blackman, *Whither You Long* (2001), by Ylva Karlsson, and *Feed* (2002), by M. T. Anderson. Since these books come from different parts of the world, I find it symptomatic that they have so much in common.

Many critics treat utopias and dystopias as two closely connected literary categories. Fredric Jameson (2005) makes no distinction between utopia and dystopia; moreover, with his political spectacles, utopia is dystopian by definition. He views utopia as a political idea, rather than a literary genre; the closest he gets to genre criteria is satire. Most of his material is science fiction in its political interpretation. A recent volume of children's literature criticism (Hintz and Ostry 2003), also treats utopia very broadly. Yet I find it necessary to distinguish between utopia and dystopia. If utopian literature depicts an ideal, albeit inaccessible, society, a dystopia is a picture of fear, a picture of a society which we would prefer to avoid, a warning. Both genres can be employed to investigate the issues of power and oppression, but in radically different ways.

Contemporary dystopias for young readers display a number of stereotypes that are gratifying to investigate from the power point of view. Stereotypes as such are strong power factors since they confirm the existing order. Dystopia is built around the double estrangement effect: while the reader is not familiar with the rules of the society presented in a novel, the characters are not aware of the "normal" world. Already this makes dystopian fiction an excellent strategy for subverting normativity. However, far from all children's writers are consistent in their use of the genre.

Nowhere and Everywhere

Since the word "utopia" means "nowhere," the reverse, dystopia, or anti-utopia, should be the opposite. What is, however, the opposite of nowhere? At least, in dystopian context, it cannot be understood as literally "everywhere," yet the global threat of a totalitarian society and in the first place totalitarian thinking is omnipresent in dystopias. In fact, it seems that totalitarianism is an indispensable feature of dystopia, and I have never read a dystopian novel depicting a democracy. Since dystopia, especially in juvenile literature, is primarily used as a cautionary tale, its starting point must necessarily be a negative development of the present society.

The chronotope, timespace of dystopia is distanced from the reader by a span of the future. This temporal and spatial isolation is already a powerful factor to create alienation. However, novels which have a stronger impact on the reader, describe a future so near that it is almost perceived as the present, something that can happen any moment, anywhere and with anyone, and maybe is happening already, as expressed in *Whither You Long*: "It is not yet, but soon, in short time, in a while. It is waiting behind the corner ... " (5; here and henceforth translations are mine). This is especially tangible in *The Denials of Kow-Ten*, which opens by the celebration of the new millennium— at the time of the publication still in the near future. Even though the story then moves sixty-five years forward, basically to account for the advancement of technology, the actors of the frame narrative are still alive and solidly present in the main plot. *Feed* takes place in a remote future, judging by the level of technology. The narrator, Titus, does not know how long ago feeds were introduced: "fifty or a hundred years ago. Before that, they had to use their hands and their eyes. Computers were all outside the body" (47). *Noughts and Crosses* is not strictly speaking a dystopia, but a counterfactual novel, the premise of which is the inverted development of human history: the black race has been dominant for many centuries, while the white race has been oppressed and actually enslaved until recently. In a counterfactual novel the action is profoundly distanced from the reader, and the actual time indications are meaningless. The futuristic setting in *Whither You Long* offers no direct temporal indication in the novel: it can be twenty years from now or longer still; yet the older generation remembers how things used to be.

Geographically, a dystopian society is necessarily isolated from the rest of the world; it is an enclave, a concept repeatedly used in *The Denials*. The implication is that the citizens are kept in ignorance about the ways and habits outside of their own community. The Kow-Ten enclave, obviously situated in Southern Africa, is surrounded by a wall onto which fake images of the external world are incessantly projected: "quietness hanging heavily in the air and the jungle thick and deep and mysterious . . . its small paths winding into tangled green shadows even in the bright afternoon sunlight" (25). The description creates a sense of idyll and innocence in which the protagonist has been brought up. In reality, beyond the fence, there is only desolate wilderness. There are several similar enclaves on Earth inciuing Lund-Sixty, Athi-Nine, Burl-Ninety-Two, Jeneev-Eighty, Kiyro-Seventy, and Mosk-Forty-Nine. Each is surrounded by a fence, illuminated by pictures of things long gone, such as the pristine views of the Swiss Alps, or the vast oceans around Toke-Twenty-Two and Syd-Ninety-Three, behind which the landscape is irreparably destroyed.

The Giver is indistinct in its timespace and does not mention how the secluded community has come into being. The dystopia in *Feed* is situated in North America and isolated from the rest of the world, known as Global Alliance; however, the enclave obviously wages colonial wars in South America and other countries that do not share its politics and ideology. *Noughts and Crosses* does not explicitly mention the place, but indirectly points at Great Britain, prominently detached from Pangaean Economic Community, where race segregation is not practiced any more. In both novels then, the dystopian enclave is opposed to the rest of the world. Beyond the fences in *The Denials* lies "Outside," a parallel to "Elsewhere" in *The Giver*. The characters are either happily unaware of the outside world or likewise happily convinced that it is evil. At closer look, the dystopia at best offers luxury for the few, while the rest of the population lives in utter misery. This feature is prominent in *Feed*, where Titus, the protagonist and narrator, lives in a sumptuous house with private climate control, including synthetic breeze and a sun that can be switched on and off.

He has an unlimited bank account, flies a posh aircraft, and goes to the Moon, Mars and Jupiter for weekends. Violet, the girl he meets by chance, lives in a poor neighborhood many levels underground; her father has saved for a year to send her on a Moon vacation, and he cannot afford proper medical care for her. In *Noughts and Crosses*, Sephy, the daughter of a rich politician, enjoys all the privileges of the ruling class, while the noughts, poor whites, carry out menial labor and serve the Crosses in their extravagant houses. Sephy contemplates her situation: "My parents' country house. Seven bedrooms and five reception rooms for four people" (30), echoed several pages further on by Callum's observation: "Every time I came back from Sephy's, I flinched at the sight of the shack that was meant to be my home" (33). The meals in Sephy's and Callum's homes are repeatedly contrasted with small, but pointed details: orange juice against low-fat milk and water, fancy dinners against constant pasta and mince. The rich Crosses go to elite schools; noughts are denied education and any status jobs. Noughts are recurrently humiliated in public transport, in shops being suspected of theft, in the news where they are presented in a negative light, and in movies in which they are portrayed as drunkards and criminals. Mutual hatred is a fact. One might believe that the society depicted in *The Giver* shows equality and absence of any class differences; on closer look, however, the strict hierarchy maintains the same social injustice as in the other novels.

In *The Denials*, Shiyle learns that the working people, who built the enclave, were betrayed by the upper-class designers of the project, and left outside the wall where the few survivals now live in misery. The outsiders are without embellishment called the Others and presented as uncivilized, not fully human, and a threat to the security of the enclave. Beyond Kow-Ten, they hide in the jungle; in Jeneev, in mountain caves in the Alps. The persistent alterity is one of the premises of the enclave project.

The landscape is pruned, leveled and unified; the weather is monitored. In the Kow-Ten enclave, the tropical sun is screened off by artificial mist, and rain begins promptly every evening at 7:00 P.M. The clouds necessary to produce the rain are drawn from the outside by weather towers; therefore the enclavists are known in the outside world as *pula-diefs*, or rain stealers. In *Feed*, nature is destroyed, oceans polluted, and forests cut down to make way for artificial air factories and beef farms, where filet mignon is grown by cloning. The cities are protected by plastic domes, and in order to go out, people have to wear protective suits and helmets. Everybody suffers from lesions as their skin peels off. The authorities turn this tragedy into a commercial gag, launching lesions as high-fashion. By contrast, the world of *Noughts and Crosses* seems to have clean private beaches and public gardens, and no ecological problems are ever mentioned. Instead, social issues are focused upon. Still more plainly, *Wither You Long* shows idyllic islets of nature contrasted to the urban decay.

The level of industrialization varies in different texts, from primitive in *The Giver* to highly developed in *The Denials* and still more in *Feed*, where superfast aircraft move in tubes all over the country and up and down connecting shafts. The common feature is, however, the amplified incongruity between high technology and ethics.

Total(itarian) Happiness?

Other distinctive features of the dystopian society include absence of hunger, unemployment and sickness, which the inhabitants of the dystopia take for granted. For the happy few, food is automatically provided. In *Feed*, food is produced in home synthesizers, and disposable plates, cutlery and even dinner tables are featured. In *The Giver*, food is delivered from communal kitchens. It is rationed and not particularly tasty or nourishing; yet because the characters know no other, they have nothing to compare. The absence of reference frames is the foundation for the authorities to manipulate the citizens.

There is no money in *The Giver*, since all necessities are provided for, albeit on a very basic level such as unified clothes or bicycles as the only transportation. Neither in *The Denials* is money an issue, since the enclavists have anything they may desire, while the population outside the enclave lives off what the bare land can give. Not much attention is paid to the everyday needs of the citizens, since they are of no significance for the focalizing character. It is only on confronting the old abandoned mall that Shyine contemplates: " . . . where were all the goods for sale? Where were the fingerprint readers?" (64), thus revealing how the needs of the enclavists are satisfied. Conversely, *Feed* excels in depictions of consumerism, and Titus's unquenchable desire to buy new expensive clothes is emphasised. In *Noughts and Crosses*, Callum's father notes that Sephy's dress must cost more than his yearly income; Sephy has a bank account and allowance from her father. Callum's parents cannot afford sending both of their children to school. Money is a tangible problem.

Sickness is eliminated by a variety of drugs, and the least injury is immediately cared for through painkillers. The absence of disease and suffering leaves the characters unprepared when they meet with these; Jonas in *The Giver*, for instance, begs for a painkiller when he first encounters slight pain in one of the Receiver's memories. Shiyne's mother takes Eezies, apparently a trade name for the future luck pills.

Full employment is achieved in *The Giver* and *The Denials* by forced assignment of life-time jobs at young age, often followed by removal from the family. Social hierarchy is thus established once and for all. *The Denials* describes the protagonist Shiyne's elder brother receiving his first employment as a Trainee Enhancer, a future member of the governing elite. His father is an engineer. Shiyne attends a privileged school for especially intelligent children. In *Feed*, large consumer-oriented corporations "keep . . . everyone in the world employed" (49). Titus's father is doing "some kind of banking thing" and his mother is "in design" (65). Sephy's father is a politician and becomes Home Office Minister.

Violet's father is a poverty-stricken university professor, which says a lot about the society's view on intellectual work. Callum's parents are menial laborers, and Callum and his brother have no bright prospects.

In *The Giver*, all children, even very young, participate in the so-called volunteer work, in practice forced labor. The text carefully avoids the depiction of actual manual labor, although presumably somebody is collecting garbage, preparing food and doing laundry. Instead, we get a glimpse of working conditions in an old people's home, a pretext to start contemplation in the young protagonist on the hierarchy of the society he lives in. Jonas's parents are, typically enough, a lawyer and a medical nurse (in inverted gender roles). The contempt for manual workers is something the society shares with many dystopias: "he didn't envy Laborers at all" (17); "Fish Hatchery Attendant. Jonas was certainly glad that *that* Assignment was taken, he wouldn't have wanted it" (53; emphasis in the original). The protagonist is assigned an intellectual, rather than menial job; none of the painful, traumatic memories he receives from the Giver involve labor, because, if anything, labor is well-known in Jonas's society. However, it is more gratifying to create smart and intellectual characters than ones that would be confined to a job as a fish hatchery attendant. Even though Callum in *Noughts and Crosses* comes from the poor working class, neither he nor any member of his family is shown at work. Instead, Callum is accepted into a privileged school.

Families are seemingly perfect in dystopias, but dysfunctional from contemporary point of view. *The Giver* portrays artificial family composition and children reared in child factories. In *Feed*, a friend of Titus was, for an incredible sum of money, cloned from Abraham Lincoln's DNA. Titus himself has been produced in a "conceptionarium" where his parents told the genetic engineers exactly what kind of a child they wanted. This is not an issue in *The Denials of Kow-Ten*, but both in this novel and in *The Giver* children only live with their parents until they are old enough to go into professional training. In *The Denials* fathers live separately from the families. Old people are placed in homes and, in *The Giver*, comfortably gotten rid of.

One of the recurrent stereotypes in depicting families is that the parents of the rich, privileged children are cold, indifferent, authoritative and often of low morals. The parents of the underprivileged children are warm, concerned and understanding, even though they may disapprove of their children's friendship with rich kids. The conflict between parents and children, in which the children see through the parents' and other adults' lies, has always been a prominent motif in children's fiction; however, combined with the dystopian setting, it produces a new type of socially conscious, ethically-charged literature. The texts maintain that future generations, anywhere from fifty to two-hundred years from now, will have the same mentality as today. In all the novels, the members of privileged social groups are mean, selfish and destructive. The rich and the powerful ignore ecological problems and perform unethical medical experiments. Human life has no value. The indignation against adults is obvious, and the adults are held responsible while the implied authors pretend to take the young protagonists' side. Yet the question remains: When does every individual's responsibility begin? Why must a twelve-year-old boy in *The Giver* take upon himself the traumatic memories when the adults cannot cope with them? Is it still the blind Romantic faith in the pure and innocent child who will withstand the world's evil for us adults? Or is it the adult authors' guilt caused by their sense of powerlessness? Frequently, at least one benevolent adult is portrayed, as if in self-defense, having the function of a mentor, who explains the truth to the confused adolescent: the Receiver in *The Giver*; the good twin Igitur in *The Denials*, or Violet's father in *Feed*.

Power Structures

Most dystopian plots are constructed around heterological concerns: ethnicity, class and gender. In *The Denials* Shiyne contemplates the different skin color of himself and his friends; it becomes clear that he is black, and his friend Blinda is white; yet ethnicity does not seem to be an issue. The Implementation of the Enclave Blueprints, as the dictatorship is called, was created by a multinational and multiethnic conspiracy. Yet women are denied access to power; as Shiyne notices at his brother's ceremony, there are no women among the leaders, and no girls among the trainees. *The Giver* is more politically correct in this respect, as the Chief Elder is female.

In *Feed* and in *Noughts and Crosses*, the conflict is based on class differences. From the start, a considerable cleft is stated between the rich, referred to as Crosses, and the poor, contemptuously called noughts—the difference in status is further emphasized by Crosses spelled with capital C, and noughts with a small n. However, only many pages later it is explicitly stated that Crosses' skin is dark, while noughts are white. A school lesson is used to explain the counterfactual development of history to the reader, a history written by Crosses just as real history is always written by the ruling classes. Class distinction, comparable to slavery in the United States or apartheid in South Africa, is never interrogated, except by the clandestine terrorist organization. In a conversation with Sephy, Callum says "us noughts and you Crosses," to which Sephy, deeply hurt, replies: "like you're in one place and I'm in another, with a huge, great wall between us" (27), which is exactly the case, even though the wall is mental rather than material, as in *The Denials*. It eventually turns out that Crosses are the bearers of a world religion and therefore closer to God. The label Crosses not only evokes the popular game, alluding to the perpetual class struggle, but also has a connection to an inverted form of Christianity, in which God is only the Crosses' god, celebrated at Crossmas. Noughts are godless.

In *Feed*, apart from pecuniary privileges, the upper class has access to life-sustaining implanted chip that the lower classes cannot afford. When Titus tries to defend the authorities by pointing out the benefits of feeds, Violet informs him, to his total dismay, that only seventy-three percent of Americans have feeds. In most dystopias, higher authorities manipulate the characters to believe they are living in luxury, since they have no other reference frames. Yet Violet is highly aware of her underprivileged position and does not share her father's idealistic philosophy, but says to Titus: "You lead this life like I've always wanted to" (267). In one of their final quarrels, Titus reprimands her for making fun of him and his friends, "all the time, having this little wish you could be like us" (271). Similarly, Callum dreams of getting education, "[h]aving a large house and money in the bank and not having to work and being respected wherever I go" (151). In visualizing his future, he constructs it according to the Cross norms. The aspirations, that young people from lower classes cherish, imply leaving their own class behind as soon as possible. Callum's sister Lynette once had a Cross boyfriend, who was killed by resentful noughts. As Lynette goes into insanity as an escape from trauma, she fancies herself to be a Cross, brought up in a nought family by mistake. Jude, the elder brother, spells out both siblings' feelings: "I've seen you hating it and hating us and hating yourself because you weren't born one of them" (53).

In all the texts there is another teenager, usually alienated from the protagonist by gender, ethnicity or class, occasionally all of these. Violet is even trying to resist the pressure of the feed, the implanted chip that gives authorities full control over her. In one of her explicit sermons to Titus, where she becomes the author's mouthpiece to balance Titus's ignorance and conceit, she says: "They try to figure out who you are, and to make you conform to one of their types for easy marketing. It's like a spiral: They keep making everything more basic so it will appeal to everyone. And gradually, everyone gets used to everything being basic, so we get less and less varied as people, more simple" (97). Violet is politically and environmentally engaged, trying to explain to Titus how the rest of the world hates Americans "for what [they] did" (111). Blinda in *The Denials* eventually becomes aware of the brainwash as she realizes that Shiyle's memory has been wiped out.

Irrelevant in *The Giver* and conspicuously absent in *The Denials,* the cross-class romances in *Feed* and *Noughts and Crosses* inevitably enhance other differences, gender- as well as race-related. *Wither You Long* takes the conflict one step further, as it also involves the issue of heteronormativity, featuring a Lesbian love story in which a young upper-class girl from the wealthy North suburbs of Stockholm meets an "ordinary girl" from the slums of South (traditionally a working-class area of the city, although at present one of the most posh neighborhoods among young intellectuals). The theme goes back to the classical literary plot, noticeable clearly in the some of the discussed dystopias, dealing with lovers from different social groups. The motif inescapably leads to conflicts, and at best, the upper-class partner becomes aware of class differences and social injustice. In *Whither You Long*, Hedvig's social indignation and engagement is, however, sustained by her infatuation with Marija, also a common dilemma in fiction. The spelling of the name, Marija, is supposed to point out that she is not only poor, but also an immigrant or a child of immigrants; thus yet another axis of alterity is involved. Not unexpectedly, Hedvig is intellectual and loves poetry, while her disadvantaged companions can barely read.

Hedvig feels no remorse toward her rich fiancé, but she is not happy when her laptop is used to access and rob rich people's bank accounts, including that of her parents. While revolting against parents is normal for any young person, loyalty to one's social class cannot be ignored too easily, as also in *Noughts and Crosses*. While living temporarily in a poor community in the South, Hedvig feels empathy with the hungry, the freezing and the unemployed; she even makes a practical contribution by placing homeless children in the care of her grandmother in a villa in the Stockholm archipelago. At the same time, Hedvig misses good and healthy food and warm showers, and as she has not cut off her links with her former life, she can anytime take a first-class train back home to enjoy a few hours in a soft bed, a bath with scented oils, a toothbrush and toothpaste, classic music, and a change of clean clothes. Even though she is ashamed of longing for comfort, aversion toward poverty is growing within her. The world of the dispossessed is described, through focalization of the protagonist, in recurrent adjectives such as "dull," "filthy," "disgusting," "broken," "stinking," and "contagious." Observing filthy children playing in the streets, old people with decayed teeth, and dilapidated shacks, Hedvig repeatedly notes that she didn't know there were places like this. Her own world is, just as the enclave in *The Denials*, fenced and guarded. Hedvig's experience of Otherness is similar to Shiyne's as he wanders about beyond the Fence. Devastation, filth, stench, violence, unbearable heat and blinding sun, bad food, poisoned water, and evil minds are his first encounters with the unknown world that he has been curious about. Moreover, he learns that the Outside has its own conflicts and power hierarchies; the harmony of the enclave is unfamiliar here. But, unlike inside Kow-Ten, the memories of the past are kept and cherished, never to be forgotten. The outsiders have not been brainwashed.

Power, Memory and Language

Brainwash is a prominent feature in any dystopian society, *Feed* being the most extreme case where the authorities have complete control over the citizens through the implanted computer chips. Their habits, especially shopping habits, are monitored to offer them more and more purchases; as Titus notes, a feed "knows everything you want and hope for, sometimes before you even know what those things are. It can tell you how to get them, and help you make buying decisions that are hard" (48). Education is focused on the art of shopping and consuming, since schools are run by corporations; Titus can barely read, while his mind is constantly bombarded by aggressive advertisement. Violet can read and write because she has been home-schooled, but her knowledge and skills are worthless in the world where she lives. When Titus's and his friends' feeds get hacked into and have to be switched off for a while, Titus feels totally cut away from life. During this attack, caused by an anti-feed activist, Violet's feed gets permanently damaged, since it is not only the source of constant flow of information, but also connected to brain activity itself, to body movements, and even emotions. When her feed fails, Violet turns into a package and finally dies. Her gradual loss of memory, speech and intelligence becomes a powerful symbol of the decay of the whole society.

In *The Giver*, society is characterized by the absence of memory; the traumatic memory of the past, of war, hunger and misery, but also of joy, love, friendship, of all emotions. Significantly, a lost memory of a Christmas Eve in the midst of a loving family is amplified. Christmas stands for family ties rather than a religious celebration, since yet another fascinating feature in the dystopias is the absence of religion. In *Noughts and Crosses*, the privileged classes are supposed to be "God's chosen," but faith has little influence on ideology, and religious practice is not described. In *The Denials*, the enclavists swear by "Hanran," but any memory of what this supposed deity refers to is lost. Similarly, the recurrent exclamation "Omigod" in *Feed* has lost its original implication. In *Feed*, consumerism is the religion, and in *The Giver* there is no indication of any faith. The protagonists of the dystopias never contemplate this fact, since they simply do not know what religion is; it has been obliterated from society alongside morals, conscience, and all personal convictions.

The discrepancy between the characters' and the readers' knowledge, understanding and physical as well as mental experience is the hub of any dystopian fiction, yet for a young reader, additional effort must be taken to grasp the significance of the protagonists' ethical choices. It is hardly possible to conceive of a world without color, and until Jonas realizes that he has been denied it and seen everything in black and white, there are reasons to assume it. Similarly, there is no reason to question the reality of the jungle and the lion in *The Denials*, until Shiyne, the protagonist and focalizer, begins to doubt. A keen reader will perhaps suspect that something is wrong when the lion day after day steps into the same pothole. Shiyne does not realize that the lion is a projected image; but the reader is supposed to be superior to the naïve character. Further, possessing previous information from the frame narrative, the readers have a better understanding of the background of the enclave. The citizens, however, have full confidence in the authorities that "stood guard over all the secret knowledge of the enclave" (32). The motto of the Dome, the seat of the authorities, says: "Knowledge is the key." Yet, knowledge is only reserved for the topmost elite. All information concerning the "Outside," "the Others," and the "Before," is unavailable to ordinary citizens. To his web search, Shiyne gets the answer: "Further information unnecessary." The adults are invariably given the responsibility for the present state of events. This can only be done implicitly, since the premise of dystopia is strong focalization, through which the alien society is depicted, without a narrator's discursive intervention. Yet the moral decay of the adults is the foremost insight that the young characters reach. In *The Denials*, the adults who created the dystopia are still alive, but their memories have been deliberately erased.

In a totalitarian society, denouncement is a virtue, and Shiyne, young as he is, has already practiced it, reporting his best friend Dayvid for telling him about life Outside. The society encourages loyalty and explains the necessity by the formula FGG, "for greater good." The spelling out of the abbreviation comes many pages after it is first used, but the reader is expected to understand the implication. The slogan is reminiscent of the ostensible Jesuit motto: "The end justifies the means," also appropriated by the Communist ideology and explicitly used by the terrorists in *Noughts and Crosses*. Yet deep inside, Shiyne knows that he is acting inappropriately, and on learning the meaning of the word "conscience" he realizes that conscience is what he was feeling in regard to his friend. Here, as in all dystopian novels, the episode draws the readers' attention to the manipulative power of language. *The Giver* describes a society where language has been purged of all words referring to phenomena undesirable in the eyes of authorities, and where "language precision" is used as a means of oppression. For instance, there are no words to describe human emotions and relationships. When Jonas asks his parents whether they love him, they reply: "you used a very generalized word, so meaningless that it's become almost obsolete" (127). Instead, they suggest that he ask whether they take pride in his accomplishments. Jonas has learned the word "love" from the Giver; but it has long been eliminated from the common vocabulary. When there are no words to describe feelings, the feelings themselves disappear from human mentality. Toward the end of the novel, Jonas wonders whether the people around them have actually experienced any feelings at all or whether they merely use empty words.

Similar methods of control appear in *The Denials*. The elimination of certain words implies the obliteration of the concepts these words have once denoted. Shiyne does not understand the word "conscience" when Igitur explains that he could not live with his conscience inside the enclave. The reader knows the meaning and implication of the word, but in case the message in not clear, Igitur concludes: "Yes, of course. That word's no longer part of the enclave vocabulary. My dear brother believes that if you don't have a word for something, it ceases to exist" (78).

Further, many words are used euphemistically. In the society of *The Giver*, euphemisms are practiced to conceal less attractive sides of existence. Family units denote people brought together by the authorities' will. Profession is called Assignment and imposed on every citizen, once and for all. Volunteer hours stand for forced labor. Sexual desire is referred to as "stirrings" and gets treated like a serious disease. The most striking example, however, is "release," the euphemism for execution. Release is practiced on old citizens who have become a burden to society, on babies born too weak, and not least on political dissidents. Yet it takes the reader some time, together with Jonas, to come to this realization. First, Jonas believes, as he has been brainwashed to believe, that "releasing" an erring citizen merely means that the offender is sent Elsewhere. It becomes clear later on that Elsewhere is just another euphemism. Release of the elderly is presented as "a time of celebration for a life well and fully lived" (7), and again it takes Jonas a long time to understand that his friend Fiona, who is assigned the job in The House of the Old, will soon be introduced into "the fine art of release" (153), giving old men and women a lethal injection.

Noughts and Crosses may seem devoid of manipulative language, yet at closer look the very words featured in the title are euphemisms: Crosses for the rich ruling black, noughts for the poor and oppressed white. Further, each class has contemptuous nicknames for each other: Crosses are called daggers, while noughts are called blankers. This leads not unexpectedly to conflicts, and Sephy suddenly gets an insight: "*Blankers.* What a horrible word! A nasty word. My friend Callum wasn't a blanker. He wasn't" (44; emphasis in the original). Having herself on the spur of a moment used the word, she contemplates: "it was a word that hurt my best friend . . . I hadn't fully realized just how powerful words could be" (60).

Even ordinary words can be used to denote something else. In *The Giver* Jonas calls his parents mother and father, but they have no biological bonds whatsoever. Nobody in the community knows what an animal is, but the word is used "to describe someone uneducated or clumsy, someone who didn't fit in" (5). Figurative language is banished as imprecise. When Jonas says: "I am starving," he is immediately corrected by his teacher. The phrase "I am starving" is a hyperbole, and Jonas is using it in the figurative meaning, implying that he is very hungry. But the authorities want no misunderstandings: "No one in the community was starving, had never been starving, would ever be starving. To say 'starving' was to speak a lie" (70). The correct language is important, because it assures that no unpleasant memories of starvation will ever disturb the community.

In *The Denials*, too, familiar words mean something else. A Calmer is a security police, Guides are schoolteachers, and Enhancers are the dictators ruling the enclave. To show how language has developed, some words are spelled as they are pronounced: for instance, sokka is soccer, kilometres are "kays," and centimeters "cems." The deity Hanran refers to Ayn Rand. All this enhances the readers' sense of strangeness and detachment. On the other hand, new words are coined, the true meaning of which is obscured, at least in the beginning: magroads (magnetic roads on which hovercraft bikes ride), lume-dials (watch-cum-cellphone), or nitrograms (three-dimentional images). While contributing to the description of the futuristic setting, these details also demonstrate how language works. *Feed* abides in words that are partly teenage jargon, partly futuristic idiom: lo-grav, upcar—à personal aircraft used for all transportations; units and unettes for boys and girls, meg for all shades of "good," mal—short for brain malfunction, denoting alcohol and drug intoxication.

The riches of the natural language, including synonyms, are also eliminated to manipulate the citizens. When everybody wears the same clothes, there is no need for a variety of words for the various garments. When all the food is the same, no words are necessary to refer to the various dishes. When there is no difference between individual houses or apartments, it is easiest to use the word "dwelling." Or as Jonas himself puts it: "If everything's the same, then there aren't any choices" (97). The conformity of language emphasizes the conformity of society itself.

Voice and Subject

Feed employs first-person narration and is not only written in a casual, spoken language of an uneducated teenager, but the vocabulary itself is deliberately limited. When Titus hears a word he does not know, he can immediately look it up in a feednet dictionary; in this way the text contains a slightly more varied style, but the episodes deliberately point out the poverty of Titus's glossary. The text is also contaminated by advertising slogans that Titus incessantly receives from his feed. The level of linguistic sophistication of Titus and his friends is best illustrated by the title of their favorite show: "Oh? Wow! Thing!" Visiting Violet's home Titus is struck by the presence of written language: "Everything had words on them. There were papers with words on them, and books, and even posters on the wall had words" (135). Violet's father is an expert on dead languages—not Latin or Sanskrit, but Basic and Fortran, the early programming languages for computers. Nevertheless, he is highly aware of the ongoing impoverishment of natural languages and resists it by using high-flown phrases that Titus finds completely incomprehensible: "I am filled with astonishment at the regularity of your features and the handsome generosity you have shown my daughter. The two of you are close, which gladdens the heart, as close as two wings torn off the same butterfly" (136)

In *Noughts and Crosses*, multiple personal narration is used, with alternating chapters told from Callum's and Sephy's perspective. This device creates a powerful counterpoint not only in their diverse view on things, but also in the development of their idiom, especially Callum's, as he distances himself from the world of Crosses. This use of language is extremely subtle and more effective than the explicit jargon in *Feed*.

The exploration of Otherness, through language among other things, presumably leads to protagonists' revelation. Jonas in *The Giver* is not offered any choice as he is appointed the Receiver of memories. He is selected out of many young citizens because he is evaluated by the authorities as strong-minded and immune toward dissent. Until then, he does not interrogate the society he is living in; he simply has no reasons to do so; he is wholly compliant to begin with, making the contrast all the stronger. Shiyne is inquisitive by nature: "the questions began to swirl round and round in his head . . . His head was always full of swirling questions—because there was always something amazing to be wondering about" (26). The protagonist is a potential dissident from start, which makes his final defeat still more effective. Early in the plot, Shiyne is chastised by the Chief Enhancer Gaudeamus:

> When you were a child, you were free to ask any questions that sprang into your mind . . . But you are fourteen now, Shiyne, and your childish inquisitiveness must be left behind you. Now when you ask questions, those questions must have sense and purpose. (50f)

Promised a future as a Trainee Enhancer, Shiyne decides to stop asking, even himself, pointless, from the enclave's perspective, questions. The only questions worth asking are those "that could improve the welfare of Kow-Ten" (55). This is his first step toward conformism. Yet his spirit is so far not completely broken; as a true rebel he realizes that he "didn't have to stop these questions of his. No! All he had to do was stop voicing them . . . What was hidden in his head was hidden and private" (59). Apparently, the technology of the enclave has not yet learned how to access people's thoughts, as is portrayed in *Feed* and less prominently in *The Giver*.

The dystopian protagonists' epiphany can cause several actions that all demand the reader's ethical standpoint: they may attempt to change their society, escape from it, or conform to it. Callum in *Noughts and Crosses* rebels against social injustices, but by doing so he betrays his girlfriend. The compromise is inevitable, as he has to choose between two loyalties, and the loyalty toward his class proves stronger. On orders from his terrorist organization he kidnaps Sephy, even though he later helps her to escape. Sephy is in this episode used to convey the didactic message: "If you try to change the world using violence, you'll just swap one form of injustice for another" (363).

Violet in *Feed* is intent upon changing the world, but dies because her father cannot afford adequate care. Titus has, however, betrayed her even before her imminent death, since he does not want to get involved. Forced by Violet to take her out for an overnight excursion, he is unable to make love, because in his mind her body is already half-decayed. Sitting by her bedside, he looks at his watch not to miss his date with his new girlfriend. He feels no remorse, and feed does not allow him to feel grief, instead filling his mind with new alluring advertisements. Similarly, Hedvig in *Wither You Long* abandons Marija like a discarded toy.

Jonas is not merely empowered by the intelligence that allows him to realize the hypocrisy of his world. He is the chosen one, the person who will eventually become the most influential in his macabre society. But power has its price; in fact, the adults have chosen Jonas to bear their burdens, to accumulate and preserve the traumatic memories of the past. Jonas flees when he realizes that his little brother is in danger. This selfless deed, however, leads both into death. Thus the child is used—abused—by the adults as a mental garbage bin, and for all his insights, Jonas cannot escape and must die. This is a disturbing idea, since it justifies the adults' right to manipulate and abuse the child, and although the intention of the text is to cause indignation, the disobedient child is efficiently punished. Forced conformism may occasionally take extremely violent forms; however, it can equally be a matter of simple cowardice. In such a case, moral judgment is wholly left to the reader, who must disengage from the protagonist in order to judge fairly.

Shiyle, returning to the enclave loaded with new knowledge as well as conscience, is determined to fight injustice. Meanwhile, he experiences pain and exhaustion, that life in the enclave spares its citizens. Taking himself home over the hills, nonexistent in his flat world, he firmly decides to share his insights with the highest authority of the enclave, Igitur's twin Gaudeamus. Then he remembers the blissful pain relievers, the soft bed sheets, the comfort of his world, and his previous wish to become one of the leaders himself. Most of all, he starts questioning the story Igitur has told him. Safely back in his home, taken care of, surrounded by his loving family, he feels that his experience from the Outside is fading away. He does speak to Gaudeamus, without meeting the expected reaction. And, as the perspective is shifted from Shiyle to an omniscient narrator, the reader learns that the young protagonist will be given a dose of memory-erasing drug and return to his former innocent state. The novel then circles back to itself with Shiyle wondering over the repeated actions of the hologram lion.

When Hedvig in *Whither You Long* is back in her familiar upper-class environment, the natural question is what the reader is supposed to infer. The protagonist has cautiously studied how the unprivileged classes live and decided that it is more comfortable to be rich. Love across class boundaries has ended—not necessarily because of class differences, yet Hedvig's cooling-off feelings are closely connected with the sense of filth, bad smell, hunger and misery. Her bad conscience is stilled by a bearable portion of charity work. This is a betrayal, as much as Callum's and Titus's, but this moral issue is not pursued. What are the readers supposed to think of Hedvig? Are we supposed to blame her? On the other hand, it is hard to liberate oneself from the subjectivity of the text, as we have been allowed to follow Hedvig's strong and contradictory emotions. Should we ascribe Hedvig's failing solidarity to her growing up in an exaggerated futuristic class divergence? The longing, featured in the title, is at first a longing away from her regulated life, a longing for something different and more exciting; but experiencing the forbidden fruit, she admits to herself that whither she longs does not exist. The ending feels like conventional romances, in which upper-class protagonists become poor through a freak of Fate, but eventually regain their legitimate high status and wealth. Or else it is reminiscent of the prodigal daughter, returning home to receive the father's forgiveness. In other words, Hedvig returns to her class, ethnicity and heteronormativity without ever interrogating her choice, as if her period with the poor has been an exciting computer game in an exotic setting.

Whither You Long?

Dystopia is then a powerful vehicle to alienate readers, making them aware of either the characters' naiveté or their failing morals. The ending of *The Giver* spares the protagonist the humiliation of being brainwashed all over again. Jonas's death echoes the nineteenth-century practice of killing off fictive children before they have an opportunity to sin. Callum in *Noughts and Crosses* dies a violent death that signals impossibility of reconciliation, but Sephy is carrying their child who may still change the world (there are sequels to the novel which I am not discussing here). *Feed* leaves the protagonist completely unchanged and reduced to the half-robot he was before he met Violet. The ending of *The Denials of Kow-Ten* shows the total defeat of the young protagonist. The spokesman of the novel, Igitur, states: "Unlike a story, there is no final chapter in the real world. The misery just goes on and on and on . . ." (82). Yet despite this metafictional comment, the text contains a final chapter, or epilogue, connected with the prologue, suggesting that in another, parallel universe, the fatal development on Earth has not taken place. This is the implied author's safety line to give the reader some hope, and the hideous scenario turns out to be a cautionary tale.

Each in its own way, the novels put a barrier between the protagonist and the reader, persuading the latter to adopt an independent subject position. Unless this happens, the readers will be strapped to the naïve characters who are completely blind toward their own behavior as well as the surrounding world. Among other things, the readers' resistance to disempowering endings is a common phenomenon; for instance, many real readers of *The Giver*, even adult readers, prefer to interpret the ending optimistically, claiming that the protagonist has indeed reached a better place and will live happily ever after. A more sophisticated reading of the novel excludes such an interpretation: throughout the novel, the Elsewhere, that Jonas is trying to reach, is used as a euphemism for death. The depiction of Jonas struggling with cold and hunger and having hallucinations is an accurate picture of death agony. Thus, as shown, the only way the author sees for her rebellious hero is to kill him off.

The close reading of the novels leaves one with pessimistic conclusions. Here it feels natural to return to the questions of power, as well as the distinction between utopian and dystopian children's fiction. The depiction of childhood in conventional children's fiction reflects the adult writers' view, often highly idealized, sometimes nostalgic. Paradoxically, the vision of the future in children's novels is also likely to be radically different from the ideas young people today may have of their own future. Even though adult writers may try to liberate themselves from their experience, "to give a voice" to the child protagonist, "speak in the child's name," still we mainly hear the adult voice and the adult values leaking through the young protagonists' deliberately naïve perspective. It implies that in the obvious fear of the future in contemporary children's and young adult fiction, we see the reflection of adults' own fears and their own feeling of guilt.

Chapter Six
Othering the Setting:
Orientalism and Robinsonnade

The term "Orientalism" is associated with Edward Said (1978). The phenomenon dates, however, considerably further back in time, to the period when the Western world first came into contact with the Orient and was dazzled by the completely different mentality, culture and art. The "chinoiserie" and "japonism" as the specific trends of the Western art, architecture, and partly literature, were a combination of admiration and appropriation. The latter has been severely criticized in postcolonial theory. Orientalism in children's literature has been studied with concepts and tools from postcolonial theory (e.g. Nodelman 1992; McGillis 1997, 2000), yet without an overall heterological context.

Hans Christian Andersen's fairy tales provide some good examples of overt Orientalism. In 'The Shepherdess and the Chimney Sweep,' the impediment to the lovers' happiness is the Shepherdess' grandfather, who happens to be a Chinese figure, a porcelain trinket that was much in vogue at the time the story was written. Here the traditional Western images, the two pastoral figurines, come to clash with an Oriental one. It is not crucial for the plot that the antagonist is Oriental, yet Andersen obviously introduces a figure as likely to be found in a Danish drawing room as miniature statues of bucolic shepherdesses. However, the Chinese grandfather is presented as evil, actually the villain of the story; thus in the tension between West and East, the latter is promptly othered. The most striking example of Andersen's Orientalism is 'The Nightingale,' an obvious tribute to chinoiserie. Unlike 'The Shepherdess and the Chimney Sweep,' it takes place entirely in China and emphasizes the Oriental ways and habits. However, the Oriental setting is not integral for the plot, and the underlying values reflect Andersen's recurrent credo of true versus false art.

Quite a few children's fantasy novels use semi-Oriental or quasi-Oriental settings in their alternative worlds, for instance, Edith Nesbit's *The Story of the Amulet* (1906), C. S. Lewis's *The Horse and His Boy* (1954), Lloyd Alexander's *The First Two Lives of Lukas-Kasha* (1978), Diana Wynne Jones's *The Lives of Christopher Chant* (1988) and *The Castle in the Air* (1990), and Philip Pullman's *The Firework Maker's Daughter* (1995). The overall alterity of the setting makes Oriental flavor less conspicuous.

Alexander's *The Remarkable Journey of Prince Jen* (1991) is set in an imaginary Oriental country in which, however, proper and place names point at China. There are some traits that may originate from Chinese mythology, and the idea of wandering scholars is unmistakably Oriental. Yet the setting is not integral to the plot. The novel is one in a vast number of Alexander's works featuring exotic settings, such as Ancient Greece, India, a vaguely historical Europe, and half-mythical Illyria, Eldorado, Drackenberg and Jedera. The plot and the set of characters in *Prince Jen* are easily recognizable from the other novels; its attraction is the richness of details, the humor, the irony and the language. It does portray an interesting character evolution and carries a humanistic and existential message. In other words, it is in every respect an excellent book. Yet the setting has no other function than contributing to the exotizing alterity.

In another, but similar trend, novels employ Oriental settings in historical plots. *A Single Shard* (2001), by Linda Sue Park, is set in Korea of the twelfth century and primarily involves a minute presentation of the art of pottery, more precisely the unique Korean celadon ceramics. The plot is vague. The protagonist, the orphaned boy nicknamed Tree-ear, becomes an apprentice to a famous potter, but since he is not Min's son he is not supposed to follow his master's trade. In the last quarter of the book, Tree-ear opts to deliver a sample of Min's work to the royal court, is assailed by robbers, presents a shard of a smashed vase to the court official and gets his master a commission. There is also a tension of loyalties for the protagonist between his master and an old crippled man who had taken care of him since he was a baby, an archetypal orphan—guide—father progression. The setting is essential in the sense that celadon pottery with inlaid decorations was only produced in Korea during the period described in the novel. The book thus carries a strong educational project. The protagonist is detached in time as well as in space, yet the narrative is presented wholly from his perspective. He ascends from his status as an orphan to his master's true heir and even gets a new name. It is hinted that he is the maker of the most famous vase preserved from the period.

Likewise, *The Kite Rider* (2001), by Geraldine McCaughrean, set in China conquered by Kublai Khan, is a conventional quest story with a strong Oriental flavor, and the trade that the young protagonist learns is kite-making and kite-flying.

Violence, Honor, Loyalty and Love

Katherine Paterson has written several novels in Oriental settings which provide excellent examples of the range of othering through setting. All of these novels are historical and as such detached in time as well as in space.

Rebels of the Heavenly Kingdom (1983) takes place in China in the 1850s, against the background of the native population's struggle to overthrow the hateful Manchu empire. The imported religion of the one and only God unites a group of people attracted by the idea of heavenly peace and eagerly adopts the value of the foreign creed. However, the ten commandments, or the Ten Heavenly Precepts, as the neophytes prefer to call them, match badly the ferocious intentions of the insurgents or their daily practice. The self-proposed spiritual leadership of the group, claiming to act on God's command, becomes a ruthless dictatorship. The two leaders impose rules of conduct in total opposition to Christian doctrine. Food is burned as a sacrifice to God, while people are starving. The God-worshipers desecrate and destroy the temples, and smash graven images, that is, statues of traditional Chinese deities. They preach love, but act on hatred, intolerance and disrespect for human life. In fact, they hardly behave any better than the detested enemy, the Manchu imperial forces. Looting, killing and raping become everyday practice, but it is justified by the ends: "The horrors and sufferings of the past two years would be washed away in the splendor of the Heavenly Kingdom. Soon there will be Great Peace for all in China" (199). Despite the formal declarations of equality, men and women are separated first at meetings, and later forbidden to associate at all. Families are torn apart, and husbands and wives are murdered if seen together. The sect members are encouraged to denounce their friends. Any deviation from the rules is punished with excruciating death. The tyrants thus govern by terror and violence. Whether Paterson's purpose is to present an allegory of twentieth-century Communist China is of little consequence, since the picture is much more universal, reflecting any society built on fanaticism and hatred. The allegory could just as well be of the French Revolution or the Soviet Union's Bolshevik rule.

Most of the novel is focalized through a young peasant boy named Wang Lee. Forced to join the rebels, he is at first reluctant to take on the alien dogma, personified in the brutal Lin Mei. At their first encounter, Lin Mei is disguised as a man, and Wang Lee states that she is unladylike. Her feet have not been bound, as is proper for a Chinese girl. Moreover, Lin Mei can read and write, a skill inappropriate for a woman. Wang Lee is well aware of the importance of learning, which is a rooted Chinese tradition; already as a poor peasant's son he dreams of "carrying the greatest treasure of all—he would be able to read and write" (16). Literacy is, however, an ambivalent asset. Lin Mei teaches Wang Lee the Chinese characters, but the message he gets through learning is a Christian one. Brought up by his pious parents, Wang Lee finds it hard to accept that the great Confucius is condemned by the God of the Heavenly Kingdom. He refuses to recognize that the leader of the sect calls himself the Heavenly King and claims to have been chosen to this position by God himself. The whole ideology is for him abominable and incomprehensible.

As Wang Lee successively gets infatuated with Lin Mei, he also gets more tolerant toward the new ideas, which is shown in the text with subtle methods. First he resents Lin Mei being "so manlike" (38); he loathes being "rebuked by a mere woman" (58) and doesn't "care about the opinion of a mere woman" (62). He hates her taking away his name, Wang, because it means "King" and there is only one king in the new ideology. In his opinion, quite rightly, Lin Mei has robbed him of his identity. Yet when he notices how respected Lin Mei is by the other rebels, men and women equally, he "almost forgot that she was ugly and unwomanly" (65). When she first starts teaching him the elements of the new religion, he is reluctant: "Memorizing the God-worshippers' fancy words. How could he?" (66). He is coaxed into repentance and finally into baptism. His transition becomes, in his own mind, a rite of passage: "Now, suddenly, he became a man, a soldier in the Heavenly Army" (97). The firmer he gets in his belief, the less problematic violence appears. The text informs us, matter-of-factly, that Wang Lee has killed his first man. Dozens follow, and Wang Lee now sees them as evil demons, threatening the new faith. Any human feelings abandon him: " . . . he shot the boy. Cleanly. He was proud of that" (99); "His arm no longer trembled under the weight of the sword" (104). Wang Lee becomes an executioner rather than a soldier. His fellow rebels' death is celebrated, rather than mourned, since it is perceived as a passage into paradise. When a friend very cautiously starts questioning the ideology, Wang Lee defends it passionately and denounces the alleged traitor. The collective values are put before the individual: "The Heavenly Kingdom was greater than any feelings or obligations of a single soldier" (124). Wang Lee becomes a cog in the ideological machine. Yet gradually he starts to recognize the gap between declarations and actions. There is also enough human left in him to acknowledge his true feelings toward Lin Mei, the forbidden desire that finally makes him a deserter and an outlaw.

Lin Mei in her turn has escaped slavery and sexual abuse, and the new ideology attracts her by the slogan of gender equality. "In the Heavenly Kingdom there is no difference between male and female," she tells Wang Lee (36). This reference to Col. 3:11 ("where there is neither Greek nor Jew") sounds ironic, as women are exploited by the sect leaders for their own purposes. Christianity appeals to Lin Mei because it does not condemn fallen women, but she does not realize that she is being used in another sense than the sexual. Equality means in the context equal right to die for the cause. Lin Mei is an army captain and is promoted to colonel, leading her sisters into battle and death. Participating in the rebellion alongside men, Lin Mei considers herself emancipated, but eventually encounters the worst kind of Oriental patriarchy, forced into a polygamous marriage.

Sharing alternatively the two protagonists' perspective, it is easy to take their side not only in opposition to the imperial regime, but also to the long-nosed Westerners, from which the new ideology comes. Having witnessed and misinterpreted Christian Communion, the Chinese in the novel believe that the Christians are cannibals: they eat the flesh "cut up into tiny pieces and then blood squeezed out. They drink the blood separately" (13). Wang Lee feels superior to "the long-nosed barbarians" (101). However, the distorted Christianity may decidedly alienate the implied Western reader. One may further perceive the implied author's worldview as abominable, and a most horrendous example of Orientalism, savage Chinese as opposed to civilized Christians, and the Christian values as appropriate for saving the world. The mutual othering of the two cultures is apparent. As the novel progresses, however, the situation gradually becomes more and more complex. It is obvious that the leaders exploit the new religion for their own purposes, material as well as power-related. They roll in wealth and self-indulgence. While imposing rules on their subordinates, they exempt themselves from any rules. The propagated ideas of equality, communal property, chastity and honor do not pertain to them. In the end, the only surviving leader, having got rid of all rivals, forces Lin Mei to marry him, claiming that the God has so desired.

Wang Lee and Lin Mei solve their problem on a personal level, returning to simple rural life and rejecting terror following the fanatical faith. Yet they believe themselves to be unworthy it rather than the doctrine being corrupt: "we chose a different path" (227).

In this novel, the setting, comprised of concrete space and time, is an integral part of the plot, while it is at the same time significantly more universal and allegorical. The othering works in reverse, presenting an insider perspective and engaging rather than alienating the reader. Yet to assess the protagonists' malleability, the readers must dissociate themselves from the subjectivity of the text.

Paterson's three other oriental novels, all set in various historical periods in Japan, are written from completely different artistic and educational premises. There is no conflict between alien ideologies, and the plots revolve around much more general human values and reflect recognizable patterns of children's literature. *The Sign of the Chrysanthemum* (1973) is an adventure story, featuring an archetypal orphan in search of his lost father. Typically, Muna has created a father image from his mother's fragmentary account, a phantom figure onto which he can project his adolescent revolt. In the end, he admits that his biological father is irretrievably lost and instead accepts a father substitute whom he first resented but who proves to possess all the traits that his imaginary father would have.

The Master Puppeteer (1975) is a mystery novel, in which the Robin Hood plot is somewhat eclipsed by the young protagonist's everyday experience as an apprentice in a Japanese puppet theatre, where the technicalities come into the foreground. The settings in both novels allow a richness of historical details, and add to the exotic flavor. Both male protagonists, especially Jiro in *The Master Puppeteer*, are thoroughly introduced into their professions, which also provide the readers with glimpses of an exciting world of a particular trade. The ways and traditions of Japan in the far-away epochs create a colorful backdrop; yet both stories could easily employ a different setting, including an imaginary one.

Of Nightingales That Weep (1974) is a female initiation narrative, following the conventional pattern of separation—isolation—re-emergence. The plot includes recognizable elements such as the death of the father, the mother/daughter conflict, a substitute father figure, removal from the family, first love and reconciliation. The girl is even cross-dressed for a short while. For Takiko, not unlike Muna, the dead father is a hero whose memory she fondly cherishes. She resents her deformed stepfather, whom she finally learns to respect and even love, but has to go through another separation, in order to be incorporated into female hierarchy. This, however, proves untenable, since the female community belongs to the losing side in an armed conflict. The object of Takiko's infatuation represents an enemy clan, so that an issue of loyalty is posed. With war, exile and danger, adventurous excitement is added to the plot, yet the narrative itself is unmistakably feminine. Unlike the male protagonists, Takiko lacks agency and is confined to the domestic sphere. The historical Oriental setting is used to amplify the subjugated situation of a young woman. Takiko's creativity, channeled through a traditionally male trade, pottery, is suppressed by patriarchy, and she herself eventually rejects it as childish. But she also possesses feminine artistry, being a superb musician. Music, however, as a non-verbal art, has lower societal status. Although Takiko can actually read and write, she has no use for these skill. The delicate balance between masculine and feminine is maintained throughout the novel, allowing a much deeper psychological thrust. Takiko chooses love rather than duty. Her ethical standpoint is questioned, and, in a symbolical manner, she is punished by the death of her mother, infant brother and favorite nurse. Punishment for forbidden love is a recurrent pattern in a female initiation narrative, since the young woman must learn to make right choices and see through superficial beauty and valor. In a historical setting especially, the narrative has little room for the heroine's agency. Takiko has already declined death as a way out of imprisonment. In a symbolically charged scene, she shreds her rich silk garments and dons simple peasant clothes. Through an accident, she gets an ugly scar across her face, while months of toil in the rice fields deform her body and tan her skin. She is thus no longer an appropriate object of male desire. The young Genji warrior rejects her, revealing himself as unworthy.

The heteronormative solution is closed for the protagonist, but the patriarchal norm is confirmed and questioned: a woman is only attractive as long as she is pretty and weak. Another choice is then prompted, as Takiko tries to enter a convent. An old nun, a mother substitute, denies her this way as well, suggesting instead that Takiko find her place in life through creativity, through her music. However, the world where music was appreciated, the Imperial court of Takiko's clan, has perished. The only remaining option for the protagonist is to return to heteronormativity, which may be viewed as submissiveness, yet she acts in a manner that still allows her agency. She marries her old, poor and deformed stepfather, a man inferior to her, who is a potter and lower in social status when compared to Takiko who is the daughter of a samurai. She accepts the conventional female role of nurturing, yet she is physically and mentally stronger of the two. She is further empowered by giving birth to a daughter, thus strengthening the female element instead of submitting to the male. Interestingly enough, her husband affirms the fact. When Takiko, upset to disappoint him, says: "It is only a girl", he responds with admiration: "Isn't it what you are . . . I'm no match for two of you" (170). This subtle way of interrogating norms is possible because of the Oriental setting, which in itself has an alienating effect. Without creating a too obvious anachronism, the novel presents a truly subversive message.

Male Robinsonnade

Michael Morpurgo's *Kensuke's Kingdom* (1999) combines Orientalism with Robinsonnade, or survival story, which adds a number of new heterological tensions. The protagonist is not a bearer of an indigenous culture, but a white man, in extreme terms, a colonialist. The personal narrative perspective sets up alterity from the very start, since Western values are given priority. Ignoring the complete incredibility of the novel on the mimetic level, we may best interpret it as a symbolic depiction of a male initiation rite, or else a hallucinatory dream narrative. In any case, the pattern of a novice isolated from his normal, well protected environment, guidance by a wise old man, and re-introduction into society is highly recognizable. As an intertextual reply to *Robinson Crusoe*, the novel certainly presents more acceptable ideology, and yet several slightly imperialistic traits come through. Michael is British, while the man he meets on the tiny Pacific island is Japanese. Although Michael has rather vague knowledge of WWII, he is aware, and Kensuke does not fail to remind him repeatedly, that Japan lost the war. Kensuke's deficient English makes him inferior to the protagonist, and while he makes an effort to learn the language of the conquerors, Michael shows no interest whatsoever to learn Japanese, merely stating that the characters Kensuke uses are strange. In rendering his experience, Kensuke only has access to oral language, while Michael is literate and describes his adventures through written, public discourse. Kensuke lives among orangutans and has learned his survival skills from them. He treats them as friends, has learned their body language and can communicate with them, and has given them names. He protects them from hunters and in the end chooses to stay on the island, claiming that the orangutans are his family. Implicitly, the text suggests that Kensuke is nothing else than an ape himself. This is an exceedingly harsh statement about the novel, but I dare make it to show how blurred and potentially treacherous heterological frontiers are.

On the other hand, Michael is totally dependent on Kensuke for his survival. Not only does the old man save him from drowning or heal him when he gets paralyzed by a giant jellyfish, but he also provides him and his dog with food and water, shares his supplies and finally his shelter. He also teaches him his art of painting. Further, it turns out that Kensuke is a doctor of medicine and used to have a high societal status, while Michael comes from a working-class family with limited economic means (that the two redundant lower-class workers can afford a voyage around the world should not be judged as a realistic detail). As an adult and an educated man, as well as a mythic guide, Kensuke is unconditionally superior to Michael. The carnival of Robinsonnade transforms into anti-carnival, as the protagonist is deprived of the little power he had before the shipwreck (he was after all entrusted by his parents to steer the vessel) and rendered helpless and compliant. Kensuke promptly interrupts Michael's attempts to escape by lighting a fire or sending flask post, and the boy has to acquiesce. However, Kensuke eventually admits that Michael must return to civilization which indicates that it is preferable to his savage existence of the island. Yet Michael has hardly learned anything from his initiation, and he does not return to become independent, but to be restored into the security of the family and protective care of his parents. The fact that he returns to his biological parents, not least his strong-willed mother (symbolically, a skipper on the boat), after a period with a substitute father, indicates reversal to immaturity. It is essential for a young man to liberate himself from maternal protection and incorporate himself into a male community. A transitional father figure is an important phase in the process. Instead, the protagonist is brought back into his mother's safe embrace.

Female Robinsonnades

Stories of girls or young women surviving in an extreme environment are not an unusual genre. Yet they present a dilemma for a children's writer, since they are initially a masculine genre, in which typically masculine traits of the protagonist are emphasized: strength, activity, independence, rationality, analytical and quantitative thinking, and so on. In a female Robinsonnade, the character must necessarily hover between maintaining, or even developing, masculine traits and values on the one hand, and, on the other, retaining or affirming her femininity.

Julie of the Wolves (1972), by Jean George, recounts the experience of a thirteen-year-old native girl in Alaska, who runs away from an arranged marriage and, losing her way in the tundra, spends several months on her own, near a pack of wolves. She once heard from her father that wolves are friendly and sociable, and that they will accept a human being into their community and share their food as long as you learn the code of behavior. Apart from support from the wolves, Miyax learns to use the skills of her people, including building shelters, hunting and using weapons and tools. At the same time, she acts in a typically feminine way as she decorates her provisional house with flowers and states with satisfaction that "it was cozy inside" (13).

The protagonist's identity is ambivalent. Brought up by her father in a traditional way, Miyax is snatched from this environment and claimed by the white civilization, represented by mandatory schooling. She goes through a cultural transformation closely connected with the change of name; in the civilized world she becomes Julie. She enjoys the comforts of urban life, but feels uneasy watching her Americanized classmates. On the one hand, she admires their Western education: "The girls her age could speak and write English and they knew the names of presidents, astronauts, and radio and movie personalities" (84f). Her classmates, in turn, resent her ignorance of the most elementary tokens of civilization. Her confusion is further amplified by getting a pen-pal from California, who entices her with "television, sports cars, blue jeans, bikinis, hero sandwiches, and wall-to-wall carpeting" (88). The image of the pretty pink bedroom, promised to her in Amy's house, becomes for Julie a distant, yet realistic goal. As she runs away, Julie gradually shifts into her formal self, which is elegantly conveyed by the transition back to the native name. Since her life in civilization is narrated in a flashback, and the novel opens with her first day astray, the text sets up her perspective by using indigenous expressions such as "two sleeps ago" or "many harpoon-shots away."

For her survival in the tundra, Miyax strongly depends on masculine skills she has learned from the father. Her full trust in the father's superior knowledge reverberates like a mantra: "Kapugen had taught her" (29, 42); "Kapugen had said" (36); "Kapugen had once told her" (37); "just like Kapugen said" (40); "she remembered that Kapugen … " (44). At the same time, she possesses some indispensable feminine dexterity as well, such as sewing. In her backpack, she carries a woman's knife and a man's knife (it is not explained why she has a man's knife). The former is typically described as being in the shape of the moon, a feminine symbol. The sun, a masculine symbol, is Miyax's enemy since she needs stars to orient herself, and has no help from the sun during the Polar day. Miyax regrets that she has not brought a gun.

The text refers to Miyax and her people as Eskimos: "her father, an Eskimo hunter" (6); "Eskimo children playing" (18), "the Eskimo hunters" (19). Even she herself uses the label: "We Eskimos" (34) and questions her identity: "scoffing at herself for being such an old-fashioned Eskimo" (59). While the word may feel politically incorrect today, it was acceptable at the time the novel was published. Yet it is more important that the bearers of a culture seldom use labels for themselves, instead dividing the world between "us" and all other peoples and cultures. The white population is in the novel referred to as gussak, and their ways and beliefs are constantly interrogated. This lays the perspective with the protagonist. Yet the objective narrator, focalizing Miyax, nevertheless recurrently slants into didactic omniscience, coming with explanations such as:

> Not a tree *grew* anywhere . . . Only moss, grass, lichens, and a few hardy flowers *take* root in the thin upper layer that *thaws* briefly in summer. Nor do any species of animals *live* in the rigorous land . . . Swarm of crane flies, one of the few insects that *can* survive the cold, *darkened* the tips of the mosses. (9; emphasis added)

The passage is obviously addressed to the non-native implied readers, unfamiliar with the environment, which for Miyax should be self-evident. The emphasized verbs exemplify how the narrative voice recurrently lapses into present tense, abandoning the character's narrative time and speaking in the general edifying manner, more appropriate in non-fiction.

The lengthy external description of the character is especially questionable:

> Miyax was a classic Eskimo beauty, small of bone and *delicately* wired with strong muscles. Her face was pearl-round and her nose was flat. Her black eyes, which slanted *gracefully*, were moist and sparkling. Like the beautifully formed polar bears and foxes of the north, she was slightly short-limbed. (8; emphasis added)

Since this block description appears in the beginning of the novel, as the protagonist is starving and totally focused on obtaining food, it is unlikely that the passage represents figural discourse, that is, her own reflections on her looks; she is too preoccupied with survival. The emphasized words are evaluative in a manner a person would hardly use about herself, while the simile reveals a mature linguistic and cognitive skill. The statement about her being short-limbed is an outsider's view, since for a native, the observation is pointless. Rather, the extradiegetic narrator is scrutinizing the Other, noting, presumably for the benefit of the implied reader, the deviant features of the protagonist. The narrative swings between the desire for authenticity and the necessity to be elucidatory and instructive. The authorial description becomes all the more problematic as Miyax several pages later watches herself in a pond: "She was pleased, for she looked almost like the gussak girls in the magazines and movies—thin and gaunt, not moon-faced like an Eskimo" (28). This self-evaluation shows the inerasable impact of civilization.

As the story develops, Miyax rejects her Julie self and becomes intent on staying true to her native culture. The content of her pack, needles, knife and boots, becomes "more wonderful . . . than airplanes, ocean liners, and the great bridge" (122). The tundra turns in her eyes "even more beautiful" (123), she realizes that the "old Eskimo customs are not so foolish" (126), while "civilization became this monster that snarled across the sky" (141). She decides to live in a native village: "Perhaps she would teach children how to snare rabbits, make parkas, and carve . . . she would live as her ancestors had, in rhythm with the animals and the climate" (156). Identifying completely with the wolves, as well as the plover she has tamed and named, Miyax is appalled at the episode with ruthless hunting, and all the more when she discovers that her adored father has adopted the hunting ways of the white men. He has even married a white woman, an act of betrayal that Miyax can neither grasp nor forgive. Initially, "it never occurred to her that anything that Kapugen decided was not absolutely perfect" (83). Now she starts to doubt. Typically, her stepmother immediately tries to impose civilization on Miyax by telling her that she must go to school and learn English. As usual, literacy turns out to be the most essential mechanism of power. Exercised by a woman, this power is based on age and ethnicity.

Although Miyax's first reaction is to escape, in the last sentence of the novel "Julie pointed her boots toward Kapugen" (170). In the sequel, *Julie* (1974), the protagonist has returned to civilization, firmly adopted her Julie identity and reconciled with her stepmother, even though she continues her ecological engagement and finally redeems her father. This compromise is inevitable if a somewhat credible framework is maintained, which is not necessary with a more symbolic, or even mythic, interpretation of the first novel. In the third part of the trilogy, *Julie's Wolf Pack* (1997), the narrative perspective shifts over to the wolves, creating a completely different othering effect.

The pattern of *Julie of the Wolves* is repeated in several of George's novels, for instance *My Side of the Mountain* (1960) and *The Talking Earth* (1983). In the former, an urban boy runs away from a dysfunctional home, surviving in the mountains where a falcon and a weasel supply him with food. The resolution shows the family reunited and starting a new life in the environment discovered by the protagonist. In the two sequels, the plea for natural life continues, and the final novel is told from the falcon's perspective. In *The Talking Earth*, an adolescent girl of the Seminole tribe survives in the Florida Everglades during a self-inflicted banishment from her village. An otter supplies her with food, and she also befriends a panther and a turtle. The ecological message of both novels is reminiscent of the *Julie* books, emphasizing and idealizing the simple and healthy life of the native population. In *The Talking Earth*, Billie turns from a doubter into a firm supporter of traditional values, not least because they actually help her to survive. In the novels with female protagonists, the text creates alterity by using native focalizers. A male protagonist is already othered from the implied author, and interestingly enough, not detached further by ethnicity.

This gender-based alterity is a recurrent strategy, reflected in several other female Robinsonnades, not least written by male authors. *Island of the Blue Dolphins* (1960), by Scott O'Dell, is claimed to be based on a true story, but just as *Robinson Crusoe* is based on a true story, it is its fictitious representation that is of interest. In the novel, narrated in the first-person, the young native girl, Karana, is unintentionally left behind by her tribe on an island off Californian coast in the beginning of the nineteenth century. Alterity and power position in the novel are extremely intricate. The protagonist is detached in time and in space; she is also alienated from the implied author by age, gender and ethnicity. These factors make her exotic and othered, while the personal narrative voice is supposed to create authenticity and a sense of insider experience.

The narrative situation is vague. The novel opens: "I remember the day" (1), which indicates retrospective narration, but it is unclear whether remembrance takes place while she is still on the island or has left it after twenty years. In the final scene, the narration presents a prolepsis: "Not until I came to Mission Santa Barbara and met Father Gonzales did I learn" (180). The question of the narratee is crucial. It is possible that Karana tells her story to Father Gonzales; there are, however, no direct textual markers. The author's postscript mentions that the real "Lost Woman of Nicolas Island" never learned to communicate other than with signs. Although we should not attach too much importance to this extra textual information, we can assume that Karana lost her verbal capacity during the many years of isolation and is unlikely to learn English or Spanish, as may be, to tell her story to a white man. There is no indication of her being literate to believe that her story is a written account. On merely one occasion, the text contains an invocation of a narratee: "Perhaps I should tell *you* about our island so *you* will know how it looks and where our village was" (9; emphasis added). The narratee could probably be Karana's own children or grandchildren who certainly need a description since they have never seen the island. Further, the narrator explains some things that she would hardly need to explain to someone from her own culture: "apples that grow on the cactus bushes and are called tunas" (27). The explication is reminiscent of similar passages in *Julie of the Wolves*, not least in the shift to present tense. Karana also repeatedly stresses the ways and habits of her own people. Thus as a narrator she deliberately creates her narratee as the Other; or rather the (masculine) implied author lets the female narrator express his values in terms of alterity.

If the narratee is a white man (or a white woman for that matter, or any other outsider), it is highly unlikely that Karana would in her narrative reveal her sacred and secret name, especially since she has seen her father lose his life by doing so. She does reveal it to the Aleut girl she has secretly befriended, but even then she need not reveal it to the narratee. Since she does, we may infer that the narratee is someone she fully trusts, and after all the betrayals she has encountered, who would she trust except the dumb beasts around her—or herself.

The most reasonable interpretation of the narrative perspective is that the text represents mental discourse, retrospective rather than simultaneous, thus creating yet another power hierarchy, that between the narrating and the experiencing self. Even though the narrative can further be judged as consonant rather than dissonant, the power tension of the novel is created on the crossroads of these different alterities.

After the dramatic opening, when the majority of men on the island are killed by Aleut otter hunters and the rest are taken away by white men (for unclear purposes, presumably for slavery), not much happens for the rest of the story. Years go by at high pace, and the narrator does not dwell on the psychological aspects of survival. One could assume that a young girl's thoughts during twenty years in total isolation would focus more on her emotions. Naturally, the large temporal span of the story does not allow much detail, but the narrative is conspicuously devoid of self-reflection. Karana mentions occasionally that she grieves her father's and her little brother's death; that she misses her sister and later the Aleut girl. Yet these feelings are stated rather than artistically represented, told rather than shown. Instead, the narrative concentrates on physical survival, getting food and drinking water, building shelters and canoes, and not least making weapons. Karana is highly ambivalent about this action. "The laws of Ghalas-at forbade the making of weapons by the women of the tribe" (51). She returns to this argument repeatedly; "I thought again about the law that forbade women to make weapons" (80); "I suddenly remembered my father's warning that, because I was a woman, the bow would break" (82). Yet she also knows she is dependent on breaking the laws: "I made up my mind that no matter what befell me I would make the weapons" (54). One may argue that Karana is adopting an anti-patriarchal attitude; but it may be equally assessed as the character constructed as quasi-feminine, not least because she is so explicitly goal-oriented. In her use of language, she does not hesitate to repeat the verb "kill."

Karana is not a "green-world" girl who finds strength in nature and feels part of it. On the contrary, she is, in a typically masculine way, intent on conquering nature and making it serve her purposes; on setting up goals and achieving them. In other words, her performative gender is, at least initially, masculine.

As the story develops, Karana's attitude gradually changes. Her first shift toward femininity is marked by her hesitation to kill the leader of the wild dogs. She has been determined to kill off the pack to revenge her brother. The leader, an Aleut dog, also represents the human enemy, the Aleuts who have murdered most of her tribe. Yet when Karana sees the leader fighting another dog, an episode foreshadowed in the combat of two sea elephant bulls, she feels compassion and, wondering at her own behavior, brings the wounded dog home to nurture. The action is not unequivocal. By taming the dog, she gains power over him. By naming him, she obtains still more power, as is emphasized in her contemplation on secret names. Just as Miyax totally identifies with the wolf leader, Karana identifies with the dog, consistently referring to them both as "we." On a more symbolic level, both male animals are the female protagonists' respective Animus, or, to borrow a concept from a recent novel, daemon.

Further, Karana tames, or vanquishes, birds, an otter and a fox. She says that the animals are her family, the children "so different from the ones I always wished to have" (153). This is a typically feminine way of expression; yet behind it a masculine power order is hidden. Karana's total mastery over nature makes her a social androgyne. Yet the shift toward the feminine progresses. After securing her safety with weapons, Karana gets an interest in her looks and makes herself new clothes and jewelry, showing a good deal of female vanity. After making friends with the young otter, she feels that she will never be able to kill another animal. The nurturing attitude toward nature overpowers the drive to subjugate it; eventually, a truly ecological message is preached: "this is the way I felt about the animals who had become my friends and those who were not, but in time could be" (156).

On espying the white men's ship, Karana hurries to make herself attractive and appropriate to what she believes to be her rescuers' expectations:

> I went down to the ravine and bathed in the spring and put on my otter cape and my cormorant skirt. I put on the necklace of black stones and the black earrings. With blue clay I made the mark of our tribe across my nose. (177)

The mention of the bath is especially illuminating. The narrator has never before referred to washing or any other form of hygiene. The circumvention of female bodily functions is especially telling, as in her development from a twelve-year-old girl to a mature woman, Karana would logically contemplate the changes in her body. Yet bathing in anticipation of white men signals Karana's awareness of her own imperfection. In contrast, she puts on her best clothes and paints her face in a manner that, in her culture, indicates her status.

After twenty years of growth and independence, Karana is prepared to shrink back to her disempowered initial position. Her readiness for acquiescence to white men does not only accentuate her own inferior status, but also points at the Aleut (and their Russian leader) as barbaric, disreputable and unworthy.

In the end, after, in terms of the nineteenth century, a life-time on the island, Karana is discovered and removed. Her rescuer is presented, with a truly estranging effect, as:

> ... man in the gray robe had a string of beads around his neck and at the end of it was an ornament of polished wood. He raised his hand and made a motion toward me which was in the shape of the ornament he wore. (178)

A string of beads is something Korana can relate to since it is customary among her people. The crucifix and the blessing are signs of otherness, and the redeemer's gender further emphasizes the opposition between the two. Yet

Karana is captivated by the sounds of the men's voices and is willing to follow the white men to the mainland. At this point she still hopes to find her own people. But already this decision shows her total submission to the masculine and "civilized" world. The first act of socialization implies a superficial make-over, as Karana is forced to give up her pagan dress, that she has been so proud of, and wear something that her deliverers think more appropriate: "dress . . . made of two trousers just like those the white men were wearing" (179). Three aspects are reflected in this short statement: gender, civilization and race. Karana does not like her new attire: "I wanted to wear my cormorant skirt and my otter cape, which were much more beautiful" (179). By now, Karana has developed a strong sense of gender and ethnic identity, and is reluctant to be forced to reject it.

White man's ideology, represented in the first hand through Christianity, triumphs over Karana's "primitive" values. The power polarities are not in her favor: gender, race, illiteracy (moreover, muteness), paganism, lack of Western etiquette and so on. The resolution shows a white "civilized" and educated man's supremacy. If the ending is supposed to be ironic, the irony is thoroughly disguised. Instead, the novel asserts the common stereotype of socializing the savage, even though the socialization process remains beyond the text. The protagonist's gender amplifies the message.

The text demonstrates clearly the pattern examined by postcolonial theory: appropriation of voice. The narrative pretends to be constructed from the perspective of the oppressed, yet the inevitable alterity creates an insurmountable clash.

A factor that strongly contributes to alterity in *Island of the Blue Dolphins* is the gender imbalance between the (implied) author and the narrator/protagonist. The problems of voice performance will be investigated in a later chapter; yet first a more general discussion on gender is necessary.

Chapter Seven
Othering Gender:
New Masculinities, New Femininities

From the previous chapter, it should be clear that there is a difference between masculine and feminine plots and between strategies of othering in young adult (YA) fiction, as compared to literature for younger readers, where genders are more interchangeable. Since male and female rites of passage, whether archaic or modern, follow different patterns, it should be anticipated that fictional representation of masculinity and femininity reflects the actual situation, yet at the same time is affected by other power hierarchies. Since masculinity is traditionally given priority in power relationships, it would seem natural that in YA novels male protagonists must confirm their masculinity, while female protagonists must negotiate their power position in compliance with patriarchal rules.

Although feminist approaches to children's literature have been prominent for many years, we still lack a more precise metalanguage to discuss gender-related issues and too often get entangled in rigid definitions of female/male, feminine/masculine, which frequently depends on the scholar's essentialist or constructivist approach respectively. The issues raised by feminist and queer criticism go far beyond the concept of gender, toward general questions of power and alterity. Further, the terminology provided by feminist and queer theories is limited since it is focused either on the binarity female/male (alternately feminine/masculine) or heterosexual/homosexual. Postcolonial theory provides yet another binarity: (ethnic) majority/minority, or imperialistic/indigenous, yet another aspect of power hierarchy. Therefore I choose in discussions of gender speak of heterological rather than feminist or queer analysis. The culturally dependent term masculine, as opposed to the biological male should henceforth be understood as normative and empowered, while feminine equals disempowered, oppressed, deviant and silenced.

This statement is based on a number of preconceived opinions about masculine and feminine writing. I am using these exclusively as a point of departure for my discussion and do not in any way maintain that these prejudices are indeed true. Yet the premises come from previous gender-related studies of general and children's texts, in which certain generalizations have been made, including gender stereotypes and gender-related textual features (Gilbert and Gubar 1977; Showalter 1989; Spender 1998; Stephens 1996 Trites 1997; Hourihan 1997; Wilkie-Stibbs 2002). I use the concepts of convention to refer to statements about what literary texts "normally" are and do. A convention implies that a majority of texts within a certain culture or timeframe follow a certain pattern. For instance, by convention, male authors use male protagonists while female authors use female protagonists. By convention, male protagonists appear in action-oriented genres while female protagonists appear in character-oriented stories. Some other preconceived opinions claim that masculine writing includes external focalization, open narrative space, goal-oriented plot, linear time, and logical, structured language, while feminine narration implies internal focalization, closed space, diffuse plot, circular time and fragmentary language.

It is trivial to point out that gender construction in fiction for teenage readers reflects societal changes and expectations. Boys and young men are exposed to societal pressures just as much as girls and young women, merely in a different manner. While girls, in reality as well as in literature, have been forced into silent and submissive roles, young males have always had the pressure on them to be strong, aggressive and competitive. Similarly, while real and literary girls have relatively successfully insisted on their right to be strong and independent, the masculine stereotypes turned out to be much more tenacious. The masculine stereotype has been dominant in juvenile literature because it has prevailed in Western culture at large, going back to myths and classic literature. Recent YA novels frequently present a new male, encumbered by the social pressures and uncomfortable in his conventional gender role. The first-person perspective, frequently employed in YA literature, attempts to convey the loneliness and confusion of a teenager in the world of adults. However, since the textual agency conveying ideology is the implied author rather than the narrator, there is always an empowered adult behind the young disempowered narrator.

The New Male

Aidan Chambers' *Dance on My Grave* (1982) entered the history of juvenile fiction as one of the first books that explicitly and candidly discussed homosexuality. But it also became a trendsetter in a different manner, introducing the new kind of male character in YA novel, the new "way of being male" (Stephens 2002). It is therefore an appropriate text to start the discussion of gender and the transformations of masculinity and femininity.

On the surface, *Dance on My Grave* may appear a typical masculine narrative in terms of genre. It starts with a dramatic sailing adventure in which the hero saves a "damsel in distress" (that the damsel happens to be a young man is another matter) and includes a number of spectacular motorbike rides, one of which results in a violent death. There is a confrontation between the hero and a hostile gang from which the hero emerges as a victor (true, through cunning rather than strength, but this is allowed in heroic stories). Further, the novel is constructed as a thriller: a crime has been committed, the criminal has been arrested and put on trial, and a detective—in this case, a social worker—is investigating the case. As readers, we are allowed to get ahead of the investigator since we take part of Hal's written report before Ms. Atkins. As she is helplessly trying to put the jigsaw bits together, we follow Hal's self-exploration, which only partially coincides with Ms. Atkins's in its goal.

On the other hand, the novel is definitely about relationships and the protagonist's feelings, features normally associated with feminine discourse. Hal's way to identity does not go though heroic deeds, but a thorough examination of his own emotions. In fact, in the relationship with Barry, Hal does not play the hero's part. Barry is the strong, intelligent, "macho-man" hero, while Hal is insecure, emotional, and vulnerable. Viewing the novel in this light, it appears to be a typical feminine narrative, a romance, in which the protagonist is inferior to the stronger and more dominant male, and which is focused on the protagonist's confused feelings about this male. The almost compulsory ingredient of the romance, the rich/poor contrast, is present as well.

In accordance with the masculine stereotype, Hal finds home restrictive and tries to spend as much time as he can outside it. He seeks open spaces such as the beach, and undertakes dangerous adventures symbolizing the conquering of the elements, such as sailing in rough weather. His high-speed motorbike rides with Barry also imply triumph over vast spaces. In fact, the motorbike is a kenotype, as opposed to archetype, a modern-time transformation of the mythical hero's horse, the attribute that enables fast and efficient movement in space, inherent to the male hero. At the same time, the physical and emotional bonds between Hal and Barry emerge and develop at home, in the traditional feminine space.

Hal's coming to terms through writing is a feature often pointed out in heterological studies as a liberation strategy. Many classical and modern girls' novels show young women struggling for recognition as writers and either finding their voices or becoming silenced by patriarchal structures. Hal's writing is affected by several power positions. He is empowered as male, but disempowered as young against the adults, as homosexual against heteronormal, as a working-class boy against the socially privileged, and as a criminal against the socially acceptable. His writing is therefore an extremely important weapon not only in his direct self-defense, but also in terms of power negotiation. Here several tensions emerge. By seeking education, Hal crosses the class border; by asserting his sexual orientation he challenges heteronormativity;

by being acquitted through his written plea he reenters the social norm. All these aspects collaborate in constructing his performative gender.

The sixteen-year-old Hal is telling his own story, and the purpose of his written account is in the first place to produce a basis for a trial against him. Hal is accused of having vandalized the grave of his friend Barry, who was killed in a motorbike accident. Hal's story is told in self-justification, to explain why he has acted the way he has. His voice is thus a public one: the narrative is meant to be accessible to a broad audience of strangers. Public discourse, especially written discourse, has stronger societal authority than private and gives Hal more power. Although Hal describes highly intimate events, the public addressee of his confession affects the tone and style of his writing. In its purpose, or the illocutive function, the narrative is affected by the narrator's attempt to gain something through narrating. It is possible to consider Hal's narrative as self-therapy, which would render the narration private. Yet the strong presence of the public voice prompts to view Hal's private voice as subordinate.

Hal is presented in the novel—by himself as well as his surrounding—as an intellectual, literate and verbal young man. Although coming from a low-educated family, he shows a great interest in studies, especially English, and is in fact encouraged in writing his confessions not only by the social worker Ms. Atkins, the direct narratee of his story, but also by his English teacher Mr. Osborne, the indirect narratee. It is not stated explicitly from the beginning that Hal's story has any particular recipient. Yet the fact that the narratee is covert rather than overt does not mean that there is no narratee. The first invocation of the narratee does not appear until halfway through the novel: "I was going to write pages more about those seven weeks. I wanted *you* to understand what we were like together" (163; emphasis added). The repeatedly invoked "you" is eventually named: " . . . you, Ms Atkins" (173). But also Osborne is addressed indirectly, since Hal knows that the teacher will peruse his story. The double narratee accounts for the self-irony of Hal's narration, as he is deliberately teasing the female social worker and at the same time exchanging internal jokes with the male teacher.

Hal repeatedly tells us that he is writing down his story and how much trouble he is having in this endeavor. Every now and then he corrects himself, trying to find a more adequate expression of his thoughts:

> That was how it was.
> *Correction:* That was how it was not. (42; emphasis in the original)

He also rewrites some episodes of the story, as well as "replays" the events in slow motion (a device from film and TV, widely adopted by juvenile authors after Chambers), and constantly questions the possibility of a trustworthy narrative. The narrator is also allowed to alter his story, but the purpose is not so much to illuminate the gap between experience and narrating as to show the narrator's interrogating his own capacity of finding adequate linguistic means to convey his experience. In other words, the text illustrates Lacan's thesis about the inadequacy of language in conveying complex mental states. Concerning the gap between the experiencing and the narrating self, it is important to bear in mind that the time span between the events and the narration is relatively short. The temporal frames of the novel are marked by the newspaper clipping referring to "yesterday" when a nameless youth was charged in court for vandalizing a grave. The clipping informs the reader that "the case was adjourned until a social inquiry report could be prepared" (n.p.). We can determine the day of the trial as the beginning point of the discourse (but not the story), since it is apparently the same day that Hal starts recording his confessions as an appendix to the social worker's official report. The analepsis, taking us back to "that first day" (9), "last June" (11), begins seven weeks prior to the trial, although we will not know this until halfway through the novel:

> From beginning to end was seven weeks.
>   Forty-nine days from me being soaked in seaweed to him being dead. He becoming It.
>   One thousand one hundred and seventy-six hours.
>   Seventy thousand five hundred and sixty minutes.
>   Four million two hundred and thirty-three thousand six hundred seconds. (155)

The poignantly exact time account emphasizes the intensity of Hal's experience, when each second was significant. Hal's memories are quite fresh, and he is eager to describe the events as accurately as possible. He does not win anything by lying or explaining away his actions, but on the contrary tries to sound as candid as he can. By the end of the novel, story time and discourse time are synchronized, that is, the gap between experience and narration diminishes and eventually disappears.

It would seem that the novel presents an explicit feminine structure, with its short, fragmentary, impressionistic sketches and observations. Yet there is a difference between plot, implying the chain of events, and their discursive organization. The plot of the novel is quite conventional, with a logical beginning (Hal's meeting with Barry) and end (Barry's death and Hal's desecration of his grave). The plot is focused on external events: Barry saves Hal, they go out together, ride the motorbike, get involved in a fight, and so on. It is on the discourse level that Hal's reflections emerge, and the text becomes fragmentary.

The protagonist himself is far from stereotypical. Hal shows considerably more conventional feminine traits; he is passive, non-aggressive, dependent, and vulnerable, which is especially emphasized through contrast with Barry. He is also fixed upon his looks, which is repeatedly conveyed as he views himself in a mirror, a scene reverberating in many classical novels with female protagonists. On one occasion, Hal is disguised as a girl:

> He was gazing at a girl with fluffed, slightly frizzed blonde hair that ha-loed a tanned face touched with a blush of colour on high cheeks. She had a wide, generous mouth, perhaps a too prominent chin. She wore a loose white summer dress . . . (213)

Hal has for a short time adopted a female identity, but he studies himself as if from outside, as he would have gazed at a girl. He even wonders "whether this girl would attract him" (214). Since Hal is homosexual, the use of feminine characterization device is appropriate and efficient. By the end of the novel, Hal has become more masculine, which confirms the masculine stereotype. Even though homosexuality in itself is an interrogation of the heterosexual script as a norm, Hal becomes a more "normal" male figure in his development from object to subject, toward an active sexual agency.

While in *Dance on My Grave* gender alterity is amplified by class and sexual orientation, other combinations can be employed. *Winter Bay* (1993) by the Swedish writer Mats Wahl, introduces several alteriries, including a strong aetonormative conflict, which all contribute to an intertwined set of norms and deviations. The protagonist/narrator is extremely violent and a part of a strong homosocial group. His moral qualities are dubious, and the text successfully alienates the character by these traits. Yet at the same time, John-John is sensitive and vulnerable. He is also creative, participating in a school theater production. The text goes so far in its ambiguity that only half-way through the novel do we realize that the first-person narrator is colored, son of a black immigrant; thus the ethnic alterity is touched upon. For the protagonist of *Winter Bay*, it is just one of many psychological plights. The character is doubtless othered, but ethnic identity is not his foremost issue. Alterity is created by the synergy of various power hierarchies: black/white, male/female/, rich/poor, strong/weak. John-John is talented and creative, yet his race and social background are against him. Entangled in the world of crime, he retains some basic ethic values and convictions. The solution, if there is any, is on a personal level rather than in collective achievements. John-John is a complex, elusive and ambivalent character, not a stereotypical second-generation immigrant.

Creativity is for John-John, like for Hal, a part of his maturation process. Moreover, his writing is not an ordered, structured, logical masculine discourse, but dreamlike, fragmentary poetry. Interspersed throughout the text, the poems, reminiscent of Walt Whitman, create a sharp contrast with the rough rendering of external events, revealing the character as significantly more contradictory than the rest of the narrative might suggest. The poems feature John-John's father, yet not the real father, but an imaginary, phantom father emerging through words.

While new masculinities evolve towards a more ambivalent mix of conventional masculine and feminine features, the development of new femininity often goes quite radically away from stereotypes. Typically, several of the first really rough girls in Swedish YA fiction were created by a male author, the same Mats Wahl, first in the historical novel *Anna-Carolina's War* (1986) and then in *Little Marie* (1995), in which both characterization and voice of the first-person female narrator appear a simple gender permutation. Wahl supplants a seemingly female character for his favorite male hero, the confused and therefore violent teenager, best shown through John-John in *Winter Bay*. Anna-Carolina acts within a traditional cross-dressing plot, when she takes her brother's place as a conscript during the Thirty-Year War. Engaged in active combat, the protagonist not only performs externally in a masculine way, entering a homosocial community, but soon internalizes a masculine mentality, referring to other women as "them" and even participating in a collective rape. Her agency is typically masculine, and she enjoys the power her masculine status offers. Yet, as it has been noticed in several studies of cross-dressing, the outcome of the carnival is predictable. Unless the girl in disguise perishes, she is inevitably reintroduced into the stereotypical feminine matrix. As soon as Anna-Carolina meets a man that she, or rather the implied author, deems suitable, she happily changes back to female attire, and presumably also regains her feminine way of thinking, although the latter fact is never touched upon. From an independent subject, albeit on patriarchal conditions, the young woman voluntarily becomes an object for the strong and protective male, and by extension, for the voyeuristic male implied author.

The female character-narrator of *Little Marie* is a "hero in drag" in a subtler manner: masculine mentality, behavior and sexuality put into a female body without superficial disguise. Marie is extraordinarily strong and extremely aggressive, demonstrating all the deviant features of the feminine stereotype. Her domain is outdoors. Violence is her way to power, and she consistently constructs herself in opposition to societal expectations of girls. It is socially accepted for men to be violent, while aggressive women are viewed as deviation from norm. The question is whether Marie interrogates norms or confirms them by her violent performance. She is definitely not the conventional tomboy girl who is subsequently tamed and returned to patriarchal order.

An easily recognizable set of patterns appears in the novel. Marie is a result of rape, and she desperately attempts to find her father in her identity quest. Her working-class mother is weak, and her stepfather tries to abuse her sexually. While Marie herself is violent, she is exposed to violence in her capacity as a girl; she is open for male desire. However, she strongly rejects being a victim and a sexual object. As a consequence, she seems to lack any sexual identity and clearly dissociates from other girls until she meets a girl to whom she is erotically attracted. But the masculine Marie does not take initiative, she remains passive, while the feminine, sexually experienced Katrin acts a seducer. As a character, Marie is queer, but she does not find liberation in queerness. The implied author does not allow her to deviate from heteronormativity and kills off her girlfriend. Unlike Hal, Marie does not acknowledge and affirm her homosexuality, most probably because the heteronormative order does not approve of it. In other words, the masculine ideology of the novel eventually denies Marie agency on equal premises. The way she is constructed, there is no room for complexity or ambiguity. Personal narration limits character assessment. As a character, Marie is simply inconsistent and unconvincing, an artistic failure. Masculine femininity, created by the masculine ideology, is projected onto a female body.

Not unexpectedly, creativity is explored in the novels as a part of identity quest. Yet when Marie is assigned to express herself through writing, she writes a romantic story with erotic undertones, in line with prejudices about feminine creative abilities. Compared to John-John's imaginative poetry, Marie's attempts are flat and do not open vistas for liberation. Yet, it seems that Marie paved the way for a vast number of literary sisters molded in the same pattern, using male stereotypical traits to create a new stereotype of strong and violent quasi-girl.

Girls Take Over

It would seem that contemporary women writers would be extremely sensitive to the issues of gender, not least in works addressed to young readers. However, a new trend in Sweden during the 2000s shows a considerably more palpable borderline between YA novels for male and female audience. The old gender-oriented publications from the 1930s and 1940s seem to break through the postmodern covers of newly published YA novels, and, not unexpectedly, we witness the new, but vaguely familiar phenomenon: books about female characters written by female writers for female readers.[1]

Johanna Thydell's *The Stars Are Shining On the Ceiling* (2003) was awarded the prestigious national August Prize as the best juvenile book of the year and received enthusiastic reviews. Obviously the critics have been misled by a side theme of the book, a young girl coping with her mother's terminal cancer. Given the autobiographical background to this subplot, the adult readers' fascination is somewhat understandable. Yet the mother's painful withering behind the scenes, in a hospital where the protagonist dutifully visits her every week, is totally eclipsed by the main plot, which can be used as a master plot for the new feminine stereotype. In fact, the novel presents every possible cliché, without ever attempting to question them. On closer examination, the thirteen-year-old Jenna has two major concerns in life: how to get hold of strong alcohol for the weekly parties; and whether to sleep with the boy who fancies her.

The dying mother in the background feels like a convenient—and for juvenile literature, conventional—way of getting rid of parental protections and allowing the character to taste the temptations of adult life all on her own. In traditional girls' novels, such as *Little Women*, the father was at war and the mother had to go and take care of his wounds. Alternatively, both parents would be permanently removed, giving a free way for substitute and phantom parental figures. In a contemporary realistic novel, it is not so easy to kill off a parent. *The Stars Are Shining* needs the mother to be comfortably absent to allow the heroine freedom of action. Whether there is an autobiographical source to this fact is of no aesthetic significance.

Judging by this novel and others appearing during the last few years, urban girls in Sweden normally get blind drunk every Friday when they are twelve, have their first sexual experience at thirteen, and are daily subjected to rape, incest and drugs. Of course, these horrible events occur in real life, and of course it is more exciting to write about drugs and violence than about ordinary, uneventful life in a harmonious family. Yet the new stereotype is provided by the adults, apparently as a role model rather than cautionary tale.

Jenna is merely one in a row of similar characters, exposing the adult writers ideas of how their young female readers prefer to see themselves. Emma Hamberg creates a self-portrait of a young girl in *Lina's Noctury* (2003). The title is a clever wordplay with "diary," since the character-narrator states initially that nobody ever keeps a diary in the daytime, so it must be called "noctury" instead. Whatever she calls it, her only problem seems to be how to get rid of her virginity as soon as possible. All of Lina's entries focus on sexuality in a rather superficial manner. She wants to have sex because everybody has it; mostly because her best friend has had it or at least claims she has. Getting drunk is high on her list of priorities. Apparently, these are the two essential components of new femininity.

Employing a first-person simultaneous narrator, the implied author has a difficult dilemma, striving for authenticity and therefore using the naïve, unsophisticated perspective, but also needing to carry the educational message through and therefore letting the character argue with herself, in a most unnatural voice for a teenager: maybe it is not so clever after all to have unsafe sex; maybe everybody just pretends it is fun throwing up after heavy drinking. When Lina thinks she is pregnant, she feels none of the anguish that her literary sisters did in the 1970s: whether to choose family or career. For Lina it is just a nuisance, and she has no existential concerns about extinguishing a life. Typically, it proves to be false alarm, and she does not have to make a choice, a convenient way of pointing out an issue without having to tackle it.

Like Jenna, Lina has no intellectual interests: she never reads, she has neither hobbies nor academic ambitions, she never talks about anything significant with her friend. Judging from what she reveals about herself, it is remarkable that she can express herself in written form, even though the language is deliberately meager and childish. Basically, she renders external events, without reflecting much on them. Here is a full-size portrait of the new femininity: ignorant, immature, solipsistic, focused on her own sexuality on a primitive, superficial level, perceiving herself as a sexual object, eager to please the male. There is a substantial difference from the conventional female stereotype we meet, for instance, in *Little Women*, but it is still a highly problematic stereotype. In a way it is more problematic, since in classical texts, a young girl's liberation through creativity is accentuated. Lina's keeping a diary is not convincing in terms of feminine creativity, it is merely a superficial device, seemingly employed to come as close to the "authentic" teenage voice as possible.

In *Sandor slash Ida* (2001), by Sara Kadefors, several heterological patterns support and subvert gender issues. The title itself announces one of the two protagonists' ethnicity. It is never explicitly said which country Sandor's parents come from, but the name is Hungarian. Apparently, Sandor has no Hungarian identity whatsoever, but his mother has all the more. The Central European tradition of upbringing is tangibly present in the text. The mother has failed in her career as a dancer and has transferred her aspirations onto her son, presumably unaware that ballet dancing has different social status and connotation in Sweden than in Hungary. Sandor is a stereotypical "new male": he lacks conventional masculine traits; he genuinely wants to be a dancer and attends a dance school, which causes his classmates to bully him and call him a "pansy." His position as a second-generation immigrant is amplified through his disempowerment as suspect homosexual. The character is structured in cross-section of different alterities, where sexual identity eclipses ethnicity. In fact, Sandor's ethnic background may appear secondary or even totally insignificant, yet it is not only amplified by his gender ambivalence, but also by the class opposites presented in the novel. The other protagonist, whose Swedish name is juxtaposed to Sandor's in the title, comes from an underprivileged, dysfunctional suburban family, in a strong contrast to Sandor's wealthy and well-educated parents. Thus yet another axis of power is added to the othering strategy of the novel.

In its narrative technique, the novel employs another enormously popular classical form revived in contemporary Swedish YA fiction, epistolary novel. Getting a pen-pal allows anonymity and the possibility to change identity that many teenagers need in their identity quest. Epistolary form—updated in *Sandor slash Ida* to e-mail—is the premise of the two characters' self-definition. Both Sandor and Ida hide behind the false role figures they have created for themselves on the Internet. These new identities reflect young people's frequent wish to be something more grand and glamorous than they are. If Sandor is a "new male," Ida is a "new female" with the full set of traits sketched above: getting helplessly drunk on Fridays, meeting boys, getting rid of her virginity, gossiping about other girls, changing loyalties, and an absent father and a sick mother are part of the package. As Sandor and Ida meet under assumed names online, the identities they take on are the direct opposites of what they really are. Sandor presents himself as a tough guy who plays soccer, drinks beer with his buddies and is remarkably popular with girls. Ida introduces herself as shy and inconspicuous, describing her quiet, idyllic life in the countryside, with the obligatory feminine hobby of horseback-riding. Both characters thus present themselves in a conventionally stereotypical manner, not necessarily because they wish to be like that, but because this reflects societal gender expectations. Not quite unexpectedly, the rough masculinity that Sandor lacks is represented by a boy named Babak. Traditional violent masculine identity is connected with the immigrant, and Sandor is thus not only invited to join a male, homosocial community, but also to affirm his heritage, "us" immigrants in opposition to "them" Swedes. Returning to his former self, he rejects both options. Yet as his alleged homosexuality is not confirmed, the novel supports conventional power hierarchies: heteronormativity, ethnic normativity, and superiority of the rich over the poor. Sandor is not only a new male, but a new ethnic stereotype: fully assimilated and basically not encumbered by the issue of origin.

Finding a Genuine Voice

One of the most illuminating ways of demonstrating the profound changes in the construction of gender is to compare books with similar themes, plots and characters written over a hundred years ago with those written today. *Little Women* has often been considered in terms of a "master text," concerning plot structure, characterization and narrative perspective in a domestic novel. Among the typical narrative features associated with feminine writing we find in this novel, for instance, is a long timespan, also a cyclical one, depicting a year in the lives of the four characters and allowing a profound change in them. The multiple character is another common narrative element of domestic fiction, an excellent didactic device allowing the author to emphasize the four sisters' most prominent traits rather than combining them all in a more complex single protagonist. The authoritative narrative voice is used to manipulate the reader toward correct judgment of each character, pointing out their weaknesses and failures as well as the desirable improvements. On the whole, the novel can serve as a perfect illustration of gender and power structures in conventional YA fiction.

Katherine Paterson plays an original and poignant variation on the *Little Women* theme in *Jacob Have I Loved* (1980). In this novel, too, a young girl wishes to be a boy because boys are valued higher in the world she lives in. Louise behaves in an unladylike manner and pursues a male occupation, crabbing, to contribute to the family economy. She befriends a clumsy, lonely boy, whom her pretty, talented and feminine sister will eventually snatch from her just as Amy snatches Laurie from Jo. Like Jo, Louise dreams of going away from the restricted and restrictive world of the little island where she is born and grown up, but has to see her sister Caroline given the privilege, just as Amy travels to Europe instead of Jo. In the end, after many years, Louise marries a much older man who reminds her of her father; like Jo, she seeks a secure father figure rather than a passionate young lover. Yet although many plot elements are similar, they are amplified and problematized in Paterson's novel. Rivalry between sisters, mild and innocent in *Little Women*, is developed into self-destructive jealousy and hatred. The March sisters' self-imposed spiritual pilgrimage becomes in *Jacob Have I Loved* a young girl's hopeless struggle against societal conventions. Not surprisingly, *Jacob Have I Loved* goes considerably further in its social indignation toward women's oppressed position.

The most radical difference between the two novels is, however, the narrative perspective. Instead of the conventional omniscient narrator, first-person perspective is used, which enables the author to focus on the character/narrator's subjective perception of the events rather than an objective rendition. Further, the authoritative narrative agency, able to comment on the characters' behavior and opinions and manipulate the reader toward proper assessment of the characters, disappears, and with it the inherent didacticism of conventional YA literature. The dilemma of employing personal narration in novels striving to convey the internal world of a young character lies in the discrepancy between the cognitive level of the protagonist and the complexity of mental and emotional states that needs sophisticated perception as well as advanced vocabulary to be expressed adequately. Here, the convention of juvenile literature as simple and unambiguous comes into conflict with the authors' striving for psychological complexity and credibility.

A possible narrative strategy for circumventing this dilemma is using retrospective self-narration. In *Jacob Have I Loved*, the narrative voice belongs to the adult Louise who in her memory goes back to the days when she was thirteen. This enables the implied author to pass judgments on the young protagonist as the adult Louise can comment on her own lack of perception, her blunders and shortcomings, her incapacity to evaluate people and events around her. In fact, the gap between the narrating self and the experiencing self is so wide that the narrative situation is almost similar to an omniscient narrator. Yet, there is a difference, since Louise the narrator still only has access to her own thoughts and feelings, and everything she tells us goes through her eyes and mind before readers partake of it. The subjective perspective in itself, but especially amplified by the gap between the events and the time of narration, makes the narrator highly unreliable. Even though she is hardly deliberately telling her story to present herself as a thirteen-year-old in a more favorable light, she may omit facts, or pass wrong judgments, or her memory may fail. Her narrative is colored by her strong empathy for her younger self, which makes her take sides against her twin sister. While in *Little Women* we have no reason to doubt the truth of what we are told, in Louise's case we can only be sure that the events are presented in the way the narrator remembers them or thinks she remembers them. The young protagonist is thus othered by the gap between experience and narration.

Not a Greek God, Exactly (2002), by Katarina Kieri, is a juvenile female Künstlerroman that once again remakes the classical heroine Jo March, placing her in the hardly exciting atmosphere of a small provincial town in Northern Sweden, as far away from the glory and the temptations of modern urban adolescents as Jo was from the perils and glory of Civil War. Unlike Jo, Laura is given very little time to discover who she is and what she is doing in this world. In fact, the compressed narrative time is one of the significant features of the novel, focusing on just a few weeks—but they are weeks full of emotional turbulence.

In a contemporary novel, it is more important to catch the young protagonist in the middle of a crisis, when the whole world is shattered to pieces, and follow her during just a few very intensive days, than to show a more natural chronological change during a period of months or years. One could think that the text squeezes too much in the very short time of the story, but such an avalanche of events is what often happens in real life when one insight leads to another in an agonizing chain reaction. This concentrated emotional state amplifies the readers' empathy. "Why does it have to take such a long time to grow up?" the protagonist cries out into the dark, cold emptiness around her. "Why should one go on for many years in order to learn how everything worked, but not be allowed to take responsibility for oneself, one's place in the universe? Why should one become part of a pattern that one would rather prefer to avoid?" The text's own response to these questions is by showing how Laura suddenly grows up within a few weeks when her ordered life changes into a total confusion. Yet rather than following her literary sisters' long and painful way toward self-knowledge, Laura wants to find her identity here and now; she has no time to wait, because a contemporary adolescent's life is much too hectic as compared to the March girls.

Like Louise, Laura is a single protagonist—collective characters seem to have disappeared completely from serious YA fiction—and she is a much more complex character than the four March sisters put together. A contemporary novel's purpose is not to emphasize one specific human trait to show how one sister overcomes her vanity, her whims or lack of feminine grace. As a character, Laura is contradictory and multifaceted. If *Little Women*, right in the beginning, provides a full description of the heroines and comments on their behavior to govern the readers toward correct judgment, it will take the reader the entire novel to get to know Laura. We cannot even be certain that we really know her the way she is rather than the way she imagines herself to be. For Laura is also the narrator, yet unlike *Jacob Have I Loved*, there is no distance between the narrating self and the experiencing self; Laura's story is unfolding before our eyes right as it is taking place. In fact, it could have been a diary, and there is not a single tiny indication that the narrator has any beforehand knowledge of what is going to happen next. She has no time to ponder or to embellish her story in her own defense; there is no temporal gap to affect her memory, and she lacks the experience of adulthood to judge what is going on within her or even around her.

One would assume that such narrative strategy is restrictive for the author, who must limit her own life experience, adapting it to the level of a fifteen-year-old, in order not to sound false. Yet Laura as a character and narrator has a great advantage as compared to Jo March. She lives in a modern Western society, she has a good education, she has access to mass media, including the Internet, which gives her much better possibilities for self-evaluation than the traditional heroine of domestic novel. This makes Laura plausible as a narrator. Unlike the diary writer Lina, she is verbally talented (she is the editor of the school newspaper and writes poetry) and receives a lot of stimulation at school. This allows the text to use advanced vocabulary and sophisticated, ironic self-reflection without resorting to retrospection as in *Jacob Have I Loved*.

The main conflict of the story revolves around Laura's infatuation with her new young male teacher, not a Greek god exactly, yet handsome, multi-talented—he writes in the local newspaper and plays saxophone—but most important, he encourages Laura's dream to become a writer. He even helps her get a book review published. Laura misinterprets the signals she gets from him. She is fifteen, has never been in love, is waiting for the right one, so it is natural for her to fall for the charming male. In her daydreams about the teacher, she does not notice a classmate who is obviously attracted to her, even though she is pleased to share his interest in poetry and music.

There is thus both a Professor Bhaer and a Laurie in Kieri's novel, both a Captain Wallace, doubled by Joseph Wojtkiewicz, and a Call. But their roles in the construction of modern femininity are radically different. While it was perfectly normal for Jo March to marry an old professor or for Louise to marry an old widower with children, Laura, the sensible and self-ironic narrator, is well aware of the absurdity of a fifteen-year-old being in love with an adult man. To emphasize this, a side plot is introduced that has a completely different function than the subplots of the four sisters in *Little Women*. Laura's best friend Lena unexpectedly reacts negatively to Laura's cautious reflections over her infatuation, and eventually Laura learns why. Lena's father has just left his family to live with a very young woman. "It's your like who ruin families," Lena accuses Laura, in fact quite unjustly. Laura feels heart-broken, not only because Lena has always been her soulmate, but because Lena's family has seemed so perfect as compared to her own, emotionally cold and intellectually flat. Also the two girls' previous comfortable twosomeness in opposition to the provocative "new females" in school fails as they slide apart. Laura shifts toward becoming objectified; Lena retains her integrity.

As a character, Laura has no one to guide her in her attempts to understand what is going on. Instead of trying to support her friend, Laura lets her slip further and further away. This is conveyed through subtle means, without the narrator actually mentioning it directly. Since there is no authoritative, omniscient narrative agency, the reader only has the young protagonist's version of the story, not even corrected by a retrospective view. Laura is unable to judge her own paralyzed state when she never calls Lena, doesn't greet her when bumping into her in town, or doesn't talk to her in school. The vague, diffuse chill between the two girls lacks words to describe it.

Through a simple plot description, Laura's despair may seem awkwardly like the despair of dozens of other adolescent literary females, yet the text employs a new and fresh language to depict it. Language is extremely important in the novel, since it—like *Little Women*—shows a young girl's way toward her own integrity through writing. However, while Jo March is belittled and silenced by the man whose opinion she happens to value, Laura hears, on the last pages of the novel, her male classmate Stefan perform the song she has written, while the object of her fancies, the teacher, accompanies it on the saxophone. The power tension between the young girl and the adult male is subdued through their mutual interest in arts. With firm support from her male friends, Laura, a modern young woman, finds her own voice.

This ending shows perhaps better than any other narrative element the profound change in the way a new femininity free from stereotypes is constructed as compared to the models of the past. Laura doesn't get famous overnight nor does she win a song competition with her very first song. Stefan and Laura may become a couple, but not necessarily, and even if they do, they are not likely to live happily ever after, since they are only fifteen. Laura's deep disappointment in her own parents does not vanish either. The mother goes deeper and deeper into self-isolation and depression, while the father is just as indifferent and emotionally absent as before. And the typical teenage dreams of great love—what Laura herself so pertinently describes as "girl-room fancies"—softly change over into respect and gratitude for the support the teacher shows. When we say farewell to Laura, she is on a threshold, but nothing has, as if by magic, become solved and settled.

Yet it is the voice of the young narrator that most tangibly illustrates the dilemma of the contemporary juvenile novel. When the adult voice disappears, young readers are left without guidance as to understanding and judging the events and the characters. We have no hints of how to assess Laura's mental state and whether to believe that she is capable of self-assessment. While first-person narrators are unreliable by definition, in the sense that they always convey a subjective view, Laura is unreliable not because she is trying to present herself in a more favorable light, or because she has forgotten what it was like to be young, but merely because she is too inexperienced to express her own emotions or even adequately interpret other people's actions. Basically, a complete chaos is poured out on the pages letting the reader sort it out together with the protagonist. Naturally, this puts substantially higher demands on the readers than traditional narratives where the sorting out was done by the adult narrative agency.

The femininity that emerges from this chaos is devoid of stereotypical traits, even though there is a lot in common between Laura and Jo March. One of the main reasons is the complexity of the character, which allows contradictory and variable personality qualities. Laura is, in other words, too multifaceted to be a stereotype, whether of the new or the old kind. Yet the experience that the novel is based on and that it offers the readers is unequivocally feminine.

In 2004, Katarina Kieri published a novel, *Does Elias Dance? No!*, where she uses a first-person male narrator, which, not unexpectedly, presents an extreme, almost exaggerated portrait of the "new," soft, insecure and introvert boy. Both as a character and as a narrative voice, Elias feels very much a literary construction, a quasi-male, since his gender performance is feminine. It is hard to say whether it is the effect of the author's gender, but Elias performativity is reminiscent of the masculine girls created by male authors.

And in 2005, Aidan Chambers published *This is All*, the novel that is supposed to complete his multivolume exploration of the contemporary adolescent condition and that presents a female voice and a female consciousness, as a counterbalance to his previous male protagonists and narrators. The first dilemma Chambers' teenage heroine encounters is how to get rid of her virginity. The circle is closed. However, if Chambers once inspired his colleagues with his depiction of new masculinity, it seems that he now goes in the wake of women writers reproducing the new feminine stereotype.

Some basic power-related questions emerging from this chapter are: Do YA novels reflect what the adult authors believe to be the contemporary teenagers' genuine experience? Or do they provide guidance from clever adults to the innocent adolescents? Or do they, as so much of children's literature, convey the adult authors' nostalgic memories of their own youth? Whatever, they hardly seem to show the contemporary teenagers' view of themselves. The ideology that the novels convey is apparently based on alterity, the authors' perception of their protagonists as "the Other." Here we have once again the inevitable dilemma of writing for young audiences, the unequal power position between sender and recipient.

In many of the novels discussed in this chapter, first-person perspective either amplifies or subdues the effect of gender construction. The next chapter will take a closer look on how alterity is manifested through gendered narrative perspective.

Note

1. None of the texts discussed have been translated into English; there are excerpts in *Swedish Book Review* 2006: Supplement

Chapter Eight
Othering the Voice:
Crossvocalization and Performance

Call me Isabel. Some years ago—never mind how long precisely—having little or no money in my purse, and nothing particular to interest me on shore, I thought I would sail about a little and see the watery part of the world. (Lanser 1981, 3)

This eloquent commutative test shows how a seemingly minor change from the original "Call me Ishmael" in *Moby-Dick,* the narrator's name, affects our perception. A male or a female name associated with the narrator immediately creates expectations. While it is natural for the male narrator of Melville's novel to set out on high seas adventures, with the gender permutation, the reader is placed into hesitation as to the genre and tone of the narrative. Women are normally not expected to "sail about a little" when they have nothing better to do, and the reader cannot really be certain what the narrative has in store. The female voice does not match the connotation of the opening sentences.

Feminist and queer narratology (Lanser 1986; Mezei 1996) is concerned with the question whether narrative strategies are related to gender issues, including, but not limited to the implied authors', the narrators' and the protagonists' biological gender. Masculine narration, similar to masculinity in the previous chapter, represents the dominant, empowered, conservative, conformist, normative narrative voice, as opposed to the oppressed and therefore potentially subversive one. A masculine voice implies confirming the existing norms of power, while a feminine voice interrogates and subverts it. This has little to do with the authors' gender; however, feminist studies of classic and modern literature have shown that female authors have frequently been forced to employ certain strategies to make their voices heard (Lanser 1992). In the study of gender-related narration in children's literature, yet another heterological aspect that is added is aetonormativity.

Gender-related narratology poses questions about the relationship between gender and several aspects of narration, such as narrative voice, point of view and focalization. One of the central issue is whether masculine and feminine narrative strategies are indeed different, and if so, exactly how this difference is reflected in the text. One aspect is cross-gender narration, male authors using female narrators or focalizers (Lanser 1992). Interestingly enough, examples of cross-gender personal narration (heterovocalization, or crossvocalization) are scarce. In the overwhelming majority of first-person narratives in children's and young adult fiction, narrative agency of the same gender (homovocalization) appears, of which some examples have already been discussed in previous chapters (*Dance on My Grave; Kensuke's Kingdom; Jacob Have I Loved; Not a Greek God, Exactly*). Yet there are exceptions, in which crossvocalization is employed: a female writer has chosen a male first-person narrator (*The Outsiders, Does Elias Dance?, Dear Mr Henshaw*, or *The Secret Diary of Adrian Mole*), or a male writer has chosen a female narrator (*Island of the Blue Dolphins, The True Confessions of Charlotte Doyle, Little Marie* or *This Is All*). The question is, however, whether the narrator's biological gender automatically creates a genuine voice, or whether the voice is performative (in analogy with performative gender, Butler 1999). A subsequent question is whether a female crossvocalized narrator necessarily becomes subversive, and, by contrast, whether a male voice follows the masculine patterns of confirming the existing norms. In other words, a female personal narrator can speak in a masculine voice, and vice versa. Performative voice implies a narrative agency that behaves ("performs") dependently on a certain power position, either affirmative or subversive.

In terms of power, crossvocalization has several consequences. A male author who chooses a feminine voice *descends* in power hierarchy, that is, narrates from a disempowered position, amplified by the usual asymmetry existing between the adult author and the young character. At the same time, adult authors must, consciously or subconsciously, empower their child protagonists, since the basic premise of children's literature is substituting child normativity for adult normativity. This means that a male author who employs crossvocalization must necessarily compensate the double suppressed position of the young female character/narrator, firstly as a woman deviating from the male norm, secondly as a child deviating from the adult norm. Such compensation can be found in a variety of strategies that will be investigated in this chapter.

A female author who chooses a masculine narrative voice *ascends* in power hierarchy; the voice acquires greater authority. However, an adult female author has more power as compared to her young protagonist; the two power structures are in conflict with each other. The personal narrator's power position can further be enhanced by the general striving of children's literature to empower the child. In order to achieve balance, a female author may have to subdue her narrator's power. Here we can also examine what strategies are available that create and amplify the asymmetrical, hierarchic power position, or interrogate and blur it. This can be done through genre, theme, setting, composition, characterization and narrative perspective as such, including palimpsestic narration.

Public and Private Voice

There is yet another essential distinction to consider in gender-related narratology, the distinction between public and private voice, that is, a narrative aimed at a particular audience or a narrative that is primarily self-reflective and not intended for perusal by an outsider (Lanser 1992). Some examples have already been touched upon, for instance, the public narration in *Dance on My Grave* and *Kensuke's Kingdom*, and private/mental narration in *Jacob Have I Loved* and *Not a Greek God, Exactly*. Since women were historically subjected to silencing on the part of male establishment, public narration demanded certain narrative strategies that did not have to be employed in private writing. Although there are many obvious exceptions, I will consider the public voice to be predominantly masculine (although not necessarily male), and the private voice predominantly feminine.

Even though the subject matter of a novel may decidedly personal, there are frequently overt public recipients of the narrators' discourse. In *Boikie You Better Believe It* (1994), by Dianne Hofmeyr, the male narrator, Daniel, is keeping a journal, but intends it to be read: "I decided to start this book today because of [my father] and what he did yesterday. I think if I am going to have my own kids one day, they should be made to read everything I've written" (5). The narrative is thus at least partially public, as Daniel is thinking of a specific audience. It is also private since the purpose of writing is self-knowledge: "I'm writing it to try and make sense of my life" (5). Unlike many fictive diary-writers, for instance, Hal in *Dance on My Grave*, Daniel is not encouraged by a supportive adult in his writing, and he is not particularly verbal. In fact, he admits: "I'll need to borrow a dictionary from the school library. I'm not so good with words" (5). Yet just prior to this declaration, Daniel has managed to spell the Biblical names of Belteshazzar and Nebuchadnezzar, obviously fascinated by their sounds, which indicates his natural curiosity for language. Daniel belongs to an underprivileged, silenced social group. Like many women in the Western world in the past, Daniel, living in South Africa today, can hardly dream of higher education. The female author conveys an experience shared by women rather than men, apparently because she is writing from the disempowered position.

The thirteen-year-old Charlotte in *The True Confessions of Charlotte Doyle* (1992), by Avi, describes the unusual events on board a ship crossing the Atlantic Ocean in summer 1832. The title alludes to the traditionally male genre of confessions, and the adjective "true" emphasizes the honesty and reliability of the story—a stance that needs a closer investigation. Although Charlotte has attended "the Barrington School for Better Girls," we can assume that her training has not gone far beyond basic penmanship. Unlike Daniel, who starts a journal because of his need to express himself, Charlotte is forced by her father to keep a journal since this activity was considered appropriate for young upper-class ladies of the time. In Charlotte's case, it is also a matter of keeping her busy with a proper pastime during the ocean crossing, because other ladylike occupations, such as needlework, music, or dancing, are obviously hard to pursue on board a ship. The father also declares his intention to read the journal upon her arrival to Providence. Charlotte's account is public, since she writes it with the premise that it will definitely be perused by someone else. This does not prevent Charlotte from rendering the most private details of her existence, such as the sensation of wearing a loosely fitting sailor clothing. It is arguable whether a young female journal-writer would ever dare to put in such indiscrete particulars into a narrative intended for male and adult perusal. We can, for instance, compare Charlotte's account to Jerusha Abbot's in *Daddy-Long-Legs* (1912) that is also intended for an adult male addressee and therefore avoids any personal specifics. *Daddy-Long-Legs* is written by a female author, and homovocalization governs the voice to perform in a feminine manner, prudent and well-behaved toward the male narratee. The crossvocalized text of *The True Confessions* creates a different basis. Charlotte may be deliberately provocative, knowing how her indiscretion will irritate her father; he is indeed outraged by her journal, however, more by the general contents, which he views as a pack of fibs; he never gets down to the embarrassing details. Yet we can also question the degree of indiscretion a young woman would allow herself in a text intended for her father's eyes, not least a young woman in the 1830s.

At the same time, a significant detail is conspicuously absent from Charlotte's story, which can be ascribed to the author's natural lack of typically female experience. Not once during the several months of Charlotte's ocean crossing does she mention her period. Menstruation never appears in Jerusha's letters to her male benefactor either. In 1912 bodily functions were tabooed in juvenile fiction. In contemporary young adult fiction, it is natural for female personal narrators to refer to their first period as an important event in their lives, while male narrators may repeatedly refer to their wet dreams and embarrassing erections. Charlotte may be too young to menstruate; still this would be an appropriate experience to emphasize Charlotte's precarious situation in a harsh and isolated male environment. In any case, Charlotte's public voice does not refer to her menstruation in a narrative intended for male eyes.

Both in *Boikie* and *The True Confessions*, the narratives are presented as written accounts. Written discourse is more readily perceived as public, since the written word has in our culture the status of a document. It is perhaps too categorical to maintain that written culture is masculine, while oral is feminine, yet gender-related studies of language do support this condition (e.g.

Spender 1998). In Jacques Lacan's psychoanalytical terms, too, verbal, structured, especially written discourse ("symbolic") is masculine, while non-verbal, preverbal ("imaginary") discourse is feminine. Written narratives created
by male writers had in Western civilization higher status than oral narratives,
such as folktales, often preserved by women. The concept of genderlect offers
further analytical tool to assess masculine and feminine use of language.
Masculine language is ordered, rational and precise, abounding in abstract
notions, while feminine language is fragmentary, concrete, emotionally colored and rich in images. It also contains hidden subtexts, or palimpsests. It
is, therefore, tempting to state that in both novels, masculine (written and
public) discourse is used, irrespective of the protagonist's gender.

Another and perhaps more important question is how the texts present men's and women's access to language. Feminist theory has shown how
women in literature written by men are consistently diminished and silenced,
and how female writers have tried to point at different ways out of oppression.
Charlotte is seemingly encouraged by male establishment in her writing, but
she has no credibility to her narration. Charlotte's father does not believe her
story and thus suppresses her creativity. It is of no consequence whether Charlotte's narrative is actually true. The two novels show clearly that the male
narrator is empowered through language, while for a woman, verbal competence is a disadvantage. The male crossvocalizing author shows how female
narration is questioned and dismissed, which confirms the existing conventions. The female crossvocalizing author creates a male character who, like the
female figures, lacks language, yet realizes the overall significance of language
for a person's social status. Thus she breaks the convention. The perfomative
voice is decisive in these examples.

Unexpectedly many crossvocalized novels utilize the diary and epistolary
form, with their oscillation between public and private, yet decisively written. The fictive diary as narrative form presumably allows creating a genuine
child's or teenager's voice; yet as with all narrative perspectives, this does not
occur automatically. On the contrary, fictive diary is particularly demanding since there is practically no distance between the experiencing and the
narrating self, as already shown in the discussion of *Boikie*. In order to sound
genuine, the simultaneous, immediate personal voice must be adapted to the
cognitive, emotional, existential and not least linguistic level that the protagonist is supposed to possess. Much too often diary form is used without
motivation, more like a tribute to a popular tradition. If the purpose of the
device is to create authenticity, it feels superfluous in a novel concentrated
on external events. Some texts employ poor spelling, oversimplified sentence
structure, naïve comments, limited vocabulary and extensive youth idiom to
create a sense of authenticity, but the effect is often the opposite. A private
fictive diary is supposed to represent the innermost thoughts and feelings; it
should therefore be sufficiently self-reflective to justify the form. At the same
time, unlike an authentic diary, a fictive diary must have a plot, albeit hidden

behind the depiction of seemingly external events. Even a most fragmentary fictive diary contains some form of resolution and closure. Yet fragmentarity is associated with feminine writing, while structured and ordered plots are considered masculine. A diary novel intended for young audience inevitably balances between attempts at authenticity and urge of alterity.

Male diary-writers are a relatively recent phenomenon in children's literature, apparently due to the prejudice that it is mostly girls who keep diaries and journals. Female authors who employ male diary-writers follow the masculine conventions. *The Secret Diary of Adrian Mole, Aged 13 ¾* (1982), by Sue Townsend, portrays the character as slightly weird, while the content of the diaries is mostly focused on external events. Crossvocalization precludes an in-depth depiction of a young opposite-gender protagonist's psyche or a more complex subjectivity. Crossvocalization in Kevin Major's *Diana, My Autobiography* (1993; not a diary, but close in structure) achieves the effect through a strategy similar to Adrian Mole: the female narrator is presented as silly, naïve and vain. It almost seems that the implied author mocks his narrator—a tangible token of alterity—which is especially noticeable in comparison with the same author's novel with a male narrator, *Dear Bruce Springsteen* (1987).

Dear Mr Henshaw (1983), by Beverly Cleary, is one of the infinitesimally few fictive diaries that make the most of the device to demonstrate the character's intellectual and emotional development, from awkward attempts to render external events to complex self-reflective consciousness. The development moves toward internalizing the subject position. The protagonist has several feminine traits and his voice performs as feminine, no least since language and writing becomes a way toward stronger identity. Writing from a lower power position, the author succeeds in conveying the crossvocalized protagonist's empowerment.

The epistolary novel *Letters from the Inside* (1994), by John Marsden, has two crossvocalized voices that sound identical, which in itself is credible when two teenage girls exchange superficial renditions of family life, school and boyfriends. However, the question of verisimilitude becomes superfluous through the metafictive ending of the book that compels a total reassessment of characters, events and narrative perspective. The postmodern play with fluctuant subjectivities allows the voices to perform arbitrarily since there is no substance behind them; they are purely verbal constructions. Metafiction makes characters flat and eliminates demands on integrity: the gender of characters and narrative voices becomes totally irrelevant.

Reliability and Authority

The argument above points at the conclusion that public, and especially written, narration has greater authority than private, oral or mental. The question of the narrator's reliability and authority is a matter of the relationship between the narrator's and the character's discourse. We perceive the narrator as more reliable when the narrator's discourse is clearly separated from the character's discourse, for instance in direct and reported speech or thought. Further, an omniscient narrator's access to rendered information is not interrogated. In blended forms, such as free indirect discourse and especially psychonarration, when it is difficult or occasionally impossible to decide whether the source of utterance is the narrator or the character, the level of the narrator's reliability is considerably lower. In personal narration, the situation is all the more complex since the text refers to both agencies, the narrator and the character, in first person. Personal narration is unreliable by definition, since it is subjective and affected by the narrator's permanent character traits as well as temporary moods and mental states. Holden Caulfield in *The Catcher in the Rye* (1951) presents himself as the worst liar in the world, and although this description is self-ironic, the reader's trust in the narrator is somewhat diminished. Personal discourse is less omniscient (and thus less authoritative) and more self-reflexive than impersonal narration. The metaphysical issue of the narrator's access to information cannot be dismissed in personal narration; here a variety of narrative devices appear, such as: "As I learned later . . . "

Yet there is a significant difference in degree between personal narrators' reliability. In *The True Confessions*, the relationships between the experiencing and the narrating self is somewhat obscure. In her "Important Warning," a typical fictive preface with its metafictional effect, Charlotte the narrator alerts her presumptive readers to the fact that her narrative is "no *Story of A Bad Boy*, no *What Katy Did*" (1). *The Story of a Bad Boy*, by Thomas Bailey Aldrich, was published in 1869; *What Katy Did*, by Susan Coolidge, in 1872. Charlotte, thirteen in 1832 when her adventures take place, must be over fifty to be acquainted with the books she refers to. It is possible that the reference to two juvenile classics have a metafictional rather than a mimetic function, and it is more than conceivable that the author had not really done any accurate calculations concerning his heroine's age at the time of narrating (or was ignorant about the publication dates of the intertexts). There are, however, other indications that Charlotte is telling her story long after the events took place, besides her explicitly stating so. In the same preface, the narrator says: "At the time my name *was* Charlotte Doyle. And though I have kept the name, I am not . . . the *same* Charlotte Doyle" (1; emphasis in the original). The temporal indicator "at the time" does not in itself suggest a significant temporal gap, and neither does the statement that the protagonist has changed. Finally, the preface is concluded by Charlotte telling us how she was given a notebook to keep a journal. "Keeping that journal *then* is what enables me to relate *now in perfect detail* everything that transpired during that fateful voyage . . . " (3; emphasis added). The contrast between "then" and "now" amplifies the sense of a substantial lapse of time; indeed, if the adventures had taken place relatively recently, Charlotte would not have to stress that she is relying on her journal rather than her memory for "perfect detail." Referring to an ostensibly authentic document is a well-known metafictional device that in itself subverts reliability. The narrator never returns to the metadiegetic level of the preface, but concludes the narrative by her escape from the oppressive father and return to the freedom of the high seas. The character Charlotte's situation in the "now," that is, at the time of narration, remains unclear.

Yet even though Charlotte has her journal from the voyage when she is telling her story many years later, does this make her a more reliable narrator? Unlike Holden, Charlotte declares: " . . . I intend to tell the truth as *I* lived it" (1; emphasis in the original). However, the events described in the novel do not exactly match our generic and narrative expectations. Charlotte is precisely the gender-substituted "Isabel" from Lanser's commutative test, shoved into a male plot. In fact, had the title been "The True Confessions of Charles Doyle," and the narrative agency male, we would have a stronger trust in it. Reading Charlotte's journal, her father gets furious about her wild and improper fantasies. Following the father's line, Charlotte's adventures are imaginative writing exercises, the purpose of which is to provoke her father and interrogate her own oppressed position, but more likely merely to embellish the boring, eventless existence that she is entitled to as a woman. We could argue that the ending of the novel proves against such an interpretation, as Charlotte once again dons her sailor clothes and flees through the window to return to the ship—an exceptionally subversive action directed against the existing gender stereotypes. Yet we may equally ask why this particular part of Charlotte's confessions should be more truthful than the preceding story. Since the text contains overtly metafictional elements, which always serve to subvert the narrator's reliability, we may lean toward accepting the father's authoritative accusation of Charlotte's narrative as fabulation, thus also judging the narrator as totally unreliable.

In any case, Charlotte the narrator is detached from the thirteen-year-old Charlotte the character, which gives the adult narrative agency more authority, but diminishes its reliability. Against this backdrop, the gap between the male adult, twentieth-century author and the female, adolescent nineteenth-century protagonist feels less prominent, and the obvious masculinity of the performative voice is obscured.

Daniel in *Boikie You Better Believe It* can be perceived as a more or less simultaneous narrator. I say more or less, since the narrator is not taking notes exactly while the events are happening, the way some expressly metafictional narrators do. Mostly Daniel records the events as he returns home in the evening; occasionally, he notes that some days have passed since the events he is describing. At any given time of the story, Daniel the narrator does not know what will happen next; the narrative act is intertwined with the story. Daniel is an intradiegetic narrator, while Charlotte is extradiegetic, telling the story from an outside position and knowing already the outcome of the events narrated.

The narrative situation, the relationship between the narrating self and the experiencing self, is crucial for our interpretation. Personal narrators are by definition homodiegetic, that is, appear as characters in their own narratives.

Moreover, since when the narratives focus on the narrator's own life, the narrators are autodiegetic, protagonists in their own stories. One would assume that a first-person narrator is always the main character, but this is far from the case. Personal narration can imply a wide spectrum of options, ranging from witness-narrators, who register the external flow of events or render somebody else's story, to solipsistic narrators focusing on their own feelings and experiences. Yet even autodiegetic narrators can differ substantially in their degree of introspection. Charlotte never goes beyond a registration of external events and possibly an account of her own reaction to these. Daniel primarily describes external events, yet to a certain extent he also contemplates his reactions.

Yet *Boikie* does not contain any cracks that would reveal the narrator as unreliable. As a simultaneous narrator he does not show any memory failures, there is no reason for him to conceal or distort the truth, and his primarily external description of events does not allow a too much subjective touch of his experience, which, paradoxically, gives his voice a more reliable and authoritative status. There are no grounds to assume that masculine voices are more reliable than feminine. The only argument to this effect might be that men do after all have more authority in our society; therefore their narratives are by definition more credible than stories by women. The perlocutory function of narration, that is, the effect the narrator intends to achieve, is more or less absent in *Boikie*. While Charlotte's voice is perfomatively masculine, the biologically male narrator in *Boikie* is presented as more reliable, even though he may himself contemplate on the issue:

> It's exhausting trying to make sense of my life. It takes a lot of effort to think my thoughts and then put down what I am thinking. And then how do I know that's what I am really thinking? —because I can't see my thoughts. (*Boikie You Better Believe It* 5f)

Convention associates masculine narration with external focalization and feminine narration with internal focalization. Both *Confessions* and *Boikie* employ primarily external focalization, seldom if ever going beyond the literal point of view, which does not demand the construction of complex subjectivity. In other words, the characters are opaque, even though they are narrated by themselves. Homofocalized characters are potentially more transparent, as seen in the discussion of *Dance on My Grave, Winter Bay, Jacob Have I Loved* and *Not a Greek God, Exactly*.

Gender and Genre

As already stated, the question of masculine and feminine patterns in literary texts goes far beyond the biological gender of characters or narrators. The correlation between gender and genre has been pointed out repeatedly. Authors may consciously or unconsciously choose genres that correspond to their overall gender patterns, and a crossvocalizing author may choose a genre that will allow neglecting or circumventing the discrepancy between the author's and the narrator's gender.

The common convention is that masculine writing is action-oriented while feminine writing is character-oriented; masculine writing is focused on external events and the hero's adventures, while feminine writing is preoccupied with relationships and self-reflection. Typically masculine genres include heroic fantasy, horror, crime and thriller, science fiction, war novel, pirate and robber novel, frontier and Wild West stories. Typically feminine genres include love stories, family and domestic novels. Roughly defined, the overall masculine genre is adventure and feminine is romance. It may therefore seem that the portrayal of a female character in *The Island of the Blue Dolphins*, a typical masculine Robinsonnade narrative, is norm-breaking, yet at closer examination, crossvocalization can be employed exactly because the genre not only allows, but presupposes an external perspective.

The True Confessions may appear a case of simple gender permutation, quite common in contemporary adventure pulp fiction: a female character is placed in a masculine plot and plays the role of a male hero, becoming a quasi-woman. Charlotte's situation certainly reminds one of *Treasure Island*, in which a young boy finds himself on a ship full of villains. However, the novel equally adheres to the long tradition of the female picaresque, a masculine genre employing a female protagonist and narrator. The male writers' premises in such narratives is rendering the external events rather than trying to enter the heroine's mind. Generally, a picaro is a romantic hero (in Frye's terminology), and as such devoid of psychological traits. *The True Confessions* thus employs a masculine genre, even though the protagonist is female, also without having to adapt to feminine narration. In the fictive preface to her narrative, Charlotte denies the affinity of her story with the naughty-boy as well as the naughty-girl genre. "If strong ideas and action offend you, read no more," she warns her presumptive readers (1), thus declaring that the narrative will be action-oriented and perhaps even violent. Crossvocalization is less norm-breaking in *The True Confessions*, as well as in *Island of the Blue Dolphins*, since it appears in masculine, adventure genres, presupposing masculine action-oriented plot and masculine outdoor settings.

S. E. Hinton's crossvocalizing novels *The Outsiders* and *That Was Then, This Is Now* (1971) feature the conventionally masculine "good guys–bad guys" genre. Typically, the flesh-and-blood author hides her gender behind initials. The novels are among the earliest examples of crossvocalization in young adult fiction, and since Hinton was seventeen when she published *The Outsiders*, aetonormativity is irrelevant in the overall power hierarchy. The author's blurred gender and the choice of a male protagonist/narrator raise the authority of the novels. The focus is on class differences, on friendship and love across societal boundaries, on a young person's ambivalence concerning loyalty toward his own origin and wish to climb up in society (a theme remi-niscent of mainstream working-class novel). The narratives are tangibly mas-culine, where almost all events take place outdoors, where physical strength is given priority, and where conflicts are solved through violence. Power struc-tures in the novels reflect tensions between rich and poor, upper class and working class. The narrator belongs to the oppressed group, which means that the author expresses solidarity with the marginalized. Even though the pro-tagonists could not be easily subjected to gender permutation, the voice per-forms as feminine since it narrates from a lower power position. Yet the texts avoid self-reflection and do not let the characters penetrate too deep into their own feelings, not least because at the time when the novels were published, a new stereotype of the gentle male would be perceived as norm-breaking.

Boikie You Better Believe It is a domestic story, concentrating on child/par-ent relationship, friendship, first infatuation and self-reflection. There is some violence involved, but no more than would be acceptable in a girls' novel. Typ-ically, the protagonist's reaction to violence is more accentuated than violence as such. Daniel actually does not witness the fight, but a considerable time is spent to depict his efforts to find the hospital, to which his father is taken, as well as Daniel's emotions and anxiety. Similarly, in *Dear Mr Henshaw* and *The Secret Diary of Adrian Mole*, the narrators appear within a typically feminine genre, focusing on relationships rather than actions and events. The child–parent relationship is a good example. It would be natural to assume that for a male protagonist, the liberation from his father is the most central in his psychological development, while for a girl it is the liberation from her mother (cf. Trites 2000, 100–121). As a consequence, we would expect male narrators to focus on the relationship with their fathers and female narrators on the relationship with their mothers. Furthermore, a masculine pattern includes a submissive acceptance of parental authority, while a feminine pattern pre-scribes that the protagonist, especially a female one, strongly questions the normative gender script. In *The True Confessions*, the father–daughter conflict is constructed as if it were a father–son one. *Boikie*, on the other hand, pres-ents the father–son conflict as relatively unproblematic, resolving the rela-tionship in a typically feminine, emotionally-charged manner. Similarly, the crossvocalized novel *Dear Mr Henshaw* depicts the father–son relationship as typically feminine.

Female authors frequently choose the genre of historical novel to alien-ate the crossvocalized narrator. In Katherine Paterson's *Preacher's Boy* (1999), the male narrator renders his adventures consisting of external events, often exciting and dramatic; there is little self-reflection, no complex subjectivity, and no issues of reliability. Personal narrators of these and similar stories become witnesses rather than experiencing subjects, which means that nar-ration is not dependent on the narrator's gender; the narrator is a gender-less agency, reminiscent of impersonal dramatic ("objective") narrator. It is significant that the shift from homovocalization in Mildred Taylor's *Roll of*

Thunder, Hear My Cry (1976) to crossvocalization in its sequel, *Mississippi Bridge* (1990) is effortless. Both first-person narrators are witness-narrators, presenting a detailed and emotionally neutral report about external events, and both voices sound identical. The stories could have been told in an impersonal voice, which a commutative test would confirm.

Some further conventions concerning the story level of the novels include construction of time and space, as well as plot structure. The use of narrative space is closely connected with the question of genre. Masculine space is frequently perceives as being outdoors while feminine space is indoors; masculine space is open while feminine space is closed ("imprisonment" is a recurrent trope in women's fiction); masculine field of activity is away from home, while feminine sphere is home; masculine concern is to conquer nature, while feminine concern is to "understand" and be one with nature. Male characters perceive home as restrictive while female characters perceive it as secure and protective.

Charlotte appears outside the conventional feminine space, in an environment more suitable for a boy. Not only is she confined to the exclusively male company of the transatlantic ship; she is eventually forced to leave the relative security of her cabin and enter the extremely masculine space of the deck. Charlotte is compelled by circumstances to take on a male role, therefore it seems natural that she appears in a masculine space. Daniel acts within typically feminine domestic space, even though there are quite a few scenes, including a violent one, taking place in the streets. Urban setting are masculine by definition, if we make the simple parallels such as urban = culture = masculine, while rural = nature = feminine, but despite the unstable political situation in South Africa, serving as the background for the events of the novel, the setting is rather idyllic. Daniel is happy with his space and expresses no desire to leave it. His space is narrow, never extending beyond his closest neighborhood. Unlike Hinton's male protagonists, he has no wish to gain power over his space, for instance, through becoming a street-gang leader. On the contrary, he hides from street violence in the security of a beauty parlor—an expressly feminine space, by convention unnatural for a young boy, but quite typical for the new masculinity. The narrative focuses on Daniel's uncertainty, including his obvious immaturity and reluctance for conquering vast outdoor spaces.

In terms of composition, masculine plots are moral, in the sense of a progression from imperfection toward improvement; feminine plots are romantic, from desire to fulfillment. Masculine narratives focus on external events and heroic deeds, while feminine stories are concerned with relationships and reflections. Further, masculine plots are structured, logical, chronological, strongly causal and goal-oriented; while feminine plots are fragmented and diffuse. Masculine plots are "grand narratives," while feminine plots are "little narratives" (Lyotard 1984). *Boikie* has the least conventional plot, totally lacking the standard compositional elements such as exposition, complication, climax and denouement. It is instead an unstructured string of events without causal bands, reminiscent of life as it is. Since causality is the foremost marker of narrativity, *Boikie* displays a low degree of narrativity and is therefore more subversive against the norm. *The True Confessions* is focused on the protagonist's physical trials and moral improvement.

Finally, some established opinions on temporality are that masculine time is linear, compressed and quickly progressing, while feminine time is circular (that is, taking the protagonist back to where she started), season-dependant, repetitive, and prolonged. A closer examination of temporality shows that the dominant temporality is, not unexpectedly, masculine in both *The True Confessions*, and in *Boikie*.

Androgyny, Crossdressing and Metamorphosis

It should be clear by now that the protagonists' biological gender has little relevance for masculine and feminine characterization. Masculine characterization confirms established gender stereotypes, while feminine characterization challenges them. This in turn implies that if male and female characters remain unchanged or develop toward stronger stereotypes, such characterization is masculine. This is important, since characters, not least female characters, can be represented as challenging stereotypes to begin with, but along the plot can be brought back into the prescribed gender pattern. To assess authors' attitude toward stereotypes we could use some of the existing schemata, presenting men as strong, active, violent, aggressive, competitive, and independent, and women as weak, passive, emotional, submissive, and self-sacrificial.

Looking back at herself as young, Charlotte comes up with the following description: "At the age of thirteen I was very much a girl, having not yet begun to take the shape, much less the heart, of a woman" (*The True Confessions of Charlotte Doyle* 1). The view is not only detached, but overtly objectifying. The perspective is masculine in the sense that the focalizer observes the woman rather than contemplates on her, which becomes all the more obvious by comparison with another similar, but considerably more self-ironic representation: "At thirteen I was tall and large boned, with delusions of beauty and romance" (*Jacob Have I Loved* 5).

To circumvent stereotypical characterization, several strategies can be used in crossvocalized texts. Androgyny is associated with feminine writing. Androgyny as a social phenomenon, unlike physiological ones (hermaphrodism or transsexuality), can in literature assume such forms as socially deviant behavior, choice of occupation, social transsexuality (desire to function socially as the opposite gender), homosexuality, and not least crossdressing (cf. Flanagan 2007). Androgyny is one of the most efficient ways of interrogating gender-related social norms as the androgyne's masculine performance clearly demonstrates men's superiority on every level of society. This makes androgyny as such a feminine narrative strategy, yet it can be used both for confirming and subverting stereotypes.

Charlotte finds herself in a situation in which crossdressing is her only possible survival strategy. Stranded as the only passenger on a transatlantic ship with a morally dubious captain and crew, and having involuntarily caused a man's death, she sheds her female clothes as well as her well-bred manners and joins the crew to make up for the ill she has brought about. Well before this event, Charlotte is given a set of sailor clothes by the benevolent black cook, which she accepts, yet retorts that it would improper for her, as a lady, to wear them. Later on, in the security of her cabin, she tries them on and finds them "surprisingly comfortable" (71). Although the text does not mention it, we may assume that Charlotte is subject to the torture of Western female clothing in the 1830s, including stays and tight shoes. Trying on practical, loosely fitting sailor's clothes, she is symbolically confronted with gender inequality and is prepared to take the first step toward liberation. However, when the course of events forces Charlotte to wear men's clothes, the experience is less joyful: "Slowly, fearfully, I made myself take off my shoes, my stockings, my apron, at last my dress and linen . . . The trousers and shirt felt stiff, heavy, like some skin not my own" (113). Upon arrival to Providence, Charlotte, who has managed the hard trial of being a deck hand under inhuman captain, must once again change her identity by means of clothes.

Assessment of stereotyping is, however, dependent on the general interpretation of the story. We can take sides with Charlotte's father and view her adventures as a product of her imagination, while she, like so many of her literary sisters, obediently returns to the role that her father and society has prescribed. Yet if the androgynous change in Charlotte has actually taken place, it would be too profound to be camouflaged merely by a change of clothes. Having experienced freedom and independence, she cannot accept the oppression her father imposes on her. Since she has kept her men's clothes as a reminder of her new self, she can easily slip back into this role. This interpretation would make the novel highly challenging in terms of gender transgression. There is yet another aspect to it. The narrative states without hesitation that male clothes and male behavior offer the protagonist greater freedom and stronger identity. It means that the text in fact confirms the stereotype, and that the protagonist is not a real woman, but a hero in drag. In other words, Charlotte's performative gender is masculine although she is presented as female. Moreover, she seems to reject her femininity, which is an excellent example of the concept of abjection, a woman's aversion towards her own body, which she subconsciously perceives as unfinished and inadequate as compare to a male one (cf. Westwater 2000, 65–90). Further, Charlotte illustrates the female literary archetype of "growing up grotesque" (Pratt 1981, 30); and the text emphasizes that a woman's status rises as she adopts a male role. Yet Charlotte the narrator never reflects over gender inequality.

Daniel has many feminine traits and can be viewed as socially transsexual, longing to function in a manner that society has reserved for the opposite gender. He is soft, emotional, interested in his looks, helps out at a beauty parlor and avoids conflicts. This does not, however, imply interrogating of stereotypes. On the contrary, Daniel is presented as a new stereotype of an effeminized man who feels expelled from the male community. The text demonstrates that a man who behaves like a woman has no chances to be socially accepted. Therefore Daniel's goal is to confirm his masculinity. Still Daniel is substantially closer to a female than male stereotype even though the plot brings him to the insight about his masculine identity.

Yet another conceivable strategy in characterization could be employing semiotic rather than mimetic characters, that is, metafictional characters made of words, devoid of psychological substance. Generally, as also seen from the analysis of *The True Confessions*, metafiction provides favorable prerequisites for crossvocalization, as it reduces the mimetic function of the narrative. When *The Outsiders* closes with the same sentence it opened, the effect is a considerably lower demand on credibility. Melvin Burgess's *Lady: My Life as a Bitch* (2001) may almost be categorized as fantasy in its nonmimetic representation. Metamorphosis narratives have recently been discussed as a specific mode, and its liberating as well as conventional impact has been demonstrated (Lassén 2006). The female protagonist/narrator of the novel transforms into a dog, which becomes a highly efficient device to alienate the subject. The metamorphosis precludes any issues of reliability or credibility. Even though the protagonist retains her human intelligence—which deteriorates successively as the story progresses—and even though there is no attempt to employ language as a means of conveying the protagonist's new mentality, the situation is sufficiently othered to obscure the issues of crossvocalization. In other words, since neither the author nor the reader have any experience of a dog's "genuine" narrative voice, the authority of the narrator becomes automatically stronger. The young girl's doubly disempowered position is compensated through the freedom she achieves through metamorphosis (reminiscent of Charlotte's empowerment through crossdressing). The novel also presents a rare example of a protagonist who is not disempowered at the end of a carnivalesque plot. On the contrary: Sandra becomes gradually more happy and confident in her new existence and finally stops seeking a way to transform back. She also fully enjoys her unrestricted sexuality. This is, however, only possible because a young woman turns into an animal, a lower power position than a human being. The protagonist's transformation and thus movement within power hierarchy becomes ambivalent. In the child/adult hierarchy, she grows, becomes strong and independent. Metaphorically, it is a portrayal of pubertal crisis, including sexual liberation and revolt against parental protection. A feminist interpretation would criticize the male writer's contempt against and fear of a wild and uncontrollable female. However, in the human/animal power hierarchy, Sandra descends to a considerably lower position (dogs, alongside pigs, are conventionally regarded lower than many other animals, which is reflected in the use of these words as invectives). This aspect may easily escape our attention, exactly because she is so strongly empowered on other levels. Since Sandra stays forever a dog, the plot remains unresolved and she does not return to the initial power order, which is only possible because in a canine form she does not present a threat toward the male-dominant human society.

Finally, there are texts in which the narrator's gender is deliberately obscured. *The Turbulent Term of Tyke Tiler* (1977), by Gene Kemp, uses the possibility of personal narration to conceal the narrator's gender. An impersonal narrator is usually obliged to refer to the character as "he" or "she." A personal narrator can remain ambivalent in this respect and leave the reader in hesitation, permanently or temporarily. While some crossdressing characters may deceive their surroundings as to their true gender while the reader is initiated into the secret, the surroundings in *Tyke Tiler* are aware of the narrator's gender identity, while the readers can only infer it from the narrator's gender performance. Tyke's name provides no guidance, and neither does the writer's name. Tyke's gender performance is doubtless masculine, and the voice also behaves in a masculine manner. If the narrator is a boy, there is no deviation in performance, and we are dealing with a conventional naughty-boy book. As it turns out, the narrator is a girl, which makes her gender performance challenging and norm-breaking, while the voice is still masculine. Since the author is female, the play with voice and gender becomes creative and subversive.

Subjectivity and Performance

It is extremely gratifying to compare two or more texts by the same writer with similar plots or themes, using either cross- or homovocalization, as I did briefly with *Diana: My Autobiography* and *Dear Bruce Springsteen*, and *Roll of Thunder* and *Mississippi Bridge*. Unfortunately, few authors have provided critics with such examples. There is a substantial difference in performative voice of *The True Confessions of Charlotte Doyle* and *Nothing but the Truth* (1991), depending on the different genres rather than the narrators' gender. As compared with the self-reflective, unreliable, detached female narrator in *Jacob Have I Loved*, the masculine voice of *Preacher's Boy* performs fully according to conventions, in an adventurous plot and straighforward composition, focusing on external events.

It seems that as far as homovocalization is concerned, narrative perspective is unproblematic in respect to gender. The narrator's voice does not have to be othered, and the subjectivity constructed through the same-gender narrator is relatively uncomplicated. Various genres, themes and plots can be employed; the narrator can be both detached and introdiegetic; self-reflective and an observer, with all the shades in between.

However, as soon as we move on to crossvocalization, that is, unequal power positions, deviations become obvious. A female voice performs tangibly in a masculine manner, and the other way round, unless other aspects of the text obscure the conflict. In employing crossvocalization, the subjectivity of the text is deliberately constructed as the Other. On one hand, this appears natural, as a male author would be expected to construct a feminine subject position as the Other, and vice versa. On the other hand, heterological theories point out the almost insurmountable hinders to bridge gaps between the Self and the Other in the construction of a subject position. It may turn out in further investigations that successful feminine/masculine crossvocalization is more common than masculine/feminine. There are also a few examples of novels with multiple narrators alternating between homo- and heterovocalization, for instance, Melvin Burgess's *Junk* (1996), where a close examination reveals that male and female voices perform in exactly the same way. In *Noughts and Crosses* (2001), written by a female writer from a disempowered position, the masculine and feminine narrative voices are radically different. The explanation is apparently power position. Writing from a disempowered perspective, women authors have vaster experience of alterity and can show more solidarity with a young character as such, and an opposite-gender narrator in particular. Female authors subjectify the narrating self, they confirm its position as a strong, independent subject. The power hierarchy adult/child is more prominent for a female author than masculine/feminine, and the choice of the narrator's gender is dictated in the first place by striving to depict a maturation process, a way toward subjectivity. A novel with a male protagonist can easily be feminist, in the sense of subversive (cf. Trites 1997).

A male author writes predominantly from a superior power position and objectifies his female narrator, creating her as the Other, the exotic, the detached, the incomprehensible, the androgynous, not fully human (in *My Life as a Bitch*, literally so). The adult/child alterity amplifies the effect. This is a generalization, but the tendency is obvious. I must, however, hurry to add that I do not put any evaluative aspect in the judgment.

Chapter Nine
Othering Ideology:
Literature in Society's Service

As already demonstrated, fairy tales and fantasy have an enormous subversive potential. The nature of subversion, however, may vary radically depending on the society in which the texts appear, since they will be affected by the dominant ideology. In this chapter I will show how a certain type of fantasy functioned in the former Soviet Union, a society in which art and literature were strongly subordinated to the official ideology. In these stories, young protagonists are disempowered through their encounters with magic. I will then contrast Soviet children literature against some works of Brazilian magical realism, likewise created under totalitarian regime, but demonstrating significantly stronger subversive traits.

Literary fairy tales and fantasy written during the Communist rule (1917–1991) express the dogma of the ruling class while they at the same time often carry subversive messages for those who care to see those. Subversive strategies were an inherent feature of Soviet literature at large, often referred to as "Aesopian language," the language of a fable in which readers were encouraged to seek hidden messages between the lines. This cat-and-mouse game between authors and readers was aimed at circumventing censorship, but in the long run it affected the way writers constructed their narratives, including the choice of genre. Fairy tale and fantasy proved to be an excellent means both to propagate for and to question the official dogmas (see further Salminen 2009).

Most of Soviet fantasy is conventional in its plot structure, utilizing the motif of an ordinary child being transposed into an alternative world, and following the traditional folktale pattern: the hero comes to a country oppressed by a tyrant or devastated by a dragon and delivers it from evil. It may be argued whether the writers consciously included in their narratives elements of political satire, not least where the falsehood of the tyrant is accentuated.

A number of Soviet fantasy stories follow a pattern less exploited by Western writers: that of a magical wish-fulfilling agent appearing in an otherwise ordinary world. The only significant Western author who has consistently explored this motif is Edith Nesbit. I have chosen a few Soviet stories written between the late 1930s and the 1960s, to examine how the motif was employed by the writers to educate and foster young readers in the spirit prescribed by the regime. The examples provide good illustration of power through ideology. The child is typically constructed as uneducated and unsocialized, while adults are used as mouthpieces for "correct" views and values. Heterological analysis proves fruitful applied to these texts.

Simple Moral Lessons

The Rainbow Flower (1940), by Valentin Katayev, is a good example of a tale that applies moral lessons through the views of the adults in the story. The young protagonist, Zhenya, is sent by her mother to buy some bagels. On the way home, she is absentminded—a kind of behavior unbecoming a young Soviet citizen, so Zhenya has to be punished. The text thus immediately invites the readers to join in the exercise of power, condemning the protagonist and demonstrating their own supremacy. The alterity of the child protagonist is established from start. While Zhenya is staring around, a dog eats the bagels, and chasing it, she finds herself in an unfamiliar street. As the fairy-tale structure prescribes, the protagonist must be subjected to a test. A good fairy appears and gives the girl a flower with seven rainbow-colored petals. Each petal will grant a wish. Not unexpectedly, Zhenya uses the first petal to get safely home with the bagels. The next she is obliged to spend when she breaks her mother's favorite vase and wishes it whole again. She then decides to try and make the best out of her wishes, but just as for the folktale hero, it proves to be harder than she expects. First she tries to impress the neighborhood boys, wishes herself to the North Pole, and must resort to the flower's magical force to bring her back. Then she becomes envious of the girls' toys, wishes for all the toys in the world and has to use yet another wish to get rid of them. Zhenya has thus wasted the magic flower on silly and vain wishes; she has learned a bitter lesson. The folktale plot of the three wishes is easily recognizable, in which the last wish must be used to cancel the unexpected outcome of the first two. Exactly like the recipients of folktales, the implied readers are supposed to feel superior to the protagonist. This power hierarchy is typical of official Soviet literature at large, but specifically emphasized in literature addressed to young audience.

Yet unlike the folktale hero, Zhenya is given another chance. She still has one wish left, and meeting a lame boy, she does not hesitate to use the last petal to make him healthy. This is a typical example of a happy ending in a Soviet fairy tale, where the character who had some moral flaws in the beginning proves noble and unselfish in the end. The limited scope of this short story does not allow for a thorough character development; it is focused on the actions and events; yet the moral improvement of the protagonist is the pivotal point. The character is empowered by her socialization and serves as a role model rather than cautionary example.

Three on an Island (1959), by Vitaly Gubarev, develops the motif of reckless wish-granting into a full-length novel. The protagonist, Boris, discovers that his grandmother's old handkerchief with a knot on one corner can grant wishes. Like most fantasy characters in such a situation, Boris is overwhelmed by the sense of his unlimited power. Yet similar to Zhenya from *The Rainbow Flower*, he fails to think of any sensible things to wish for. To convince his female friend Mila that he is indeed an omnipotent wizard, he turns their classmate Yuri's skin black (in the Soviet context, there are no deeper implications of this act; it is merely an innocent prank). Then the three decide to go to a desert island. Boris demonstrates his power by creating soda-pop geysers, but his friends remain unimpressed. To enthuse them, Boris conjures a pirate ship, which causes a lot of complications, but Boris is all the time confident in the power of the handkerchief that can take them home to safety any time. When the handkerchief falls into the pirates' hands, the three friends suddenly find themselves in a precarious situation. It may seem similar to the episode in Nesbit's *Five Children and It*, in which the children have wished to be in a sieged castle; yet Nesbit's characters know from experience that magic will be over by sunset. Boris and his friends are hostages in hopeless circumstances created by Boris's vanity and his foolish, romantic lust for adventure. If anything, the story suggests that wild imagination is damaging and unhealthy, at least if you are a Soviet citizen, and the Party knows what is best for you.

Boris discovers the magical power of the handkerchief after a squabble with his mother, when he has failed to do his chores as well as his homework. He gladly uses magic to perform the tedious tasks, and his foremost motivation for going to a desert island is to evade work. As soon as the friends get hungry, Boris conjures ice cream and cakes, and when Yuri suggests fishing for food, Boris simply produces a fish from thin air. Mila is not even allowed to cook it, to her utter disappointment. Exuberated by his power, Boris is determined to create a paradise where nobody has to toil and where roast ducks fly direct into your mouth—an idea natural in the ancient legend of the Land of Cocayne, but deeply alien to the Communist doctrine. Here the didactic narrator suggests that Boris's friends are morally superior to him because they prefer to use wit and their own hands to survive. Not unexpectedly, their skills prove more useful in the long run. For instance, they know how to make fire without matches, and perform other "miracles" without resorting to magic, truly enjoying their Robinson-like adventure. Yuri's boy-scout proficiency comes especially handy when Boris loses the handkerchief.

The protagonist thus becomes omnipotent through the magic agent, yet discovers that his power only brings loneliness, since his friends get bored and abandon him. Unlimited power makes him different from the rest, therefore alienated. Official Soviet ideology prescribed total conformity; nobody was to be smarter, richer or more successful than anyone else. Work in itself may be a virtue, but it is tenfold so if performed collectively. The race- and gender-balanced Yuri/Mila entity represents the invincible community, Boris the erring individual. Power structures are explicit.

The pirates embody the inimical ideology. The narrator does not fail to touch upon the race issue, when the pirates treat the enchanted black-skinned Yuri as a slave. This is supposed to show their depraved morality; otherwise they are portrayed as stereotypical villains, drinking and swearing heavily, and not stopping at foul play. Yet in a subtle way the text shows a similarity between Boris and the pirates, since he shuns honest work, just as they do, trusting magic just as they trust piracy. The parallel between the protagonist and his enemies is all the more amplified since he is trying to defeat them with their own methods, cheating and lying. For instance, to beat the pirate captain, Boris wishes to be the strongest man in the world. It is not amazing then that the pirates offer him to become their captain. Boris is horrified and declines, yet the moral, expressed by one of the pirates, is that there is no radical difference between robbing and being a wizard: neither is an honest way of earning one's bread. In fact, the pirate, painting the carefree and comfortable future life for Boris, points out: "You must admit, sir, that it is very nice not to work at all and have everything." When Boris tries to protest, the pirate says: "Do you really like to work, sir?"[1] The reader is reminded that Boris has indeed escaped to the island from what he perceived as unbearable burden of work. The protagonist is thus not only subjected to a moral trial, but, in the Soviet context, to a political one: will he succumb to the ideas of capitalism, duly represented by a bunch of gangsters? Naturally, Boris is allowed to pass the trial in the true spirit of his Motherland, yet he needs his companions to spell some things out for him.

While Yuri is allowed to be inventive and enterprising, demonstrating the best qualities of a Soviet youth, Mila shows veritable bravery when she ventures into the pirates' camp to retrieve the magic handkerchief. It is also Mila who comes with moral lectures, describing in plain words for Boris his vanity and selfishness. At one point, when Boris is bored to death by the uneventful life on the island, Mila says: "Well, if you cannot do anything, you'll have to be idle." Mila here expresses the difference between Boris's false omnipotence ("he can do anything") and the socially beneficial labor, the cornerstone of Communist ideology. She repeatedly praises Yuri for his intelligence and skills, emphasizing the contrast between the true and the false hero beyond all proportion. As if this were not enough, Boris himself eventually starts summing up his experience in phrases such as: "These monsters cannot defeat us. Isn't it like magic?", and "I now know that work is the greatest magician in the world."

The conclusion that the readers are supposed to draw is that wish-fulfillment for one's own purposes is morally wrong, because the only way to achieve happiness is through socially beneficial labor, and since Boris cannot put his unexpectedly discovered power in society's service, he must inevitably be stripped of it. Yet it would certainly feel inadequate to transfer the magical agent to the hands of the villains, even though the pirates do not know about the magical power of the handkerchief. It would be equally inappropriate to give it to the positive characters, Mila and Yuri, since these two youngsters represent firm Communist ideology that provides power as it is and has no need for magic. The loss of magic must therefore be definite and irretrievable. Boris's grandmother, who used to possess the handkerchief, once told him that the magic was in the knot (referring to the common practice of tying knots as a reminder). When Mila unknowingly unties the knot, the magic is dissolved. Boris finds himself back home, but discovers to his dismay that the pirates have followed him. The magic of the handkerchief gone, he cannot simply wish them away. He appears to be the prisoner of his own imagination. Here the narrator resorts to the convenient device of the protagonist waking up, familiar from less sophisticated children's fantasy and interrogated by J. R. R. Tolkien.

Although the plot is more complicated than in *The Rainbow Flower*, the message of the story is basically the same. Boris has learned that omnipotence does not make you happy, that you have to pay a price for careless and self-ish wishes, that work is preferable to idleness, that only the products of your own labor yield pleasure, and that true friendship is more important than power. Yet, like Zhenya, Boris emerges relatively unchanged by his adventures, because he is conveniently liberated from the consequences of his actions. In fact, he never considers the possibility that his friends are left on the island, or that Yuri will forever stay black. Since the adventures are supposed to have been a dream, all results of Boris's wishes are simply canceled. This is a comforting thought; yet the impact of Boris's experiences is considerably diminished or even demolished. He does not even, like Zhenya, has to prove himself worthy by a final unselfish deed.

I have argued elsewhere that Soviet children's literature was primarily Utopian in the sense that it presented childhood as safe and happy, and moreover, that this happy state, provided by the Communist regime, was portrayed as eternal and imperturbable (Nikolajeva 2000, 61–78). The wish-fulfilling motif amplifies the overall Utopian theme by empowering the child with the mechanism of becoming virtually omnipotent, a typical carnivalesque device. In children's books, empowering the child by means of a magical agent interrogates the adult authority, and by extension, authority at large. It would seem that Soviet fantasy has the potential to be exceptionally subversive since it is written within a totalitarian society. Yet in a paradoxical way, the conventions of children's literature, demanding the submission and socialization of the child, come into conflict with the liberating effect of the carnival. The plots of Soviet fairy tales and fantasy serve exclusively didactic purposes, and in the end the characters must learn moral lessons, the essence of which is not to single out from the masses or, in some cases, adapt to the masses if you originally did not belong to them. The lesson learned from temporal omnipotence, as seen clearly in *Three on an Island*, is overtly negative, and the subversive effect of carnival is annihilated by the didactic messages of the books.

Reversal of Normativity

Another strategy to subdue the carnivalesque impact of the story is to reverse the roles. *Old Man Hottabson* (1938), by Lazar Lagin, is loosely based on the central premise in *The Brass Bottle* (1900), by the British author F. Anstey, featuring the appearance of a genie in a modern surrounding. The rest of the plot is formed partly to suit the young audience (Anstey's protagonist's concerns rotate mostly around his girlfriend), partly to teach the lessons dictated by the Soviet educational doctrine. The thirteen-year-old protagonist Volka (Vladimir) finds a mysterious sealed jar when swimming in the Moscow River. As he opens the jar, a genie appears, bursting with gratitude toward his rescuer. The genie, who has fallen out of favor with King Solomon and has been punished by imprisonment, introduces himself as Hassan Abdurahman Ibn-Hottab, and proclaims himself as the lifetime servant of his young master.

The plot evolves in several directions, probing into a number of issues equally momentous for Soviet children's literature. The first is the most conventional and easily recognizable from other stories: Volka making stupid wishes with catastrophic aftermath. The misadventures start with Hottabson ("Hottabych" in Russian, literally "the son of Hottab," or Ibn-Hottab) offering to assist Volka with his oral exam in geography. Volka has no reason for anxiety: he has studied diligently and feels quite confident. Yet he cannot resist the temptation, and when he is assigned a question about India, Hottabson, speaking through him, amazes the teacher with a medieval, Oriental, half-mythical account, including the view of a flat world resting on six elephants and a giant turtle. Hilarious for the reader and highly embarrassing for the character, this scene proclaims the simple moral that cheating is wrong. Like the Psammead in Edith Nesbit's stories, Hottabson often misinterprets his master's wishes, however, unlike Psammead, he does not do it out of spite, but rather because of his own ignorance or inaptitude. After so many centuries in the jar, his magic has become a bit rusty. Much like Nesbit's characters, Volka also discovers that fairy-tale marvels are out of place in modern world. Among other things, he finds out that flying carpets are not as comfortable transportation means as fairy tales present it.

However, the conflict between magic and reality is taken much further, bringing into it transparent moral and political implications. The process of socialization is in this novel shifted from the child protagonist onto the genie himself. The first thing Hottabson must do to survive in the modern world is change from the Oriental attire with a turban and pointed slippers into more proper and inconspicuous clothes. He is thus compelled to give up an essential part of his individuality in order to adapt to the society into which he is involuntarily introduced. Thus conformity is once again prescribed as a foremost virtue. Apart from the general connotations, this episode may also refer to the many Asian nations incorporated—ostensibly of their own free will—into the vast Soviet empire and forced to surrender their customs and heritage for the sake of the declared Soviet multiculturalism, in practice ruthless imperialism.

The urban, modern lifestyle represented by Volka is clearly portrayed as superior to what Hottabson is likely to be familiar with. He is introduced to modern technology in the form of buses, trains, cinema, telephones and other wonders, which he, typically, takes to be the evil deeds of the Devil himself. Yet Hottabson proves to be a quick and eager disciple to his young friend. Not only does he get used to horseless carriages and moving pictures, but he also learns to read and write, thus getting fully integrated into the civilized society. The Soviet regime claimed that it had provided the illiterate Central Asian population with proper education, comfortably forgetting that Oriental culture produced masterpieces of literature centuries before the existence of the Soviet state. On the contrary, traditional Oriental literature was looked down upon by the authorities, and the Central Asian nations were forced to adopt Cyrillic alphabet instead of their traditional Persian and Arabic lettering.

Yet Hottabson gladly enters the culture of the glorious Soviet Union. Typically, one of the first written texts he peruses after he has mastered the primer is the newspaper of the Young Communists, which means that he imbibes ideology alongside grammar. He becomes an eager newspaper reader and collects both facts and opinions from them. He learns the rules of his new community and is anxious to obey them. Step by step he abandons his high-flown Oriental speech and adopts both the colloquial style of modern teenagers and the official rhetoric. The numerous lapses into his old ways are accidental on his part, and are obviously preserved in the later part of the novel for the humorous effect.

The superficial clash of cultures is, however, less important than the deeper ideological misunderstandings. Hottabson comes from a society governed by the rich and the mighty. Wishing to thank his rescuer in a proper manner, he bestows Volka with three palaces full of gold and jewels, and a caravan of elephants, camels and slaves. Apart from the gifts creating a major chaos in the street, Volka is appalled and tries to explain to the generous donor the abolishment of private property in the Soviet Union and the immorality of slavery. In our country, he says, all palaces belong to School Districts (for an enlightened reader, this is an ironic comment, since all palaces and mansions in Moscow and elsewhere were indeed confiscated and became state or municipal property soon after the Bolshevik coup d'état in 1917). However, Hottabson is not convinced. School District may be a great and noble person, he retorts, "but did School District rescue me from the jar?" Hottabson thus honors the individual's right to recognition, while Volka tries unsuccessfully to explain the society's priority over the individual. Inadvertently, the author brings forward a conflict that many Soviet citizens have struggled with. On the one hand, young readers, together with Volka, are certainly fascinated by the prospect of having all their wishes fulfilled and are allowed to let their imagination run free with visions of material wealth. On the other hand, it is the text's intention, dictated by ideology, to show that lust for property is incompatible with good morals. In fact, while Volka repeatedly resorts to the genie's help both to set out on adventures and to get safely out of them, he never contemplates asking for any worldly possessions, thus proving himself an exemplary representative of Soviet principles. When Hottabych tries to convince him that money means power, fame and friends, Volka proudly declares that friends cannot be bought for money, and that the only fame worth having is the one received through honest work. He patiently explains to his benefactor that there is no point in buying the factory where his father works, since it is already owned by his father together with the whole Soviet state.

The conflict between the widely separate worldviews continues throughout the book, yet Hottabson makes tangible progress and eventually embraces at least the most basic elements of the Communist dogma. The introduction of the magical agent is thus used not so much in order to provide the protagonist with an unlimited number of fulfilled wishes, but to create a mode of estrangement through which the superiority of the Communist morals can be demonstrated.

The circumstances in which Hottabson finds himself are reminiscent of several motifs widely explored in fiction, not least children's fiction. It is the situation of a savage or a feral child brought to civilization; or that of a time traveler displaced from the past to modern world. In both cases, civilization is frequently shown to be preferable—a stance recently strongly interrogated by postcolonial criticism. In the novel, the whole concept of civilization is closely connected with the victorious Communist state. Further, if fictional visitors from alternative magical worlds to our own reality often find it boring and pale, Hottabson is truly fascinated by the wonders he discovers in the twentieth-century Moscow, ending up as a passionate radio amateur.

Finally, the central spin of the plot is provided by the fact that Hottabson has a brother who, like himself, was punished by King Solomon through being encapsulated in a jar and thrown into the sea. The quest for the brother takes Hottabson and his young friends over the world, providing encounters with world injustices, to which Hottabson soon starts reacting with the true Communist indignation. Among other things, a confrontation is depicted between Hottabson and a grotesquely stereotypical American millionaire, from which Hottabson emerges a moral as well as physical victor (he interprets Volka's wish of "Go jump the puddle" literally). By this time, Hottabson represents the Soviet Union and its ideology. Returning to my earlier reference to the conquered Asian nations, the "backward" (correct Soviet idiom) Muslim

Hottabson has fully adapted to the new times and the new customs, proving to be a faithful champion of world Communism. He also shows solidarity with the oppressed working class of Western Europe. When the lost brother is miraculously found, the readers witness the striking contrast between the reformed Hottabson and the ideologically backward Omar. Hottabson now acts as the enlightened guru, while Omar remains firm in his old-fashioned Oriental worldview and finally receives his deserved punishment, also being comfortably removed from the story.

Thus although the child protagonist is unquestionably empowered by the presence of the magical helper, it is the helper rather than the protagonist who is subjected to the subsequent disempowerment. It is never mentioned in the end that Hottabson loses his magical power, but it is implied that he does not use it very often and in the first place does not use it for silly and vain purposes. Neither is Volka ever seen actively and consciously rejecting his helper's magical assistance, as do Nesbit's children in *Five Children and It*. Yet it is to be understood that he has matured through his adventures and is prepared to live without magical help, since there is nothing he may wish for that the generous Soviet state cannot give him. In fact, Volka has been throughout the novel acting as Hottabson's guide and teacher, as well as the mouthpiece for Soviet morals. This role reversal is unusual in children's fiction. The child appears as wiser and morally superior, while the adult, through the special circumstances, is disparaged and given the role of the ignorant and confused. In this respect, *Old Man Hottabson* differs not only from its direct model, *The Brass Bottle*, but also from Western children's novels featuring genies in modern times.

Condemning Yesterday

Both *Three on an Island* and *Old Man Hottabson* are explicitly didactic, even though didacticism is carefully packaged into adventures and nonsense. In contrast, *The Wizard Walked over the City* (1963), by Yuri Tomin, achieves a considerable psychological depth and leaves more for the readers to contemplate. It starts in a conventional way, by the protagonist, Tolik (Anatoly), finding a magic agent, a matchbox, each match granting him one wish. The ingenuity of this device is once again reminiscent of Edith Nesbit's clever restriction of magic. On discovering the magical power of the matches, Tolik, like many fantasy characters before him, also immediately realizes that the number of wishes is limited and that he must use them wisely. His first actions show the usual carnivalesque excesses in selfish and immature desires, including an ice-hockey stick and other material possessions valuable in a young boy's eyes. Tolik also wishes to be best in the world in ice hockey and in chess, to tame a lion in the Zoo, and to know his homework without studying. Tolik's wish to achieve success without effort has much in common with Boris' desire to escape work, which in the eyes of the official Soviet "state of workers" was an unpardonable sin.

So far, the story is banal and predictable. Yet there are ethical dimensions that make the book different and the character more complex. Deep inside Tolik knows all along than he is doing wrong. Becoming a world champion by magic is cheating, and Tolik is not unequivocally happy about it. He also makes himself guilty of lying, boasting, and abusing power on innocent victims just for fun. More important, he knows that he ought to tell his best friend Misha about the matchbox, and in fact share the matches with him. Yet something prevents him, and it is easy to put labels on this "something": greed, selfishness, vanity—the unacceptable qualities we have already seen condemned in the protagonists of other books. Finally, Tolik comes to the horrible realization—not unlike Boris—that although formally omnipotent, he is helpless as it comes to human relationships. He has quarreled with Misha, he has lost the respect of all his classmates, and his father does not trust him. Powerful as he is, Tolik is profoundly unhappy. Yet as readers we are perhaps not sure whether we are supposed to feel sympathy or to censure the unfortunate hero. Since Tolik is a more contradictory character than Boris, our feelings are ambivalent, and we anticipate that Tolik will soon be subjected to some terrible punishment. The second part of the novel shows more subtlety and inventiveness than the previously discussed ones. We must, however, go back to the beginning of the story and to the way Tolik got hold of the magic agent in order to understand the implications. Escaping from an unfriendly policeman after he illegally crossed the street on red, Tolik finds himself in a strange place, confronted with a mysterious blue-eyed boy surrounded by mountains of matchboxes. Thus the true villain is introduced into the story, although we will not meet him again for quite a while. Snatching a box, Tolik runs away and never gives the boy another thought until he is summoned to his opponent by magic and has to surrender the half-empty matchbox.

The blue-eyed boy, who never acquires a name other than the self-imposed Wizard, and is therefore perceived as universal evil, has succeeded with something fairy-tale heroes normally fail: on finding the wish-granting agent, his first wish was to secure an unlimited amount of wishes. He had wished for a million wish-granting matchboxes, which he was meticulously counting when Tolik took him by surprise. The encounter was highly unlikely, since, as it turns out, the boy lives in yesterday.

The implication of yesterday is transparent for anyone familiar with the Soviet Union. Yesterday stands for the pre-Communist past, and "a person from yesterday" would encompass all the alleged negative qualities of this past: individualism, greed, conceit, contempt for other people and so on. The blue-eyed boy becomes the epitome of this (officially) hateful past: a ruthless capitalist whose actions and morals are totally subordinated to his material interests. Having finished counting his assets—a rather lucid symbol—the boy fills his empty world with artifacts that would be attractive for young readers. The boy does not stop at providing himself with a hockey stick or a bicycle; he thinks globally, wishing for the largest children's department store, the best ice-cream parlor, famous palaces and museums. As a monument to his own vanity, the boy lives in a forty-four-floor house with a hundred rooms on each floor, which he keeps filling with new possessions. He has thirty cars and as many racing boats. The novel thus castigates consumerism, one of the worst vices in the Communist doctrine. At the time when private cars were rare, and few families had apartments of their own, much less houses, the luxury of the boy's existence could only cause irritation.

Yet the blue-eyed boy goes much further than providing himself with material wealth. He also secures peace of mind by erasing the memory of his parents and friends, and of his former life at large. He thus exists not only outside time, but outside society, any social network or social obligations. He has deliberately cut himself off the rest of the world. The lust for material things becomes interconnected with spiritual poverty. For even such a rational and cold-hearted character as the blue-eyed boy lacks something that cannot be bought for money: a friend. Therefore he wishes that Tolik be brought to him, hoping that Tolik's foolish behavior with the matchbox reveals a soul mate. "I like you," he says repeatedly, "because you are just like me, greedy and selfish." He offers to take away Tolik's memory as well, but since the plot demands that the protagonist's desire to return home remains intact, this does not happen. As a more tangible link with his real life, Tolik's best friend Misha is also captured in yesterday. But the blue-eyed boy has no doubts about Misha's high moral qualities, and uses him as a hostage to win Tolik's affection. Yet, as in *Three on an Island*, a companion is used as a contrast to the protagonist's unstable ethics.

In this confrontation Tolik gets a chance to show himself a true young Communist: he rejects the boy's gifts and his friendship, and after a lot of complications manages, together with Misha, to escape from "yesterday" to "today," that is, from the dubious temptations of the Capitalist past to the promising present and future of the victorious Communism.

The moral and psychological lesson Tolik learns is more complicated than those of the characters in the earlier discussed novels. He does not voluntarily surrender his power, neither is he accidentally deprived of it. He must succumb to a more powerful opponent and therefore has to come up with stronger moral qualities to win the combat. The confrontation is between the material and the spiritual wealth, and as in all Soviet children's books, the spiritual proves more vigorous. The blue-eyed boy is left with his riches in yesterday, in the past which Soviet literature encourages its readers to contempt and condemn. Unlike Hottabson, the blue-eyed boy seems to be beyond redemption. I find it significant, though, that the villain of the story is a young person and not an adult, which would perhaps be more natural for subversive purposes (as illustrated by the pirates in *Three on an Island* and the greedy American in *Hottabson*). Apparently, the text warns its readers that among the young generation there can also be individuals whose mentality belongs to yesterday. "Beware of the people with the blue color of greed in their eyes," the didactic narrator says explicitly in his afterword to the book. Naturally, it is possible and fully legitimate to interpret the blue-eyed boy in psychoanalytical terms, as Tolik's "Shadow," his dark side that he has to overcome. Yet I prefer a more mimetic, maybe even allegorical interpretation since it makes more sense in the Soviet context. The two readings actually complement each other.

Moreover, after Tolik has successfully won over his enemy and returned home, he is subjected to yet another trial. In the very beginning of his empowerment, he made a disastrous wish that his mother comply with anything he wants. He truly enjoyed her total support as she cooked his favorite meals, made his bed and packed his school bag, bought him expensive presents, gave him plenty of pocket money, approved of all his actions, and took his side against the father. But on return from yesterday, when things, according to the genre conventions, should have gone back to normal, Tolik discovers to his horror that his mother is still under the enchantment. This gives the narrator yet another opportunity to remind the readers about the fatal results of careless wishes, in this case more disturbing than in any of the previously discussed books, since the wish involves the most vulnerable relationship a child can possibly have. Unlike Boris, Tolik is not fully freed from the responsibility for his actions. Still he is given the final chance to show that he has indeed morally improved. There is one last magical match miraculously stuck behind a sofa cushion. Without a moment's hesitation, Tolik uses it to eliminate the consequences of all his previous wishes—once again, much like the folktale hero or a fantasy character.

Trying to find a common denominator for these (in many respects) very different stories, apart from the superficial similarity of the wish-granting motif, we can state that they all present exactly the opposite pattern from the carnivalesque Western fantasy. While normally, carnival empowers child protagonists and gives them self-confidence necessary to cope with problems after the time-out of the carnival is over, in the Soviet fantasy I have discussed, the impact is the opposite. The temporary empowerment through magic wishes forces the young characters to discover their faults, prompting them to adjust to societal norms and subdue individual desires. If "normal" carnivalesque hero develops personality through magical adventures, the Soviet heroes learn that individuality and self-concern are detrimental qualities that lead to no good and have to be gotten rid of. While a sophisticated reader would perhaps still be able to discern some subversive elements in these stories, interpreting their straightforward messages as ironic, I would argue that such interpretations are largely "in the mind of the beholder." Soviet fantasy clearly reflects the ruling ideology and propagates the values inherent in it. As such, it faithfully served the purposes of the society in which it was created.

Ideology and Magical Realism

In contrast, Lygia Bojunga and Ana Maria Machado, two highly appraised Brazilian children's authors, are extremely and consciously subversive. Writing within the tradition of magical realism, both authors use genre conventions in the same way some North American and European authors use fantasy: a condition of carnivalesque, suspended reality where the child has more freedom and is empowered in a way strict realism would not allow. Both stretch our normal sense of time and space, of the everyday and the uncanny. Ana Maria Machado makes wide use of native mythology and folklore, mixing tunes from oral storytelling with the most exquisite literary language, full of allusions, metaphors and complex imagery. The character of *Eyes on the feathers* (1981), who at the age of eight has already lived in five countries because of political persecution, is allowed through a mixture of dreams and imagination encounter his ancestors, real and mythical, and witness the cruel destruction of the native population by European colonizers. His personal fate is presented as closely interconnected with the fates of whole peoples. The story brings across its subversive message through the disguise of a fairy-tale-like dream.

On the other hand, *The Upside-down Story* (1978) takes place wholly in a fairy-tale realm, featuring a king and his queen, a valiant prince and a stubborn princess; but the society depicted is easily recognizable, with its self-conceited despot, his compliant servants and the ordinary people who have to cope with the ruler's follies. Reality and fairy tale easily change places in Machado's literary universe; in fact, they are just two side of the same world. Even her protagonists know it very well: it is natural for the young girl in *Magic Kisses* (1992) to believe that her new stepmother is a witch, because stepmothers are always wicked witches in fairy tales, and isn't it obvious that her father has been enchanted? And as readers, how can we be sure that Nanda is mistaken? Perhaps her stepmother is a witch after all. And how can we really feel certain that the imaginary friend in *Pedro and his Flying Bull* (1979) is indeed imaginary when he is so real for the boy? With Machado, we are always in the marginal zone between reality and imagination. It is in this liminal space that a child can be empowered.

Likewise, in Bojunga's books we meet young children empowered by special vision, who see things and creatures that the adults cannot see, as does Rachel in *The Yellow Bag* (1976) who makes unlikely friends with two cockerels, a safety pin and an umbrella. The book demonstrates, though Rachel's insights, that adults have more power than children, and Rachel's desire is to grow up as soon as possible, in the same manner that she wishes to be a boy. Yet she is strong and independent because she is a child and a girl. Notably, like her many literary sisters, Rachel also discovers the liberating power of writing. Writing and written language has more authority and is therefore usually usurped by the adults. Rachel learns to use her writing for subversive purposes.

Alexander in *Granny's House* (1978) also conquers the injustice of adult world through imagination. In this book, the adult power is most tangibly shown through the indoctrination that Alexander's peacock has been subjected to in school. Like the cockerel with his thoughts sewn up in *The Yellow Bag*, the peacock becomes a symbol of the oppressed child.

Bojunga's characters, each in her or his way, struggle against the rules and regulations that adults have imposed on them. In *Six Times Lucas* (1995) Lucas' foremost dilemma is his complicated relationship with his authoritative father and his fear of not being able to live up to adults' expectations, while he also sees the faults and insecurity of adult life. Maria in *Free Rope* (1979) is made to forget the traumatic memory of her parents' death, but dreams help her come to terms with the circumtances. Through dreams and imagination, reminiscent of Ana Maria Machado's work, she learns to explore her inner landscape and liberates herself from her grandmother's tyranny. In *My Friend the Painter* (1987) Claudio contemplates an adult man's suicide. Again, the child proves stronger than the adult in his very capacity of being a child. A deep penetration of a child's psyche is the foremost characteristic of Lygia Bojunga, who manages to use simple and accessible language to convey complex mental states, unspeakable truths and most secret emotions. Each book is a study of human fate drawn with precision and tremendous empathy; a sophisticated portrait of a child working through loss, pain and sorrow.

One particular book by Machado, *Few-letter Words, Many-letter Words, Four-letter Words* (1998) makes use of the conventionality of language and the power that language gives adults over children. The book causes us to ask "How can a young child understand why words like 'cock' and 'ass' are fine when they denote animals, but not otherwise?" And how does she feel when confronted with big and incomprehensible words such as REPRESSED AGGRESSIVENESS or MANIFESTING ANXIETY. Oppressed by the insensitive adults, the girl decides to stop talking at all, a persuasive metaphor for silencing dissidents. Even though young readers may not immediately understand it, the adult co-readers will. However, young readers will certainly understand the protagonist's feelings of resignation and abandonment, especially since she believes that all her language troubles come out of her not being a boy: boys are allowed to use bad language, but girls are not. In this simple manner, the narrator makes us aware of the gendered nature of language in society—something that sociolinguists know well, but also that young children confront daily.

Brazilian writers' subversive impact depends on the use of the synergy of heterological conditions, including race, gender, class and age. Yet another prominent feature in Bojunga's as well as Machado's works is strong female protagonists, young as well as old. I have already mentioned Rachel and Maria, the inquisitive and determined character of Machado's *Few-letter Words* and the suspicious stepdaughter in *Magic Kisses*, as well as the brave and clever Shepherdess in *The Upside-Down Story*. Machado's *Grandmother*

Bia, Grandmother Bel (1982) is a piercing, compelling magical exploration of the invisible links between generations of women. It goes far beyond the conventional motif of imaginary companion. The photo of Isabel's great-grandmother mystically transubstantiates into a part of herself, a real, living person inside herself, who in reality has been dead for many years. Moreover, and perhaps more disturbing, there is a third voice which suddenly appears within Isabel and which proves to be her great-granddaughter from the distant future almost impossible to imagine. These links with the past and the future help the protagonist to find her own place, her own identity, but only in relationship to others, as a part of a larger whole. Multiplicity, heterogeneity, ambiguity—all the labels of the so-called postmodern literature—are easily recognizable. This is an example of how a child can be empowered rather than disempowered through bonds with adults, but it can only be done within the conventions of magical realism.

Note

1. The texts have been accessed on the web and therefore lack pagination. All translations in this chapter are those of the author.

Chapter Ten
Othering the Species:
The (Ab)use of Animals

Narratives about animated toys and humanized animals that live in symbiosis with a human child have excellent premises for the carnival effect. Animals and toys are usually inferior to children in strength and intelligence. This includes both the fictive children in the narrative and the young readers. It is not accidental that the most common animals in children's books are small: such as mice, rabbits, guinea-pigs and kittens. In the company of toys and small animals, the child can feel strong, clever and protective. No overview of children's literature can ignore the fact that animal characters appear significantly more often in children's books than in mainstream books. Apart from myths and fables, merely a handful of adult novels feature animal protagonists. E. M. Forster claims that "actors in a story are usually human," and continues: "Other animals have been introduced, but with limited success, for we know too little so far about their psychology" (Forster 1985, 43). Forster was hardly acquainted with children's literature, yet he is right in one respect. When animals appear as literary characters they are ascribed human traits, both behaviorial and intellectual. Even when animals are presented in their natural habitat, their emotions and thoughts are patterned according to human models.

Such anthropomorphism can, however, vary significantly. Different species can exist in an unnatural symbiosis, endowed with human speech and mind, communicating with each other as the plot demands. Animals can be portrayed in close relationship with humans, or a least one human who can understand the animal, talk to it and have it as a personal friend. Within children's literature, such characters, alongside toys, are typically interpreted as the child's imaginary friend, a compensatory figure, a projection of the child's inner conflicts, as already shown in the discussion of *Winnie-the-Pooh*. However, the most complex stories show animals as hybrids, where the boundary between animal and human is fluctuant.

It is a common view that animals, especially anthropomorphic animals, are suitable characters in children's literature. This is based on the vague assumption that "children love animals." I have never seen any empirical research about real children's attitude toward animals, nor about young readers' preference for animals in their stories, so the assumption must be one of many ungrounded prejudices. Some scholars have been rather skeptical about this stance, pointing out the contemptuous attitude of bundling together animals and children as "small," "inferior," and basically "not human" (e.g. Schwarcz and Schwarcz 1991, 9). Another explanation can be pedagogical: animal shape distances the conflict, making it easier for the reader to deal with it. Animals thus become estrangement devices, similar to the fantasy mode, and indeed animal stories are frequently treated as a subcategory of fantasy. In the vast majority of stories, animals are used to empower the human child, the character as well as the reader, who feel superior to beasts. This statement is confirmed by the fact that among the most popular animals in books for children we notice the prevalence of small creatures, such as mice, rabbits, kittens and monkeys. A possible explanation is that small and helpless characters empower the child who feels big, strong and capable, but an equally plausible reason is that small animals, just as stuffed toys, are "cute" and therefore considered suitable for children's books. There are some exceptions such as Jean de Brunhoff's *The Story of Babar, the Little Elephant* (1931)—note the epithet "little," even though applied to a large animal. A hippo, yet another large and far more dangerous beast, cannot compete with Babar in popularity, yet also hippos feature in children's books as cute and lovable characters. What is the attraction of these huge, clumsy and, frankly said, quite ugly quadrupeds?

Veronica (1961), by Roger Duvoisin, starts with a true, but unexpected statement: "Hippopotamuses can sometimes be very conspicuous" (n.p.). The colorful image shows a giant hippo surrounded by a group of children. We can accept this *licentia poetica*, although hippos normally do not allow humans to cuddle them, but the point is that one can hardly miss a hippo if you come across one. However, as the text continues, Veronica was an inconspicuous hippo since she lived among hippo mothers and hippo fathers and hippo uncles and hippo aunts and hippo brothers and hippo sisters and hippo cousins. Like many other characters in children literature, Veronica is not content being one of many; she wants to be different and preferably famous. Like many other characters, she leaves home in search of a place where she would feel unique. This beginning is reminiscent of the first *Babar* book, and precisely like Babar, Veronica comes to a large city. There she is indeed conspicuous, and causes a lot of commotion. The solution comes, just as in Babar, in a nice rich lady. Yet in *Babar*, the encounter leads to the elephant's socialization, including walking upright, wearing clothes, eating at tables and driving cars. In *Veronica*, the hippo is returned to her own world; yet she is no longer indistinguishable among the crowd. She is standing on her hind legs and telling about her adventures to a large audience of admirers.

Veronica is depicted in her natural surroundings, even though she is bestowed with human mind and makes a short visit to civilization. The hippos in James Marshall's *George and Martha* series are fully anthropomorphized: they wear clothes, walk on hind legs, live in a house and eat human food. The plot consists of short, unsophisticated episodes which best illustrate a central issue of using animals in children's stories, Normally it is assumed that animals, as well as animated objects, represent children, that is, are child characters in disguise (as Veronica no doubt is). However, this is far from universal. The use of animals allows circumventing some aspects inevitable in a narrative with human characters, such as age and social status. Are Martha and George two children playing together, or are they adults, perhaps two happy seniors who visit each other and have a good time? The options do not change anything in the stories, yet the question remains unanswered. Further, we can wonder whether the hippo form is significant or whether the characters could just as well be dogs, cats or bears. It is only the illustrations that make jokes of the clumsy bodies, for instance, when Martha takes a bath in a tub which is apparently too little for her. If anything, this is a reminder of the existence of obesity, and some young readers may feel hurt, even though the characters seem totally happy with themselves. There are no other characters who could laugh at them or bully them for being overweight. George does play a trick on Martha when she looks at herself in a mirror, but he could do this even if she weren't fat. The hippos are fully interchangeable in these stories.

These examples illustrate two approaches to employment of animals, both allowing the child reader to feel superior. In the rest of this chapter, I will explore the significant alterity of animal characters by a discussion of some famous and less-known literary cats that have different functions, from dumb beasts to magical helpers to heroes in their own rights. Portrayal of cats as creative and wise is reflected, for instance, in E. T. A. Hoffmann's philosophical novel *The Life and Opinions of Cat Murr* (1820). In children's literature, whether cats represent the child or act as helpers or antagonists, they are frequently shown as inferior to human beings.

Cats as Props

Domestic cats appear in the earliest known myths and folktales as representations of the highest deities, such as the Egyptian goddess Bast, the cult of which was connected with joy and merrymaking. The cat was also featured in Egyptian mythology as one of the many incarnations of the solar god Ra, who struggles against and kills an evil serpent. The amalgamation of the cat and the dragonslayer has left traces in Oriental as well as European folklore, where the motif often got inverted and the cat, especially a black cat, became one of the many transformations of the antagonist, while the hero can also in some situations metamorphose into a cat. This ambiguity results in the twofold status of cats in folklore, where they feature both as benevolent and evil (see Briggs 1980; Holmgren 1996)

The practical uses of domestic cats as mousers contributed to their positive reputation, which is reflected in the folktale of Dick Whittington. Dick is an orphan and a kitchen boy in the house of a rich London merchant. He has to endure all kinds of hardships, including hoards of mice in the attic where he sleeps. With his last and only penny he buys a cat from a street girl and can thus sleep calmly. However, the merchant soon demands that, as the custom prescribes, everyone in the household send an item with his ship. Dick has only his cat to send, and this makes his fortune. The ship ends up in Africa, where a local king pays most money for the wonderful animal who can deliver his country from rodents. The cat never gets a name, and Dick has no sentiments toward it; the cat has a solely pragmatic purpose. When the cat is taken away from him, Dick does not lack his companion, but merely laments that he will once again be troubled by vermin.

During the Middle Ages in Europe, cats became connected with evil powers, which was based partly on the popular beliefs about cats' lewdness, partly on their Christian association with Satan. Such attitudes led to cats' connection with witches; indeed, black cats, together with ravens, frequently appear in folktales as witches' familiars, and witches also turn into cats, a fact reflected in the *Harry Potter* books when Professor McGonnagal occasionally takes the shape of a cat. An evil cat monster appears in King Arthur stories. The view of cats as evil led to incredible cruelties toward them. During witch hunts, cats were burned together with their mistresses. At the same times, there is evidence of cats being put into walls of newly built houses to bring luck.

By the beginning of the nineteenth century, the cat's reputation was exculpated, and cats became popular pets in upper- and middle-class families, which is, among other things, reflected in numerous nursery rhymes, fables, cartoons, children's stories and picturebooks. Cats became benign and often sweet characters, adapted to children's and family reading. Most of modern cat stories are picturebooks portraying anthropomorphic cats, representing humans. The shape is, just as in George and Martha books, arbitrary and interchangeable. It is hardly worth mentioning the abundant felines rubbing against their owners' feet or purring on their laps, merely to create an atmosphere. In hundreds of books, a child gets a kitten for pet. Occasionally, a black cat may prompt, most often erroneously, that its owner is a witch.

In James Joyce's *The Cat and the Devil* (1957), the cat seemingly plays a minor role. Yet on closer consideration, the story appears a parodic play with the Faust myth, where a cat rather than a woman is presented as sacrificial; besides the cat's action is not voluntary and therefore less sublime. The Devil claims "the first person who crosses the bridge", but, as in many folktales, he is outwitted. Had he said "the first human being", the Lord Mayor would have to offer him one of his subjects. Instead, the cunning man sends a cat across the bridge, which presumably makes no difference, as cats are supposed to have no souls and thus have nothing to fear from the Devil. In the 1980 edition of the book, illustrated by Roger Blachon, the last doublespread shows the cat joyfully playing with the tip of the Devil's tail, much to the latter's annoyance. Yet the story certainly accentuates the association between the Devil and the cat, even though Blachon chooses to depict the cat white rather than black.

Cats as Cats

Rudyard Kipling's etiologic story 'The Cat who Walked by Himself' (from *Just So Stories,* 1902) depicts the nature of cats as unreliable and independent as opposed to dogs as man's true friends. The cat is, in his own words, " . . . not a friend, and . . . not a servant," he is "the Cat who walks by himself, and all places are alike to him." The bargain between the cat and the humans, according to this story, includes the cats' obligation to keep the house free from mice, to be nice to babies just as long as do not pull his tail too hard. For this, the Cat is allowed to be inside the house when he pleases, sit by the fire, and "drink the warm white milk three times a day for always and always and always."

Many stories represent animals as animals, demonstrating typical animal behaviour and only occasionally ascribing them intelligence, comparable with that of human beings, or even less frequent, human emotions. An early forerunner of this line was the poignant story by Ernest Thompson Seton 'The Slum Cat.' The author writes in the Preface to the collection *Animal Heroes*:

> A hero is an individual of unusual gifts and achievements. Whether it be man or animal, this definition applies; and it is the histories of such that appeal to the imagination and to the hearts of those who hear them. In this volume every one of the stories . . . is founded on the actual life of a veritable animal hero. (n.p.)

The cat is used as a focalizer in the sense that it is its perspective the narrative follows, but it is never ascribed any human traits, and its innate behaviour is depicted accurately. Narrative estrangement is employed to pinpoint the perspective, as, for instance, a train is described through the cat's perception, without being explicitly mentioned. Characteristically, the Slum Cat has no name, although her owners would be expected to give her one; yet the text underscores her point of view by referring to her merely as the generic Pussy or Kitty. It is also speculated on what emotions a cat *may* experience in certain situations, translating them into human terms. Thus, with her first litter of kittens, the little Slum Cat "felt all the elation an animal mother can feel, all the delight, and she loved them and licked them with a tenderness that must have been a surprise to herself, had she had the power to think of such things" (n.p.). Further, the text attempts to convey her awareness of sight, sound, touch and especially smell in a way that is felt as authentic as a literary text can get to the interior of a fictional character, animal or human. This exemplifies the cats' asserted independence and love of freedom by dwelling on the Slum Cat's longing as she is pampered in a rich home:

> She had all the food she wanted, but still she was not happy. She was hankering for many things, she scarcely knew what. She had everything—yes, but she wanted something else. Plenty to eat and drink—yes, but milk does not taste the same when you can go and drink all you want from a saucer; it has to be stolen out of a tin pail when you are belly-pinched with hunger and thirst, or it does not have the tang—it isn't milk. (n.p.)

The quote can naturally be interpreted allegorically, as applicable to human beings; yet it is more likely to be a genuine attempt to penetrate the animal nature.

Cats as Tricksters

Of greater interest are perhaps those texts in which specific feline traits are featured in combination with certain human traits, in the first hand intelligence and speech. These abilities create the hybrid human-animal character in which both aspects are amplified. In fairy tales and stories where cats appear as the hero's helper, they are initially empowered as compared to their masters, but eventually bring them to power.

The most famous fairy-tale cat is undoubtedly Puss in Boots, a trickster figure featured in Charles Perrault collection, but also known in other cultures, where a similar role is occasionally played by other animals, for instance, a fox in Slavic folktales. The story has strong Oedipal undertones. The young man must symbolically kill his father, represented by the ogre, to reclaim his inheritance, stolen from him by his brothers. The animal helper's role is to assist his master by cunning and wit. The young man, cheated by his brothers, does not see the potentials of his lot, but the cat surprises his master by being able to talk. Further, the remarkable Puss immediately shows another ability that puts him closer to human beings: he can walk upright. He also asks his master for a pair of boots. This is an unusual request especially since the cat's explanation is "that I may scamper through the dirt and the brambles." Obviously, the reason is quite different: clothes make the person, and human clothes turn the animal into a human. Indeed, with this seemingly simple transformation, Puss is empowered beyond imagination, even though, or perhaps exactly because he retains his feline cunning, agility and hunting skills. Notably, he kills the ogre in the shape of a mouse using his natural animalistic skills, rather than human ones. All this underscores the mysterious, double nature of the cat. At the end, when Puss has become a great lord, alongside his master, we are told that he "never ran after mice anymore but only for his diversion." This ironic commentary shows that there is still an animal behind the fine gentleman in rich clothes.

'Puss in Boots' is by far the most popular version of the tale, reappearing in picturebooks, fractured stories, movies, cartoons and stage plays. Yet this version is predated by several centuries by others stories, in which the cat is female and often an enchanted princess, who pursues her own goals in making her master rich and socially established. The story is thus connected with a cycle of fairy tales featuring a magical bride/bridegroom motif. It is not accidental that in 'Puss in Boots' the gender of the magical helper is revered. A tomcat is expected to be adventurous and mischievous. She-cats are, as earlier mentioned, associated with feminine witchcraft, shape-shifting, mystery and sexuality (see von Franz 1999).

The male trickster cat has, however, remained in the focus of writers' attention. Lloyd Alexander's collection *The Town Cats and Other Tales* (1977) is another good example. Here we meet cats who assist humans against malevolent intruders, cats as confidants of maidens in distress, cats who challenge powerful rulers, cats who manage daily chores for their owners, cats who assist great painters (including the use of their tails for brush), and a cat who proves unfit for his apprenticeship precisely due to his feline traits. In all the stories, the margin between cat and human is emphasized by clothes. Like Puss in Boots, Pescato the town cat gains power by dressing up as the mayor and stages a true carnival by letting cats perform as people and the other way round. Once again, the dual nature of cats is played upon.

Because of their trickster nature, cats can be easily employed as carnivalesque figures, turning order into chaos and interrogating higher authorities. The most famous American cat is *The Cat in the Hat* (1957), by Dr Seuss, who incorporates both the trickster and the magical helper aspect of the folklore cat. In this dynamic story, chaos invades the everyday order, all rules are abolished, and the whole house is literally turned upside down. This is carnival in its purest form: wild, uncontrolled and nonsensical.

The Cat can be interpreted as the child's playful imagination set free as soon as the adults leave the house. The Cat interrogates all the norms of the adult order. He can do the impossible balancing acts. His use of language is intricate; yet he does not play with sheer logic. Instead, he demonstrates the arbitrary nature of language, which is one of the main instruments of power that adults employ to oppress children. For instance, the Cat promises to show the children two things. The word "thing" is a so-called linguistic shifter, that is, an expression the content of which can only be determined by the situation ("a thing" can denote almost anything, although most often an inanimate object). However, on turning the page, the word acquires a concrete and tangible signified, as it refers to two living creatures. The word "thing" ceases to be a shifter and becomes a regular signifier, while the signified, Thing One and Thing Two, are portrayed in the picture, thus visualizing the concretized abstraction. Not least, the Cat and the two Things intrude into the Holiest, the mother's bedroom, where the children most likely are not allowed to be, and turn it upside down too—a perfect symbol for the attack on parental authority.

Typically, the adult world is present and tries to supervise and prevent the chaotic invasion, in the form of the fish. Perhaps the fish can also be seen as the voice of the children's conscience, their adult rationality, as he says: "You should not be here/when *our* mother is not" (emphasis added). Yet this adult presence seems too weak to stop the wild games; the fish is literally dethroned as the Cat drops him, he falls down and gets stuck in a tea-pot. However, as soon as the mother once again is in sight, the Cat and all the consequences of his breath-taking capers disappear, as if they had never existed. Yet this is not the same device as waking up from a dream. In fact, the child becomes aware of the danger and suppresses his own imagination, literally by catching the two Things in a net. He then gives order to the Cat: "Now you do as I say./You pack up those Things/ and you take them away!" And the Cat not only does this, but brings everything else back to order. This is the child's acknowledgment of adult power, of the ordered adult world in which there is no place for the Cat or the two wild Things. Although the revolt is sanctioned (mother did leave the children alone to play) and thoroughly channeled it has an emancipating effect. "And Sally and I did not know/what to say./Should we tell her/the things that went on there that day?" By having secrets from the mother, a secret world of their own, the children have seriously subverted the mother's authority.

Cats as Guides

In modern fantasy, cats are widely featured as magical helpers and bearers of magical powers, especially assisting the hero in transportation between the everyday and the magical realm. Cats are depicted as nightly characters, secretive, mysterious; half animal, half divine. This fact puts them in a superior position toward humans. The saying about cats having nine lives is used imaginatively in Lloyd Alexander's *Time Cat* (1963), suggesting that a cat may travel into nine different historical periods, which the black cat Gareth does, taking Jason, the boy protagonist, with him. Time travel is deliberate: Gareth takes Jason on nine time-shift adventures, naturally to the times when cats were important, such as Ancient Egypt, Roman Britain, early Christian Ireland, Japan, medieval Europe with witch hunts, and so on. They even witness the creation of the first painting by Leonardo da Vinci, the cat acting as an ample model. Most episodes focus on the events introducing domestic cats in a particular culture, such as first cats in Peru during Spanish conquer. Almost everywhere, the cats' practical skill as mousers is emphasized, but also the superstitions against cats are brought forward:

> There's no kind of worriment or wickedness they won't put on cat . . .
> Cats bring on hail storms, they say, and winds. Cats have an evil eye, to
> bewitch whatever they look at. They can turn themselves invisible or fly

through the air. They take the shape of a witch, and the witch takes the shape of a cat. (152)

The novel becomes a short handbook in cat history, but it also demonstrates the special mystic powers that cats possess, such as their remarkable ability to disappear and reappear. At the same time, typical fantasy devices are ascribed to the magical helper: Jason has always adequate clothing wherever he arrives; he is also able to understand any language: "Perhaps this was all a part of the cat's strange powers" (13). As a character, the boy is rather flat, used merely as the recipient of knowledge, alongside the reader. For instance, his explicit inference is: "If the days in Egypt had been the greatest times for a cat . . . the days in the [medieval] village must be the worst" (156). The cat is employed as a magical agent, which could just as well be a magic wand. He does, however, take active part in the adventures and occasionally seems to have changed the flow of history, yet he warns the boy: "You'd be on your own, you wouldn't have any kind of protection . . . . What happens, happens. And you couldn't change your mind in the middle" (9). Jason becomes, indeed, involved in many dangerous adventures, but finally the cat brings him safely home. A rational dream explanation is offered, yet there is, as in many fantasy novels, a little indication that the time travel has been true after all.

Plurality of cat lives is echoed in the title of *The Lives of Christopher Chant* (1988), by Diana Wynne Jones. One of the ideas recurrent in Jones' fantasy novels is heterotopia, the infinite multitude of alternative worlds, separate worlds which may recall our own, but are different, sometimes slightly, some substantially, depending on the development of each particular world. The point of departure is that some time, during an early period in history, the worlds grew apart; no world is thus more "real" than any other world. The difference between worlds implies that in some of them magic is a common trait. Although the mechanism of travel between worlds in *The Lives of Christopher Chant* seems obvious and, not unexpectedly, reserved for the child, it soon becomes apparent that a cat plays a significant role in the magical transportations. Christopher's evil uncle uses his magical ability to transport valuable merchandize from other worlds, such as dragon blood, mermaid flesh, hallucinogenous mushrooms, but also deadly weapons absent in his own world. At one point Uncle Ralph sends Christopher to bring a sacred cat from the Temple of Asheth, a goddess worshipped in one of the parallel worlds (and obviously inspired by the Oriental cat deities). Christopher, in his child innocence and naiveté, believes that his magician uncle merely experiments with transposing objects and living beings between worlds; however, it soon becomes clear that Uncle Ralph has other pursuits: magicians in his world will pay fortunes for intestines, claws or eyes of Asheth's cats. The ginger cat Throgmorten escapes and later reappears in the story, becoming not only Christopher's companion in his quite lonely existence in Chrestomanci castle, but eventually turns out to be a powerful magician in his own right. Typically for Jones, the cat is initially depicted as vicious and bad-tempered, while the real villain is amiable and generous. The actuality that appearances are deceptive is just one of many lessons the protagonist learns. Christopher has nine lives, a quality only granted to the highest order of magicians. Throgmorten, who obviously also has nine lives, is thus equal not only to Christopher but to Chrestomanci himself. Yet in some mysterious way Throgmorten seems to be involved each time Christopher loses a life, so his true nature is more complex than can be described in terms of good and evil. After all, he is the cat of Asheth, the goddess of vengeance.

Neil Gaiman's *Coraline* (2002) is a dialogical response to *Alice in Wonderland,* with every indication of postmodern literature present. In this novel, we encounter, similarly to *Alice,* doors and keys, mirrors, pretty gardens, murky passages, and bizarre creatures. While *Alice* may be considered dark, *Coraline* is darker, and while Alice comfortably wakes up from her nightmare, nightmare pursues Coraline into her reality. Alice encounters her symbolic evil (step) mothers, the Queen of Hearts, and the chess Queen, but how these might reflect her real mother/daughter conflict remains to guess and is perhaps of little significance. For Coraline, the other mother is a perfect reflection of her real mother, but a reflection in a sinister mirror. The other world is not merely absurd, but virtually terrifying; and while Alice in all her vulnerability is not exposed to moral choices, Coraline's life is wholly dependent on the right decisions. Yet not even then can she feel safe and secure. Who is then the figure providing the guidance such as offered to Alice by the Cheshire Cat? The patron figure is introduced in the very first chapter as Coraline moves into a new house: "There was also a haughty black cat, who sat on the walls and tree stumps and watched her" (5). The cat's elevated position is reminiscent of the Cheshire Cat as well as Humpty Dumpty. Further, the cat belongs to both worlds, the real and the mirrored, created by Coraline's evil other mother. Unlike the other inhabitants of the other world, but like Coraline herself, the cat is not a reflected double, he can in fact move between worlds: "I'm not the other anything. I'm me . . . You people are spread all over the place. Cats, on the other hand, keep ourselves together" (36). Upon Coraline's inquiry, the cat explains that cats don't have names, commenting it further: "*you* people have names. That's because you don't know who you are. We know who we are, so we don't need names" (37; emphasis in the original). The integrity of the cat is contrasted to Coraline's identity confusion, as she, much like Alice again, "did not know where she was; she was not entirely sure *who* she was" (67; emphasis in the original). Not unexpected, the cat can talk in the other world, but not in the real one, although Coraline wonders "whether cats could talk where she came from and just chose not to" (38). The cat's natural skills prove advantageous when he kills an evil rat. Although black, he is not the witch mother's familiar and does assist Coraline, even though he initially, like the Cheshire Cat, is vague about locations:

"Please, what is this place?
The cat glanced around briefly. "It's here," he said.

"I can see that. Well, how did you get here?"
"Like you did. I walked," said the cat. (37)

Thus the cat may seem quite a conventional liminal character, but this first impression proves wrong. As the passages back to reality are closed by the other mother's will, the cat is rendered helpless, and eventually it is Coraline who saves them both. Yet in this novel, as in many others, cats' ability to breach fluctuant boundaries between alternative worlds is masterly exploited.

Cats as Confused Teenagers

The most complex images of animals are those in which animal and human traits are amalgamated to the extent that challenges simple categorization. Eugen Trivizas's *The Last Black Cat* (2001), one of the relatively rare cat stories employing first-person perspective, is an allegory of the Holocaust. On an unnamed island, a secret society decides to exterminate all black cats. The reasons are conventional: superstitions about black cats bringing bad luck; yet the significance is transparent and may, naturally, even be applied to other genocides and racial discrimination. When all black cats are murdered, the next step is to decimate all grey cats, then all cats with black spots, and finally every single cat on the island. Having miraculously survived, the feline narrator tells his story as a warning to the coming generations. While it can be argued that cats are interchangeable with any other species in this novel, it is cats' alleged connection with the evil, their otherness and people's prejudice against cats that make the story plausible. Naturally, the novel can also be read as plain adventure, about love and friendship, loyalty and betrayal; yet its ideological intentions are obvious.

During the last few years readers have witnessed a conspicuous trend in juvenile novels about feline communities, from Sonya Hartnett's poignant *Forest: Journey from the Wild* (2001) to S. F. Said's tragicomic *Varjak Paw* (2003) and not least the captivating mixture of feral child story and mystical fantasy, *Warrior Cats,* by Erin Hunter, starting with *Into the Wild* (2003). The series can also be read as an allegory, or rather metaphor, following the typical storyline of an adolescent gang novel, such as S. E. Hinton's *The Outsiders*. The master plot adds up to the following: A young man from a respectable family dreams about the freedom and independence of street life. He encounters some youngsters from a street gang that lives by stealing and fighting other gangs. Without much consideration, our hero exchanges his carefree and secure life for the romantics and sexual liberty that gang life has in store. At first, he is bullied and treated as an outsider, but soon learns the ways and the jargon of the gang; he gains some friends and one enemy, and the wise leader of the gang is on his side. In a decisive confrontation with a rival gang he shows himself worthy and is fully accepted into the new community.

To counterbalance the harsh social realism, in *Warrior Cats*, strong elements of the occult are woven into the story, such as adoration of the celestial ancestors, an eventful journey to an ancient cult place, divine trance, and the figure of a shaman ("medicine cat"). These features, frequently found in high fantasy, would scarcely be displayed in a realistic gang story, but they pay tribute to the blend of genres common in contemporary literature. The hero, initially called Rusty but adopted by the wild cat community by the name of Firepaw (the naming also an archetypal element), has few psychological traits. He feels no remorse about leaving home and never regrets it. He is the sole focalizer of the novel, but occasionally the reader is allowed to make inferences before the character. He is intelligent and he does have some inner argument concerning loyalty and honor; yet his considerations are markedly focused on actions. From a mimetic viewpoint, it is ludicrous to expect cats to have a rich spiritual life, yet with the general premises of the novel, that is, its allegorical dimension, the character could have been more round to encourage empathy. On the other hand, flat orientation of the character is a norm rather than exception in a gang novel, so young Firepaw is far from unique. In fact, he continues the long row of archetypal heroes that have to go through initiation to be accepted into a given community. Both the setting and the quest are glorified without question. The deviations, or rather the specifics of employing cats rather than human beings, lie in detail. Instead of stealing, cats go mousing; they use claws and teeth rather than knives and guns. The young tom's castration fears are not pursued further after the wild cats explain the consequences, yet they may be translated into an adolescent's restricted sexuality within the family's constraint. Otherwise, battles for territory, rivalry, loyalty and treachery, strict hierarchy within the clan, honor codes, rewards and punishments are highly reminiscent of the numerous novels with human protagonists. The book is an example of (ab)using cats as a disguise for human beings, since the feline appearance is not inherent to the plot. It certainly adds excitement and not least novelty to the well-trodden narrative, appealing to cat lovers and adventure lovers equally. Yet it necessarily alienates the reader by the exterior and life conditions of the characters, which may be attractive as well as repelling.

By contrast, *Forest*, while superficially similar to *Warrior Cats*, signals the decisive difference already in the title: Fireclaw's journey is *into* the wild; Kian's *from* the wild. Kian's loyalty lies wholly with the domesticated world, and his quest, against all odds, is to return home. Thus the character is doubly othered, first as an animal, then as an animal betraying his nature. By describing the human world through a smart animal's mind—a distinctive case of estrangement—the narrator allows the reader, familiar with this world, to circumvent Kian's perception and infer that the cats' owner is dead and that no welcome awaits them when they return to the house they once called home. This shift in subject position by no means impedes the reader's empathy, but, paradoxically, amplifies it. The readers realize that the protagonist has no chance in the fictive universe of the novel; unlike the young kittens he is in charge of, he will not be able to adapt to life in the wild, not so much because he is used to comfort, but because of his firm convictions. Significantly, Kian dies after being shot by a human, his end coming from the same agency toward which he had shown unconditional loyalty. The character's totally unexpected death, portrayed with a heart-piercing detachment, inevitably shifts the point of view for the few remaining pages of the novel, further alienating the reader; yet the new, neutral, or omniscient, perspective is never established either. Even though the readers earlier felt compelled to share the protagonist's subjectivity, by the end they are expected to view him from aside and literally leave him behind, as his more fortunate companions make their way toward the forest. The matter-of-fact closure casts a retrospective shadow on the construction of the whole text, magnifying the alienation effect without encroaching on empathy.

Forest is a rare example of the use of animals in fiction where a perfect balance is achieved between zoomorphization of the human and anthropomorphization of the beast. The novel is neither an allegory, nor a simple transposition of the human world into an animal one. The human/animal equilibrium contributes to the right proportion of estrangement and empathy so that a strong independent subject position is incited.

Chapter Eleven
Othering the Visual:
Power Structures in Picturebooks

Picturebooks have great potential for subversion of adult power and interrogation of the existing order. The two narrative levels, the verbal and the visual, allow counterpoint and contradiction between the power structures presented by words and images. Far from all picturebook creators deliberately employ the dynamic word/image interaction, but even when the relationship is seemingly duplicative, the images can expand and enhance ideological statements of the words. In this chapter I will explore some picturebooks in which the tension between words and images amplifies the position of the text toward power hierarchies.

In Maurice Sendak's *Where the Wild Things Are* (1963), during his imaginary journey "through night and day and in and out of weeks and almost a year to where the wild things are" Max is crowned as "the most wild of all" and "king of all wild things." As he is from start powerless and oppressed—denied food and exiled to his room—the ascension is a perfect illustration of carnival: the lowest becomes the highest. In the end, he is brought back to the world where his mother has the power of providing or denying him food. Max has mastered the monsters (his own aggressions), but as a child, he is at his mother's will. In the last picture, he has not only lost his crown, but is losing his wolf suit, the initial device of his empowerment in becoming a wild thing. The conflict remains unresolved; the adult superiority is confirmed.

When Max starts "the wild rumpus" the verbal text suddenly gets silent. Instead, three wordless doublespreads reflect what happens in a little boy's imagination when his wild aggressions are replayed in his inner world, after he has been sent to bed "without eating anything." The images take over when words are no longer sufficient to convey strong emotions: anger, anxiety, loneliness, fear and joy. Certainly, words could *describe* what Max and the wild things are doing on the wordless spreads, yet they would not affect the reader's senses in the same immediate and efficient manner as the images. It is exactly senses, in the plural, as we can hear Max's shouts as well as the wild things' roar of admiration; we can smell the steaming jungle and sweaty fur; we can feel the rough grass under our bare feet. Max is totally empowered by his imaginary journey to the land of the wild things. In his fantasy he uses the same mechanisms of power that his mother has used on him: he sends them off to bed without supper. The oppressed becomes the oppressor.

The picturebook as a special art form is able to express emotions that the young protagonist himself as yet lacks language to articulate. When Max's mother, irritated by his mischief, calls him "WILD THING!" he retorts with: "I'LL EAT YOU UP!" With this phrase he is trying to express a wide range of emotions, from "I hate you—right now" to "I love you and I know that you will always love no matter what" and everything in between. Max is too young to be able to verbalize his contradictory feelings, and instead of using an omniscient narrator who would explain how Max feels and why, the text resorts to visual narration, translating anger and disappointment into images that lack direct correspondence in words. Significantly, the wild things respond in the same manner to Max's exercise of power as they plead with him: "Oh please don't go—we'll eat you up—we love you so!" Playing out his emotions, Max tries to explain that "I'll eat you up" equals "I love you." The pose of the monster closest to Max on this spread is reminiscent of Max's pose during one of his pranks in the beginning of the book.

Max is depicted in an open conflict with his mother who has the power to give or deny him not only food, as we are told explicitly, but also what food symbolizes: warmth, attention and love. At the end of the story, the mother, although giving in with warm meal, can still deny her son care and love, as he is once again alone in his room, which, incidentally, does not look like a child's room, with its gloomy colors, a gigantic bed, and absence of any toys. The image reflects Max's subjective perception of the room as a prison rather than its real appearance; yet if the last picture is supposed to convey reconciliation, the setting does not support it. As has been repeatedly observed, the mother is only present in the verbal text, as a shouting voice, passing a judgment on the boy's improper behavior. We can infer, however, that she has given Max his wolf suit to play and thus initiated his wild games. Calling him "wild thing" she provides a verbal image that he will use to create his compensatory mind-scape. Apparently, she is too busy to notice that her son is using inappropriate playthings: a curtain, hammer and nail, and a couple of thick books. She has likewise failed to observe that the boy has hung his teddy bear—a sign of emotional disturbance; or that he has drawn a monster and nailed up the drawing on the wall. All these details are depicted visually. The mother is thus portrayed as an omnipotent, omnipresent, but indifferent authority. Her power is especially threatening through her visual absence. Max's father is not mentioned at all, neither visually nor verbally, unless we interpret the action "was sent" as coming from the invisible father. In some interpretation, the father is represented symbolically as one of the Wild Things that has human toes rather than claws. If so, the horned monster is not a flattering father image in the boy's mindscape, and in one of the wordless doublespreads Max is actually riding on his back, the monster stooping grudgingly but submissively. The missing father is conquered.

Sendak's *Outside Over There* (1981) is another book in which child/parent conflict and the child's inner world is presented with a complex and nuanced visual language. It demonstrates an exciting counterpart to Max's masculine aggressions, showing a girl's terror connected with a typical feminine theme. Ida's parents have abandoned her: the father literally, as he is "away at sea" and the mother, emotionally. The text informs us that the mother is "in the arbor," which should not in itself feel dangerous, yet the image reveals her emotional absence. She has turned her back to both Ida and the crying baby; she is deaf to the world around her. Yet we may ask whether this is an objective characteristic or Ida's inner picture of her mother, and if so, a permanent image or one at this particular moment. It is quite in accordance with a young child's perception of reality to equal the father away at sea to the mother in the arbor, since in both cases it is an issue of a subjective feeling of parental rejection.

As it has been repeatedly pointed out, the story takes place during a few moments between the images on the half-title page and the last page of the book. Like Max, Ida undertakes an inner journey. The figures and landscapes she encounters on the way reflect her deep dive into the subconscious, which cannot be expressed by words. In *The Wild Things*, the dominant emotion is anger, which eventually turns into reconciliation and longing, expressed verbally as longing for "good things to eat," but also for being "where someone loved him best of all." Max's longing is solipsistic, which is emphasized by the fact that apart from his visualized rage there are no other actors in the story. The dominant emotion in *Outside Over There* is anxiety, a substantially less selfish feeling, projected outwards and embracing Ida's nearest people: the father at sea, the mother in distress, and the helpless baby sister. Unlike anger and even fear that have a particular target, anxiety is vague and diffuse. Max's anger acquires the visual appearance as huge, hairy creatures with enormous eyes, horns, teeth and claws. Yet exactly because of these concrete shapes, horrible as they are, they can be mastered. Max tames the Wild Things "with the magic trick of staring into all their yellow eyes without blinking"—a physical battle of power that Max has learned from his mother. Ida's despair over her father's absence at the dangerous seas, over the mother' passivity and the baby's vulnerability takes the shape of formless, faceless figures—there are no eyes to stare into. The goblins do not attack or threaten to eat Ida up. They sneak on her behind the corners, hide in their loose grey capes, crawl into the window and assail someone that Ida is most worried about, the baby. When the mother ignores her daughters – and this is still Ida's subjective view – Ida feels total responsibility for her little sister, while she also feels guilty when the goblins snatch the baby away and leave a changeling instead. The text says nothing about Ida's feelings, except a matter-of-fact statement: "Ida played her wonder horn to rock the baby still—but never watched." In the previous pages Ida holds the baby tight in her arms, glancing uneasily at the approaching goblins, who first appear in the verbal text on the page where they kidnap the baby. The plot, however, starts on the half-title page, title page and dedication page, in which the goblin images represent Ida's discomfort.

Ida, a girl, does not get any tangible reward in the form of good and warm supper, as does Max, a boy. Instead, her consolation is a letter from the father saying: "I'll be home one day, and my brave, bright little Ida must watch the baby and her Mama for her Papa, who loves her always." The girl is supposed to babysit not only her little sister but her own mother, since the patriarchal authority orders her to do so. Empowered by her journey, having shown exceptional courage and wit, Ida returns to her mother in the arbor. True, the mother has changed her stale, indifferent pose and opens her arms to her daughters, and on the last doublespread she holds her arm around Ida, yet without looking at her, engrossed in the letter. The images tell us that after Ida has played out the horrible scenario with the goblins, she has regained her sense of security and her faith that the parents will always be there and love her (at least the father will). But while Max's security is connected with the warm meal, which his mother can use as a power implement, Ida's security lies wholly in her own self-esteem: when she holds her toddling sister in the last page, the goblins have disappeared. Max's story is focused on himself; Ida's story is about care, responsibility and sacrifice. Few picturebooks have captured the difference between masculine and feminine perception in such a subtle way.

Heroism, Disobedience and Conformism

In Beatrix Potter's *The Tale of Peter Rabbit* (1902) the little hero ventures, naturally breaking his mother's prohibition, into a new, unknown, and exciting territory. He does what every folktale hero did before him, and what many children's literature characters have been doing after him, with various results. The narrator anticipates the protagonist's failure by condemning him from start: "Peter, who was very naughty . . . " This is the voice of adult normativity speaking; from the adult point of view, the three sisters, Flopsy, Mopsy and Cotton-tale, "who were good little bunnies, [and] went down the lane to gather blackberries," are behaving according to the prescribed norm, while the naughty Peter, who "ran straight away to Mr. McGregor's garden," breaks the norm and interrogates adult power. In the illustration he is depicted in the center of the image, occupying most of its area, with proud posture and contented smile. However, upon entering the enemy's territory, he is not, as the mythical or fairy-tale hero would be, allowed to revenge his father's untimely and horrible death. He is not allowed to show courage or wit, he does not find any treasure. On the contrary, he is repeatedly humiliated, first being sick because of his gluttony, then chased by Mr. McGregor, caught in a net, and finally, and perhaps most significantly, losing his clothes, which transforms him from an intelligent, anthropomorphic creature into an ordinary dumb animal (cf. Scott 1994). The body language of this animal-human hybrid, shown in the illustrations, reflects his inferior status. He is smaller than his enemy; his face is distorted with terror. In several pictures he is depicted upside down, a symbol of inverted power; and he is repeatedly squeezing in a most undignified manner through tight openings. The images significantly enhance the sense of the character's degradation. Instead of returning home as a glorious hero, he returns exhausted physically and defeated morally; and what does he get from his mother: not a word of consolation, but still more punishment, bed without supper, and supposedly abominable chamomile tea to cure his upset stomach. This is a full triumph of adult normativity: the child is not even allowed the tiniest taste of freedom and power during his excursion, while his obedient sisters are rewarded by "bread and milk and blackberries."

Curious George (1941), by H. A. Rey, is the story of a happy little monkey who is by force and without further consideration removed from his natural surroundings and introduced into a society where he does not know the rules, yet is expected to obey them. The story does not tell us whether George has been separated from his biological parents, yet it does say that he was initially happy where he was. The interaction of words and images is decisive—and delusive. The establishing page of the book shows George in an omniscient, but neutral perspective, as he is portrayed at the same level as the viewer. He is neither inferior nor superior to the narrator or the viewer. This neutral position is confirmed by the words: "This is George. He lived in Africa." The change in tense immediately signals a distance between the narrator and the narrative and prepares for the transition into a more didactic mode of the following three sentences: "He was very happy. But he had one fault. He was very curious." The statement "He was very happy" is ambivalent. It may equally be the protagonist's self-evaluation ("George considered himself happy"), an omniscient narrator's statement ("I know that George was happy") or an objective narrator's inference ("I believe that George was happy"). Since the picture shows George indeed smiling happily as he is swinging from a branch and eating a banana, the last interpretation is the most plausible. The statement "But he had one fault. He was very curious" is evaluative. The adult voice has put a judgment on the child, condemning him as naughty and stubborn. This disapproving attitude clearly reflects the implied adult author's conservative view of childhood. Today we would most likely encourage a child's curiosity, treating it affirmatively as inquisitiveness, while in *Curious George* the quality is undesirable. In the revised edition from 1969, the text has been changed into: "He was a good little monkey and always very curious." The explicit happiness is gone (in the picture, George is still smiling), perhaps to diminish the adult's violent action. The narrator now ascribes George positive qualities, yet with certain condescension, amplified by the derogative "little." Curiosity is no longer presented as a fault; rather it is a component of being good.

Still, it is the child's curiosity that the adult figure in the text employs to deceive him. The verbal text on the next page says: "One day George saw a man. He had on a large yellow straw hat." The words "George saw" express the character's literal point of view: we share his perspective and see the man in the yellow hat together with him. The visual perspective of the picture is reverse: although slightly shifted, we share the man's literal point of view, looking at George from a considerable distance. This corresponds to the next sentence: "The man saw George too." The images reinforce the change of perspective from the child through the omniscient—presumably adult—narrator over to the adult man, a bearer of civilization, an interpretation amplified by his carrying a gun, a camera and binoculars, symbols of power and knowledge. Moreover, we are also immediately allowed to share the man's thoughts: "'What a nice little monkey,' he thought." By sharing the man's thoughts we are involved in his plan to capture George; thus we have been manipulated to abandon our initial subject position and are now on the adult, civilized man's side. The next two spreads, in which George is caught, bring us back to the character's level of perception, especially as we only see one foot and the hands of the man. However, since we are aware of the man's conspiracy—we have been given his thought "I would like to take him home with me"—and see through George's carelessness and naiveté, we virtually share the authoritative, ironic perspective of the adult narrator.

The man in the yellow hat commits himself to being a surrogate parent for George. It would be natural to expect that the man, who never gets a name in the story, keeping him away from any closer bonds, would show affection toward his foster child and make him happy and comfortable. Instead, the man catches George by cunning, takes him away from the world he is used to ("George was sad," the text informs us, and the pictures confirm this by showing George's facial expression), takes him on board a big ship—a dangerous and unfamiliar place for a little child, and after a short talk dismisses him by saying: "Now run along and play, but don't get into trouble." How would a little child know how not to get into trouble in this situation? The text says "[I]t is easy for little monkeys to forget," but should not the adult have some responsibility for the child he has so casually adopted? Although the rest of the verbal text in the book focalizes the character both externally and internally (mentioning George's feelings of curiosity, fear or joy), and the pictures duplicate the words, the overall sense of the omniscient, didactic perspective is persistent. The narrator's ideological position lies firmly on the adult's side. Over and over again George is forced into situations he is incapable of handling, and each time he is abandoned by the adult, culminating in his being shut in prison. This may be perceived as a humorous detail, but it reveals the relationship between the adult and the child. After George has escaped from the prison (thanks to his ingenuity) and been involved in a number of further pranks, the man in the yellow hat still takes no responsibility for George's socialization, but puts him behind bars with the hypocritical and self-contented comment: "What a nice place for George to live!" (meaning: "I know that George liked the Zoo because it was a nice place"). Rather than taking care of the child he has so light-heartedly withdrawn from his natural environment, the adult places him in an institution, acting on the conviction that he is pursuing the child's best interests. The naughty child is socialized, and the adult narrator expresses his content. Because the child, George, is disguised as a monkey we may believe that the power structures we meet in this book are of no relevance; yet they definitely are, and it is essential to identify and assess them.

In Jean de Brunhoff's *The Story of Babar* (1931), the little elephant's mother is killed by hunters, and he is left an orphan. Like a fairy-tale hero, he leaves to seek his fortune elsewhere, gets adopted by an old, rich, eccentric lady and has to adjust to her ways of living. Babar's acquisition of human manners and behavior involves wearing clothes, living indoors, sleeping in a bed, eating at a table, and using tools and machines. In all these activities he shows dexterity quite opposite to George's carelessness. When in *The Travels of Babar*, the former savage is stripped of these tokens of civilization and treated as a dumb beast, he feels deeply humiliated. Upon returning to the jungle Babar brings along his newly acquired ways and values. He is empowered by the knowledge and experience of the adult world; and let us add, Western, white, male, middle-class world. Like George, Babar is introduced into civilization. Unlike the resisting George, Babar not only embraces it, but imposes it on the others. In a key scene he stands upright and wears clothes, while his subjects are still unclothed and on all four. In *Babar the King*, Babar must cut down the jungle to build a city for his subjects (some editions omit the picture where this ecologically offensive act is shown), the result being a boring, regular settlement with identical huts and two monstrous public buildings: a Bureau of Industry and an Amusement Hall. School is among the top priorities, alongside a number of other social institutions. The movement of the *Babar* books propagates the development of the character from savage to civilized, from colonized to colonizer, or, applying the heterological tools, from abnormity to norm. The former abandoned and oppressed child, Babar is crowned king, gets married and has children of his own. Power has once again reproduced itself.

In all the books just discussed, adult superiority is unquestionably confirmed. Even though Max is empowered and enthroned through his creative imagination, he is still wholly at his mother's will. Even though Peter shows courage and intelligence, besides having a good deal of luck, he is brought back into a dependent position toward the adult. Even though George is clever and enterprising, he is deprived of his freedom. And Babar becomes an adult himself.

(Dis)empowering Dreams

Bedroom stories have been subjected to a variety of interesting studies with different approaches (see e.g. Moebius 1991; Galbraight 1998), but not explicitly from the point of view of power relationships. The classical Danish picture-book *Paul Alone in the World* (1942), by Jens Sigsgaard and Arne Ungermann, shows how adult norms are promptly restored after the child has experienced unlimited power in a dream. The story starts with the young boy waking up in his room. Nothing in the words or in the pictures suggests anything else than the events depicted actually take place: a realistic setting, normal human character, and no verbal or visual details designating anything extraordinary. There are no graphic codes to imply that the boy is still asleep and dreaming. Yet it turns out that Paul is alone in the whole world and can do whatever he wishes—a situation of total empowerment of the child, used for overtly didactic purposes. Paul discovers that he can drive a tram and a fire engine, fly an airplane, eat as much candy he wants in a store, or take as much money as he wants from a bank and do whatever he wants with it: "He can buy a knife and a mouth-organ and a crane and a little bicycle and a spade and a wheelbarrow and a car and a plane and everything in the world." The images duplicate and amplify the gratification of desires.

On the last spread, the words inform us, emphasizing the impact by using capital letters, that Paul's adventures have been a dream. The story poses a number of ethical questions: is it morally correct to take money from a bank or sweets from a shop even though you are all alone in the world? When the protagonist wakes up from his dream, he is free from responsibilities for his actions, and the subversivity of the carnival is toned down. In terms of power, the omnipotent child of the dream narrative is brutally brought back to reality where he is powerless. Paul discovers through his dream that he is incompetent to manage on his own. The very last image shows Paul weeping desperately in his bed. In a revised edition from 1954, a new final image was substituted in which Paul plays happily in a park with some children, the very park where he was alone in the dream. The two images take the story in different directions. The first expresses disappointment at failed expectations; the second depicts relief that the nightmare is over. The later edition, that has become standard, teaches a more adult-normative lesson than the original one.

Another bedtime story, *Hey, Get Off Our Train!* (1989), by John Burningham, offers a significantly more subtle way of interrogating adult authority and presenting the empowered child. In *Paul Alone in the World*, adults are only present indirectly, as a didactic voice. The first page Burningham's book shows the boy's mother pointing at him in a highly authoritative manner and saying: "You aren't still playing with that train are you? Get into bed immediately. You know you have to be up early for school tomorrow." There is nothing to indicate that the boy has been sent to bed without supper, like Max in

Where the Wild Things Are, yet the mother is presented as harsh and insensitive. The pajama-case dog, who will soon accompany the boy on his imaginary train ride, is hanging from the mother's hand, probably hinting that the mother disapproves of her son's attachment to this typical transition object. She goes on with her nagging: "Here is your pajama-case dog. I found it under a cushion in the sitting room." The mother is dissatisfied with the son invading adult territory and tells him to go to sleep. There is no sign of affection between mother and child.

The words as well as images suggest that the boy actually goes on a journey, accompanied by his dog and picking up one animal after another: an elephant, a seal, a crane, a tiger and a polar bear. However, unlike the previous book, the images prompt a dream interpretation, because the situation depicted—a little boy driving the engine, and a number of talking intelligent animals—is beyond the scope of everyday experience. If we accept Paul driving the tram and the fire engine, it is exactly because his actions show his natural inaptitude. The toy train featured on the first page of Burningham's book immediately signals the nature of the adventure to come. There are several other ways in which the words and pictures mark a passage from reality to dream which occurs in the course of several spreads. When the mother gives the boy his dog, the words draw our attention to this detail which would otherwise remain unnoticed. Two spreads later, the pajama-case has come alive, and the dog is portrayed the same size as the boy. An intermediate spread zooms onto the toy train, but still has the boy's bed in the background. The tiny figure of the boy is visible on the engine, but it is unclear whether he is at the same time asleep in bed. The hazy, imaginative, symbolically charged landscape on the wordless spreads during the journey emphasizes the dreamlike nature of the events. Unlike *Paul Alone*, there are no dramatic events leading to the sudden awakening, the narrative is quiet and poetic. Except for the repetitive pattern, the plot is vague and lacks structure or resolution.

The verbal text consists exclusively of dialogue; thus there is no overt narrative agency, manipulating the reader to adopt a certain interpretation Such narrative agency informs us in authoritative manner that Paul has been dreaming. The last picture in *Hey, Get Off Our Train!*, showing the boy awake in his bed and his mother in the doorway hurrying him up, amplifies the objective interpretation. The toy train is again in the foreground, confirming the safe and secure passage back from dream to reality. Without the verbal text, there would be no doubt that the story has been the boy's dream. However, the mother suddenly asks the boy whether he has anything to do with "an elephant in the hall, a seal in the bathtub, a crane in the laundry, a tiger on the stairs, and a polar bear by the fridge." The mother's power over the boy and her dissatisfaction with his childish playfulness is seriously subverted by the products of his imagination coming true.

Power and Ambiguity

The examples already discussed clearly reflect the view on the child and childhood prevalent in their respective time and culture, as well as practiced by their respective authors. All confirm adult power, even though some are slightly subversive. In the following sections, I will consider some Scandinavian texts, to demonstrate how adult normativity can be illuminated through words and images.

"What shall we do with little Jill?" ask the little girl's parents on the first doublespread of Fam Ekman's book with this title (1976). "All day long Jill sits in a chair," the text informs us. The chair is huge, taking all the space on the recto, the little girl disappearing in its corner, turned away from the viewer in a pose suggesting fear and insecurity. A single building block and a shoe on the carpet may symbolize the scarcity of the girl's life; yet rather it can be interpreted as her futile attempts to penetrate the adult space. The chair is a piece of furniture intended for adults, and the block and the shoe, parts of the child's space, have tentatively intruded into the adult's domain. The parents' figures, standing hesitantly in the doorway, are tiny as compared to the chair. They are disproportionally far away from the child, alienated and insignificant, in spite of their concern.

The parents decide to give their daughter something to amuse her and put up a painting on her wall. On the spread, Jill is not portrayed; obviously she is not participating in the decision or the action; the picture is not something she desires. On the verso, the parents talk to each other; on the recto they are fully occupied with hanging the picture. They demonstrate no interest in their child, and are far from any thoughts of giving her warmth and love instead.

The painting shows a lonely girl sitting on a bench under a tree. The image does not directly suggest that the girl is a mirror reflection of Jill, even though the oval form of the picture does remind one of a mirror; but it suggests a reflection of Jill's state of mind, the girl's loneliness corresponding to the absence of parents in the image. Jill is standing with her back to the viewer, so that we do not see her face and cannot guess whether she is happy, pleased, confused or sad. Her arms hang passively down her sides. On the next page, however, she has put her hands behind her back, in a more resolute pose, and she is tapping impatiently with her foot (incidentally, reminiscent of Max's pose in *Where the Wild Things Are*). The verbal text conveys Jill contemplating what the painting can be used for. Irritated, she states that the painted girl cannot even talk. Not unexpectedly, the girl answers that she surely can talk whereupon Jill asks what she can do for her. Here, Jill has verbalized her own lack of attention and comfort, transferring it to her mirror reflection (I refrain from lacanian connotations). As in many other books, the solution lies in a pet; yet the painted girl does not desire a cat or a dog, but a horse: a much more powerful and perhaps masculine animal, often a heroic attribute.

The following spreads show Jill searching for a horse. She is depicted small against the image of the city, and appears lost. The setting may be her mindscape, even though nothing supports this interpretation. As evening comes, Jill finds shelter in a museum. Most existing analyses of the book have focused on this part, showing famous pieces of art in a typical postmodern play with intertextual, or rather intervisual, interpictorial links. For my examination, it is more important that Jill is still alone; she tries on a new identity, shedding her own, symbolized by her clothes, which, in a most down-to-earth manner, makes her freeze. She walks easily into a number of paintings and is invited to take a cup of coffee, borrows a blanket from a lady, and is directed further down the hall to find a horse. The painting frames dissolve as Jill enters them: the border between Jill's world and the painted worlds are fluctuant. Finally she finds an equestrian statue and brings the horse home to her painted friend. Now the sculptured horse from the museum gets into the painting in Jill's room. Jill is still swept in the blanket he got from the pained lady in the museum. All frames are broken, although there is no indication of the story taking place in Jill's imagination. Yet in her reality she is still abandoned. Invited by the painted girl to join her, Jill does not hesitate, and the two girls happily ride the horse away, into the landscape beyond the painting.

The last spread duplicates the first one, except that Jill is gone from the chair, and to the repeated question, "What shall we do with little Jill?" the father replies, "We have done what we can." There are several possibilities to interpret the ending. A child literally turning invisible because of parents' neglect is a recurrent motif in Scandinavian children's literature. Yet the question remains whether the parents have totally subdued the child or whether the child is empowered by her imagination escaping from the adults' oppression. Unlike Max, Jill does not return to find herself in her parents' indifference. Instead, she gets emerged in her inner world and thus defeated. On a more optimistic note, she has, again unlike Max, created a permanent refuge in nature.

Escape is, however, not the best way of dealing with problems, and few picturebook creators venture on such ambivalent endings. A more hopeful strategy is presented in Gro Dahle's and Svein Nyhus's *Behind Mumme Lives Moni* (2000). It relates the horrors of a nice little boy haunted by a monster that rides a huge sixteen-legged black horse, breathes smoke and can grow into a giant in ten seconds. The images duly repeat what the words convey; yet in dressing the monster is the same green-checkered trousers as the boy, they clearly suggest that the monster is part of the child's imagination. The book becomes a poignant story of self-exploration, in which images take over when the words are no longer sufficient. The text does say: "Inside his head, Mumme has a long corridor," while the image expands the simple phrase into a terrifying mindscape, in which the hard straight lines of the endless doors contrast the soft edges of the child's face.

No adults are mentioned by words or depicted in the images. The child has no contact whatsoever with the outside world, instead channeling his emotions inward. Yet rather than finding a helpful twin, Mumme discovers a monster. He manages to tame the intimidating horse, and the monster turns into a monkey. The monkey does not become a harmless and friendly companion; instead it threatens to come back. But the boy has conquered his fears and aggressions; he will tame the horse again and again if need be, and the horrible Moni will shrink still more and become a friend. Then, the text says, accompanied by a peaceful image, Mumme will be Double Mumme. Incorporating the monster into his self rather than projecting him outwards is a huge victory; yet the ending is ambivalent, in words as well as image. Mumme is going to ride to the moon, while Moni stays behind, waving and shouting "Good luck!" Is the child still trying to escape from the evil part of himself?

Although Mumme is not denied agency, he is objectified by the implied adult author instead of an adult character, as is the case in *Peter Rabbit* and some other books mentioned above. Neither Jill nor Mumme are created as subjects, and adult authors exercise their power against the protagonists as well as the readers. The easiest, but far from a justified way of treating this conclusion is to maintain that these books are not meant for children. In fact, they may be *for* children, but written from the adult's, not children's premises.

A genuinely disturbing example of adult negligence is Bent Haller's and Dorte Karrebæk's *The Ice Girl* (2001). The words describe the adults' approval of two obedient girls, while the images ironically show them being led on a leash on all fours, begging like a dog, and crouching covered with a frog's skin. The words and the images do not directly contradict each other, both conveying total compliance, but their interaction creates a discrepancy between the voice and the view. The title figure, literally turned into ice by the two friends' cold neglect, appears in the visual space long before she is mentioned by words. First she is isolated from the two other girls by a frame and placed on the facing page; later she is wide awake in bed with her face distorted by fear, as opposed to the other girls with hands piously folded over the blanket in prayer; and her hands passive in front of a blank notebook, while the other two have filled theirs with writing. The bullies' actions are symbolically illustrated by a pair of scissors closing dangerously on the lonely girl, as if rendered inert by their cheerful disregard. The transformation from a human being into an ice figure and finally into a puddle, extended over several doublespreads, is accompanied by the matter-of-fact verbal statement that the girl felt cold. Thus the conflict of the story is introduced visually and evolves mainly through imagery, while the text is considerably less dramatic. No adults interfere with the bullying, and the bullies demonstrate the reproduction of power: being themselves maltreated (even though the words try to show the opposite), they become oppressors. Without adult protection, the protagonist has no other way than perish.

A Child's Triumph

In Pija Lindebaum's *Bridget and the Gray Wolves* (2001), a periphrasis of Little Red Riding Hood, the shy and frightened girl is lost during a walk with her daycare group. Or perhaps, as the image suggests, she is not lost at all, but chooses herself to get away from the noisy and boisterous kids. Her meeting with the wolves in a dark forest and taming them is reminiscent of Max, apart from the monsters representing fears rather than aggressions. Her only reward, however, is her own self-confidence, emphasized by the last image of the book, where she is dancing on the top of the playhouse from which she initially didn't dare to jump. This is a great achievement for the child and a huge step toward self-esteem, but entering dark woods, especially imaginary, and climbing playhouses does not place high on the adult scale of values.

A similar example is Dorte Karrebæk's *Little Miss Pants and the Small Victories* (2004). Like so many Karrebæk characters, Little Miss Pants is a lonely child. Perhaps she is not even a child, as she seems to live all alone, but this loneliness may be a child's subjective perception. The protagonist is scared of the sky—because it may fall down; of the dark, of large dogs, of birds, snakes, bees, mosquitoes, cars in the street and the wide ocean. The words state all this calmly, while the images amplify the sense of fear by showing Miss Pants's tiny image at the bottom of an unusually tall, vertical page, or by presenting the terrifying animals so huge that they break the frame of the visual space. The narrative portrays Miss Pants slowly defeating her fears in the only possible way, by meeting and challenging them. She is still depicted as a tiny figure on a large panel, but her posture shows her as more active and confident, leading rather than being led. The horrible big dog turns into a friend and finally admits that he, too, can occasionally be afraid. In the penultimate page, two dogs walk with their tails between their legs, drops of sweat emphasizing their terror; and in the very last page, they look both miserable and apparently ashamed, while Miss Pants is laughing happily. The child has proved more powerful than the adults, if the two other characters are adults, or able to conquer her fears if they are products of her imagination.

Child empowerment is presented without interrogating adult norms, merely as an individual accomplishment. The child overcomes problems inherent to childhood, such as excessive aggressions or unreasonable fears, thus being socialized into a state acceptable in adult world. While on the personal psychological level the development is commendable, from the point of view of adult normativity the texts confirm the child's initial imperfection and subsequent improvement. This subtle underlying message counterbalances the subversivity of the books, as the adult author is still superior to the child, the character as well as the reader. By making adults invisible in the fictive world, the authors conceal their own power position. The child is objectified, since the adult author contemplated her condescendingly, from above.

Few authors interrogate their own norms, but occasionally an idea of a modern competent child is presented. In Pija Lindenbaum's *When Åke's Mom Forgot* (2005) the text states that the little boy's mother is "totally wild in the mornings," and she herself says: "I'll go crazy." The verbal text is iterative, that is, the wild mornings are recurrent events, even though depicted only once. The dynamic image reflecting the mother's literal going to pieces shows the boy wearing a dragon mask and playing with toy dragons at breakfast table. The text explains that the boy puts on the mask to screen off mother's shouts: "It is somewhat silent inside." The child's surviving strategy is, as in other books, escape into a word of his own.

In the next spread, the mother has turned into "a kind of dragon," pink, matching the color of the mother's dressing gown in the first spread, and with a bobble of hair held by a rubber band. It is a different dragon than the protective dragon mask, a softer and less aggressive one, but the image is evoked by the mask and the toys. The expression "go crazy" is expanded visually into a whole plot. Notably, the boy is not at all amazed at his mother's metamorphosis, which supports the interpretation of the images being a transposition, on the one hand of the mother's state (she is obviously suffering from extreme stress-related depression), on the other hand of the boy's perception. The other people do not find the dragon extraordinary: the ticket-seller at the terrarium merely informs the boy that animals enter for free; the children at the playground object when the dragon puffs smoke, but when she starts breathing fire, a fire engine is summoned. Granny comforts the boy promising that the mother will be back to her usual self in a couple of days. The images play cleverly with the fluctuant boundary between human and animal: the dragon walks upright and carries a handbag, while she also eats bugs, attacks dogs and sleeps curled up on the floor. In a central episode, she drops her clothes, much like Peter Rabbit, further losing one of her human attributes.

The child is empowered by acting a parent to his own mother. He takes care of his breakfast when the mother has forgotten how to cook; he calls mother's office to say she cannot come to work, and he takes her to a hospital to see if there is any medicine against dragons. He also saves her when she cannot stop breathing fire by giving her a bucket of water at a gas station.

Next morning, the mother is her usual self again. The wild carnival is over, and the child falls back into dependency. Yet the image shows a mother different from the stressed one in the first spread. The table is cleaned, two pieces of toast jump out of the toaster; the mother is eating her breakfast, smiling peacefully. The boy overhears her speaking on the phone saying that she is taking a day off and going on an excursion with her son. This idyllic ending illustrates reconciliation, at least temporarily, as the narrative is this time singulative, not iterative. Since the story is told wholly from the boy's perspective, we know nothing about the mother's experience during her crazy day, yet she has obviously got rid of the worst stress. The absurd time-out has brought the mother and child closer to each other, which means that the child's empowerment has had its positive effect.

Finally, I present an example in which adult normativity is not only interrogated, but totally disintegrated. In Dorte Karrebæk's *The Girl Who was Good at Many Things* (1996) the world of adults is genuinely repulsive, and the adults are portrayed as irresponsible and unreliable. The inventive play with frames creates an ingenious sense of confinement and misery. The closed visual space of the first spread, with wide borders, suggests captivity, emphasized by the protagonist's passive and downcast body language. In the subsequent spreads, she has escaped through the constraining frame into a space of her own, occupying the border where she can perform the actions necessary to care for herself. However, the developments inside the frame, depicting the parents' drunken quarrels, intervene into her visual sanctuary, as earsplitting sounds, visualized by jagged color lines; as feathers from pillows that the parents fight with, and finally a an empty bottle falling through the frame into the girl's quiet starry night. Robbed of her childhood and acting as a parent to her own parents, the nameless girl sees no other way out of the situation than to grow up. She literally steps out of the frame and the border, and the last spread shows her walking out of the book (the image actually shows the lower part of her body in the right top corner). The restrictive frame has disappeared, and the white negative space suggests opening and freedom. Unlike many other characters of children's literature, who grow up only to be integrated into the adult order, the girl steps out of the adult world that has become too restrictive and goes further to find her own way. The story does not tell us whether she succeeds or perishes, like her many literary sisters; yet presumably we are supposed to believe in her potential.

There is, however, an aspect of the book that adds some uncertainty to the narrative. The front and back cover of the book create a distinct conflict. While the front cover mirrors the optimistic ending, the back cover shows the character petrified as a doll, the way she is portrayed in the beginning. The words on the back cover, easy to dismiss as the publisher's advertising text, say: "It is never too early to find a good place to stay, where there are flowers to pick." This is the *sens morale* of the story, but can we trust it when the image points back at the initial situation? Or does the gloomy back cover encourage us to turn the book over and start reading again? Or, contrary to the overall optimistic spirit of the book, is the liberation merely an imagined escape? If so, even this genuinely subversive book is compelled to acknowledge adult supremacy.

Chapter Twelve
Othering the Reader:
Identification Fallacy

It is habitual in teaching literature to young people to encourage them to "identify" themselves with one of the characters, normally with the protagonist. A schoolteacher may express this urge by asking: "Who would you like to be in this story?" Students of children's literature warmly embrace texts that offer identification objects. This perplexing phenomenon can be called identification fallacy, in analogy with the famous intentional fallacy of New Criticism (Wimsatt and Beardsley 1954). Perhaps more than any other critical stance, identification fallacy reveals a striking inconsistency between children's literature research and literacy education. The conviction that young readers must adopt the subject position of a literary character is, however, ungrounded and prevents the development of mature reading.

Contemporary scholarly studies, especially those leaning on narratology and reception theory, emphasize the importance of the readers' ability to liberate themselves from the protagonists' subjectivity in order to evaluate them properly (see e.g. Stephens 1992, 47–83). This ability is an essential part of reading competence, which enhances sophisticated readers' ideological and aesthetic appreciation of the text. Interestingly enough, identification compulsion is seldom, if ever, discussed in general literary studies. How could we possibly read Dostoyevsky if we were supposed to identify with Raskolnikov? How could we evaluate Shakespeare if we were to identify with Macbeth? How could we enjoy Kafka's narrative irony if we were to identify with Gregor Samsa? Berthold Brecht strongly interrogated identification compulsion in his theory of estrangement. Why then do teachers and even some critics insist that young readers must necessarily find an identification object in the text? Why do children's book reviews so often include in their evaluation something like: "This book is very good because it is easy to identify with the main character"? There is no empirical research about how and at what age identification fallacy is surmounted, yet young readers must be extremely resistant to adults' pressure to be able to switch from object to subject, from the passive acceptance of the literary character's fixed subjectivity to an independent and flexible one.

Similarly, children's writers must develop intricate strategies in order to deceive adult critics, teachers and librarians and, behind their backs, subvert identification compulsion. Moreover, literary texts certainly teach young readers how to feel *empathy* with other people. Yet to be able to feel empathy, readers must separate themselves from literary characters, just as they in real life must learn to abandon solipsism and start interacting with other individuals. It is therefore essential to understand how subjectivity is constructed in literary texts and how children's writers can either promote or hamper the readers' deliverance from identification compulsion.

The opposition between the literary and the pedagogical approaches is reflected in the terms used. Pedagogy speaks about identification *object*, a passive role, following whatever the text provides. Literary studies emphasize the *subject*, the reader as an active participant interacting with the text, but independent of its imposed ideology. The difference can further be described in Mikhail Bakhtin's terms as monological versus dialogical construction of subjectivity (see McCallum 1999; Wilkie-Stibbs 2002). We often subscribe to teaching children to be critical readers, but as long as they are encouraged to be objectified alongside literary characters, they can hardly be expected to learn to be critical toward what they are fed with.

In previous chapters I have shown how alienating strategies affect subject positions. Yet the subjectivity provided by a literary text is seldom fixed and tied to a character or even a number of characters to choose from. Rather, subjectivity is tied to the narratee and especially the implied reader, and these agencies manipulate real readers in interpreting the text. The word "manipulate" is not used in pejorative meaning; manipulating can imply assistance as well as interference, and further, both assistance and interference may be more or less desirable from different viewpoints. In any case, the subject position of the text is played against the textual construction of the implied reader.

One of the favorite texts in the identification argument is *The Lion, the Witch and the Wardrobe* (1950). If you are oldest, brave and responsible, choose Peter. If you are careful and reasonable, choose Susan. If you are gullible, joyful and loyal, Lucy is your figure. If you are nasty, evil and have a sweet tooth—click on Edmund . . . This procedure is indeed reminiscent of the choice of your character in a computer game.

In pedagogical contexts, multiple characters are proclaimed desirable in children's literature, since they—to quote a generic example—"provide identification objects for readers of different ages and of both genders." Translated to a more advanced terminology, the text allows a variety of subject positions, each firmly tied to one of the characters. A closer investigation of collective characters in children's literature demonstrates that they are used mostly as pedagogical devices. Instead of portraying one complex character, the author splits the personality traits between several actors, getting the brave Peter, the sensible Susan, the treacherous Edmund and the honest Lucy rather than one character possessing many, and sometimes contradictory features. While collective characters may be viewed as a part of the conventional poetics of children's literature, this does present a difficulty because the subject position of the text is steadily attached to one of the characters. Particular real readers may, for some reason, choose to identify with the "wrong" character, Edmund, because they recognize some traits they possess themselves. Such a choice is not more advanced, since it still presuppose fixed subjectivity. A mature reader will create a subject position disconnected from the characters.

The postmodern concept of intersubjectivity allows readers more freedom, since it makes the subject position deliberately fluctuant, which in its turn renders the text more challenging. In the concrete example of the four children in *The Lion, the Witch and the Wardrobe*, rather than identifying with one of the characters, that is, sharing their literal and transferred point of view, mature readers are assumed to choose a subjectivity somewhere in between, which will enable them to assess all the four characters from equal premises, at the same time avoiding the trap of the narrator's subject position. For here is another problem in narrative perspective: the text can provide such strong narrator subjectivity that readers would be completely caught in it. The highly intrusive narrator judges the characters' behavior, finds excuses for Edmund's treachery, provides general comments, and in every possible way positions readers as superior to characters. Yet since the narrator is obviously an adult, young readers would hardly adopt his perspective.

Terror and Idealization

The most elementary case of children's literature that destroys rather than supports identification is the cautionary tale, such as Heinrich Hoffmann's *Struwwelpeter* (also known as *Slovenly Peter* 1845) What children in their right minds would identify with Little Suck-a-Thumb or Augustus Who Would Not Have Any Soup? Hoffmann has been severely criticized for his brutal stories, while other scholars have equally ardently stated that *Struwwelpeter* is a parody (e.g. Zipes 2001, 147–169). With the former stance, the purpose of the book is to scare readers. Since all the characters are punished for bad behavior, they are supposed to evoke repugnance rather than empathy. Readers are expected to react by: "Serves them right." The book offers no counterbalance; child characters are evil because of their deeds while adults are evil because they subject children to cruelties. The cautionary tale creates an insurmountable distance between the characters and the readers. If, on the other hand, Hoffmann's evergreen should be perceived as an ironic reply to his contemporary children's writers, young readers' subjectivity becomes still more complicated. It is asserted, occasionally based on limited empirical research, that young children do not appreciate irony, the rhetorical device in which statements mean the contrary of their face value. If this is true, young readers will be unable to grasp Hoffmann's irony in the first place. If they somehow do, they would all the more need to step back from the stories and avoid identification. As it turns out, this equally popular and despicable book efficiently challenges identification. Perhaps this is the secret of its undying attraction.

The opposite of Hoffmann's crime-and-punishment stories is the idealized children who often appear in nineteenth-century children's fiction, children that not only improve themselves, but preferably reform the adults around them, such as the beatific protagonists of *Jessica's First Prayer* (1867), *What Katy Did* (1872), *The Foundling* (1878), *Heidi* (1880), *Little Lord Faunteroy* (1886), or *At the Back of the North Wind* (1871). Heidi, a textbook example of child idolatry, is so perfect, sweet, nice and obedient that a sensible reader is rather disgusted, if compelled to identification. To enjoy this angelic child, readers are expected to shift their subjectivity so that they perceive idealization as a deliberate characterization device. The novel has been interpreted as the story of the grandfather rather than the child (Usrey 1985). Such interpretation is symptomatic. Unable to identify with the female five-year-old child, the critic starts searching for another identification object and, finding it, builds his argument against all reason.

There is, however, another tradition of superior children, an archetype widely employed in European children's literature, but less known in the English-language world, "the alien child." The concept itself goes back to a book title by E. T. A. Hoffmann, *The Alien Child* (1818). The idea of the alien, strange, unfamiliar, or even uncanny child, depending on how you choose to translate the German word "fremde," implies a figure that suddenly appears from nowhere, possesses supernatural qualities, affects the lives of other people, and frequently disappears without further explanation. Some examples of such a character are Antoine de Saint-Exupéry's *Little Prince* (1943), Maurice Druon's *Tistou of the Green Thumbs* (1958), Michael Ende's *Momo* (1973) and Christine Nöstlinger's *Konrad* (1975). The little prince appears in the middle of a desert, but he does not experience hunger or thirst; he can see invisible, imaginary things; and he has come in a mysterious way from an asteroid. In him, the adult protagonist and narrator, a pilot stranded in the desert, meets his own inner child. Tistou of the Green Thumbs is, as the epithet suggests, extraordinarily skillful with plants and flowers; he can make flowers miraculously grow overnight over tanks and canons, thus preventing an inevitable war. In the end of the book, Tistou disappears, and it is explicitly and somewhat didactically stated, in the very last sentence: "Tistou was an angel." If the reader could (with some effort) identify with the perfect boy, who can identify with an angel? Nöstlinger Konrad grows out of a tin can, ordered by mistake by a Bohemian lady. He is an early forerunner of the character in the movie

"A. I.", a prefabricated perfect robot-child, programed to be well-behaved, obedient and emotionless. As Konrad gradually grows more human, in the sense of childlike, interrogative and affectionate, he also changes his foster mother and his whole surrounding. The idea of a puppet or robot turning human may also go back to *Pinocchio*.

Finally, Momo in Michael Ende's novel, a more mysterious figure than any of those already presented, has an amazing gift of listening, and she is more sensitive to the imminent threat that any of the adults around her. Typically, her closest friends are not children. The grey gentlemen, the villains of the story, represent some unrevealed authority that apparently has realized that time is the most precious aspect of wealth, trivially expressed in the saying "Time is money." In this novel, however, adults rather than children prove gullible. The grey gentlemen cannot exist without the time they steal; their intention is to appropriate all time in the world and make humans not only powerless but completely redundant. Even children are eventually forced to comply with the new ways.

Momo wins back the stolen time and thus demonstrates her superiority over the adults. Significantly, Momo is a figure outside of space and time; as the text indicates in the very beginning, when she appears from nowhere in the poor outskirts of a big city: "no one could have told her age" (13); and further, to the question how old she is: "As far as I can remember . . . I have always been around" (14). As the Chosen, she can enter the timeless zone, where Professor Secundus Minutus Hora dispatches the allocated time for all people in the world. As often in children's stories, an innocent child, by virtue of her innocence, must take on the burden of saving the world.

The common trait of all these characters is that they reform adults, which can be interpreted in several ways. I prefer to view Konrad as affirmation of childhood; while the little prince is more of a nostalgic memory of something lost forever and as such rather an adult author's self-indulgence. Tistou is a flat character reminiscent of MacDonald's Diamond, a mouthpiece for adult ideology; while Momo is and remains enigmatic. Whatever the interpretation, these characters are not constructed in a way that invites identification.

Flying Dutchmen and Wandering Jews

The reader can be also alienated and thus encouraged to adopt an independent subject position by the genre and setting, as already marginally discussed in the previous chapters. Fairy tales are completely distanced from us in time and space, which is supported by the initial formulas such as: "Once upon a time, not your time, not my time . . . " Fairy-tale heroes are by definition superior to their listeners, and nobody could seriously identify with Jack the Giant Killer. The alienation is less in fantasy, yet fantasy, as already demonstrated, in itself works as an othering strategy and thus encourages readers to adopt an independent subject position. Just as nobody could seriously identify with Jack the Giant Killer, readers cannot fully adopt, for instance, Frodo Baggins's subjectivity, not only because he is not human, but in the first place because they lack his experience of a magical world. Readers are supposed to feel compassion when Frodo is anguished; they are allowed to make their own judgments, perhaps even try on the situation on themselves; yet identification is strongly hampered. Incidentally, if we compare Tolkien's *The Hobbit* (1937) with *The Lord of the Rings* (1954) in terms of identification and subjectivity, the former, addressing younger readers, has one main character and thus encourages identification. The latter addresses teenage and adult audience and offers a wide range of characters that split and have their own plots. Presumably, Tolkien falls into identification pit when writing for children, but not for adults.

In quite a few fantasy novels the subject position of the text promptly demands that identification is abandoned. In Nathalie Babbit's *Tuck Everlasting* (1975), the dream of immortality, a recurrent theme in children's literature, is transformed into a nightmare. While the Tucks may among themselves discuss whether their situation is a blessing or a curse, the narrator is quite explicit about the tragedy of their fate. The family members demonstrate a variety of attitudes toward their predicament. The novel thus focuses sharply on the human suffering connected with the curse of eternal life. It also underscores the alienation of the cursed: the Tucks cannot make friends or generally get involved with the outside world. Behind the narrative, a mature reader will recognize the universal motif of the Wandering Jew. The Tucks, however, are not punished for any specific wrongdoing or vice. Neither did they have any choice. This may be a disturbing thought, since the Tucks are paying a terribly dear price for a mere accident. Yet the anguish of the curse is shifted from the child protagonist, apparently to protect the reader who is likely to adopt Winnie's subjectivity rather than any of the Tuck family. This position is subverted by the epilogue of the novel that features the Tucks visiting Winnie's grave. Identification is seriously impaired, even though the text follows the children's literature conventions, allowing the child to win over evil merely by virtue of her innocence.

In contrast, in Diana Wynne Jones's *The Homeward Bounders* (1981), the text abandons earlier practices of children's literature, making the protagonist, rather than a secondary character, the bearer of the curse. The book declares its intertextuality openly: "Have you heard of the Flying Dutchman? No? Nor of the Wandering Jew?" (7), thus setting the informed reader's expectations. The twelve-year-old Jamie becomes accidentally involved in a mysterious war game played by anonymous higher powers and is "discarded," doomed to wander in all eternity between hundreds of parallel universes. In his fruitless attempts to find the way home, he meets Prometheus, Ahasuerus and the Flying Dutchman, who all turn out to be Homeward Bounders like himself, helpless pawns in someone else's war.

When Jamie finally finds his way home, he discovers that a hundred years have passed in his own universe and everyone dear to him is dead. A recognizable feature from the fairy tale of immortality, the ending is significantly more disturbing than the Tucks' visiting Winnie's grave. In fact this kind of ending is by definition impossible in conventional children's fiction since it shatters the child's intrinsic belief in the stability of the world. *The Homeward Bounders* interrogates this illusory stability, yet even there the child is allowed to win over evil, if not for himself then for those doomed before him. While the Flying Dutchman has given up, a remarkable tenacity and resilience of youth is demonstrated through Jamie's determination to outsmart his mysterious adversaries. Childhood's superiority over adulthood is maintained, and the child is used—maybe abused—as a Savior, a position hard to identify with. Jamie must shoulder the burdens that no adult could endure, which makes him such a tragic character that one can only relate to him from a distance.

The Detached Self

The most unexpected discovery in exploring identification fallacy is first-person narration as an exceedingly successful strategy of subverting identification. This may sound like a paradox: normally personal narration is considered more engaging, as it allows a total penetration into the protagonist's mind. Yet engagement is not the same as identification. Contemporary young adult novels frequently employ first-person narration, which ostensibly creates an authentic teenage voice, especially when youth jargon is used. This has already been discussed from several angles in the previous chapters. First-person perspective encourages the reader to share the character/narrator's point of view. The subject position prompted by the text becomes restricted when the narrator and the protagonist are the same agency. However, in most cases first-person narratives demonstrate a dialogical nature by the very fact that subjectivity is split between the experiencing and the narrating self. Can readers possibly understand the disturbed state of mind in which Holden Caulfield of *The Catcher in the Rye* (1951) roams the New York streets if they choose to identify with this disoriented teenager? They must certainly let the interaction with the one-year-older Holden's ironic comments come into their evaluation, as well as their position toward both of the agencies. Thus the dissonance between the narrative voice and the point of view in personal narration has exactly the opposite effect than might seem natural: instead of pushing readers into the protagonist's subject position, it prompts them to take a step back.

This dissonance is all the more prominent in retrospective narratives in which adult narrators are looking back at their childhood, with the wisdom and experience of their age, but also with the factual knowledge, since at the time of narration they already know the outcome of the childhood experience.

This is the case in the previously discussed novels *Jacob Have I Loved*, *The True Confessions of Charlotte Doyle*, or *The Island of the Blue Dolphins*. The gap between the narrator and the character amplifies all the other alterities in the texts.

In Sonya Hartnett's *Thursday's Child* (2000) the relationship between Harper the character and Harper the narrator is highly ambiguous and indistinct, which strongly affects our perception of the narrator's reliability. By the end of the novel, we are informed that Harper is twenty-one years old and she is telling the story as it took place between her age of seven and twelve. Yet even prior to that, Harper the narrator consistently distances herself from Harper the character, for instance through saying: "[Tin] was only four at that time" (9); "being almost seven years old at that time" (10): "When I was young I never understood" (21); "now, when I look back" (36); "for years I could not understand" (39); "later I found out" (88); "I think, looking back" (174); "It makes me sad now . . . I try to forgive myself" (182), "It is only now, years later" (204). On the other hand, the narrator tries not to interfere too much with the young child's immediate perception: "I was confused. I didn't understand what she was saying, I didn't know why Devon snarled, 'I'm going to kill him, I swear'" (169). Statements about the character being unable to understand come from the adult narrator and effectively distance the child character. When the narrator says: "I believed what Audrey said to me" (113), the implication is that, as she is narrating the story, she realizes that her trust was erroneous. The adult narrator, thus, comments repeatedly on the character's cognitive inferiority.

An efficient device to create a distance between the character and the narrator is the change of tense: "it *is* the horriblest, loneliest, saddest memory I *own*" (16; emphasis added). The narrator is here referring to the present narrative situation, the time when she is telling, or perhaps writing down, her story. There are other reflexive passages revealing an adult narrator, such as: "Time passes slowly when you're young, and quickens as you get old. Summer lasted forever when I was seven, but now it only visits" (36); "The world you live in when you are nine is different from the world the other people live within" (83).

More implicitly, the gap is expressed through language as such, a sophisticated idiom that would hardly be used by a seven-year-old from an underprivileged family; a rich language full of metaphors and other figures of speech, magnificent descriptions and mature reflections. We learn that already as a child Harper found consolation in writing stories and that she has resumed her writing as an adult. There is no indication that her narrative is a written account, yet there is a characteristic invocation of the narratee at the very beginning: "Now I would like to tell you about my brother" (7). Assuming that the story is written by an aspiring author, the twenty-one-year-old Harper living in excessive wealth and not having to earn her daily bread, it is quite plausible that she uses advanced language to convey her childhood experience.

At the same time, like so many first-person narrators, she is aware of the unreliability of memory:

... I never saw Tin an old man or even a young one, so he stays just a boy in my mind. Tin's bound up in childhood forever, as far as my recollection goes ... Memory is eccentric, how it stalls when it wants to. (7)

The narrator admits that she remembers some things, but not other: "I remember Caffy with the pink on his cheeks the evening we talked about Tin under the house, but I don't remember him learning to crawl" (36). The selective nature of memory is not unique for the narrator, but the seven-year-old character's fragmentary perception amplifies the narrator's unreliability. In fact, the incredibility of the central element of the plot, a child who moves to live underground and grows feral, prompts a metaphorical rather than mimetic reading. Tin digging tunnels into which he escapes from the misery of life is a perfect point of departure for a psychoanalytical interpretation. It is also plausible to read the story as Harper's attempts to translate her traumatic experience into a more symbolic form, something that Sonya Hartnett also explores in her novel *The Ghost's Child* (2007).

Further, there are situations in which the narrator's and character's discourse are ambivalent.

It must be terrible, I thought, to be such a nothing that you could be bargained away. Tin was Da's pet, of course, but it relieved me knowing ... (19).

In the previous passage, the first sentence, expressed in direct discourse, originates from the narrator who conveys the character's thoughts at the time the story takes place. The second sentence, however, is more complicated. Does the judgment "Tin was Da's pet" come from the seven-year-old character or from the adult narrator? Would the "of course" support the latter interpretation? Does the clause "it relieved me knowing" reflect the immediate experience or a distanced self-evaluation? Here, the narrator's and the character's subjectivities interplay and interfere with each other, encouraging the readers to position themselves somewhere in between.

As a seven– or even twelve-year-old, there are many things Harper does not understand, in the first hand the intricate and mystifying relationships between the adults in general, but also her father's cowardice and lack of responsibility, the perfidy of the rich neighbor, Mr Cable, and the nature of his offence toward Audrey. As an adult narrator, Harper may ascribe her younger self more maturity than she actually possessed. She dresses her young emotions into a more complex and grown-up language. On the other hand, as an adult she cannot help realizing why her father intended to kill Mr Cable, but she does not allow the character to reflect on this. It is virtually impossible to separate narrator's and character's discourse, which is the greatest challenge of this novel and many others of the same kind. In all these cases, if readers fall into identification trap and share the protagonists' inevitably limited point of view, they will never be able to comprehend what is actually going on in the novels and become so confined to the protagonists' subjectivity that they will ignore the repeated cracks that the texts offer. A mature reading of any first-person narrative presupposes liberation from the character/narrator's subject position, even though personal narration does allow the reader to enter the characters' minds and thus stand as close to them as possible.

Yet the personality split can be much more concrete and complex than detachment in time. In Hartnett's *Surrender* (2005), two personal narrators tell the same story antiphonically, an alternating chapter each, literally in dialogue, complementing the events the other had no access to, and more significantly, correcting the erroneous inferences of the dialogue partner. Time oscillates between then and now, yet neither is clearly delineated. Besides, it is apparent that both narrators omit significant parts of their stories, merely dropping hints here and there. For instance, both keep mentioning that a sensational discovery has just been made and a many-years-old crime has been literally unearthed. Both boys are involved in this crime, but it is not until toward the end of the novel that the mystery is revealed.

Further, both narratives contain elements of hesitation as to the status of one of them, the feral child Finnigan. He appears from nowhere when the protagonist, referred to in the chapter headings as Gabriel, but addressed by the other characters as Anwell, is ten years old. Finnigan is everything that Anwell is not: strong-minded, brave, dexterous and not least free from parental as well as social constraints. The boys make a pact: Anwell, assuming the angelic name of Gabriel, will be a model of goodness, while Finnigan will be allowed to do anything he wishes:

> "I'll do the bad things for you. Then you won't have to. You can just do the good things ... You will only be *good* things—you'll never get angry or fight. And I will only be *bad* things—I will always get angry and fight. We'll be like opposites—like pictures in the water—"
>
> "Reflection, you mean?"
>
> "Yeah, reflections! The same, but different. Like twins—like blood brothers! And when you need something bad done, like punishment or revenge, you'll just ask me, and I will do it—" (43f; emphasis in the original).

At this point, Finnigan may still be viewed as a somewhat sinister version of the "alien child," or perhaps a ghost, and the novel itself a subtle blend of psychological realism and mystical fantasy, in line with Hartnett's considerably less depressing *The Ghost's Child*. It starts relatively innocently as Anwell takes money from his mother's purse and—for himself only—blames it on Finnigan, a typical childish behavior indicating the testing of boundaries. A long chain of horrible events follow, including repeated arson, through which Finnigan seems to take revenge on everyone who has been mean toward his friend. Readers are successively allowed to realize that Finnigan does not exist, that he is entirely the product of the mentally sick Anwell. "Inside me . . . I daydreamed of the damage Finnigan could do. My enemies would flee like dogs" (54). It is not merely a matter of an alternative interpretation: there is no doubt that Finnigan is Anwell's dark side, created to hold his vicious dreams and painful memories. Gabriel is his perfect side, just as much a phantom. In the "Gabriel" chapters, the narrator both accounts for the events after he first met—or rather invented—Finnigan, and for Finnigan making him go still further back to his early childhood. Finnigan thus also becomes Anwell's voice of conscience, forcing him to recollect the circumstances of his mentally handicapped brother's death. The "Gabriel" narrator claims that it was an accident. Finnigan comments: "You must feel pretty bad about you brother . . . You must wish you never did such a bad thing" (42). The readers is left to decide whether the seven-year-old Anwell acted out of spite, mercy ("You'll be safer if you die," 62), or carelessness; whether he embellishes his story, remembers the details wrong, is confused at the time of narration or was already disturbed at the time of the event. Deep inside, Anwell knows that Finnigan does not exist; he must be kept a secret, and "[n]o one would believe" (41) anyway. Possibly, Finnigan is also Anwell's projection of his dead brother, thus yet another split persona. Anwell's mind, that the reader is exposed to, is in complete chaos, and it is not only the matter of putting the jigsaw-puzzle bits together, but deciding which of them are real, which are distorted, and which purely imaginary. On careful re-reading, amazingly many clues are given to the reader quite early in the text.

In the now of the narrative, when Anwell is twenty, he is dying, and from his initial narration readers may get the impression that he is dying of cancer. He refers to his aunt Sarah who takes care of him, while it finally turns out that the woman he calls Sarah is a nurse. He says that he is happy to be dying in his childhood home, while he is in fact in a mental hospital, firmly strapped to the bed as a dangerous, violent patient. Anwell is starving himself to death, since in his sick mind it is the only way to get rid of his dark twin: "I'm dying to kill you" (224); "I can't live in the terror of you" (227). Finnigan has got completely out of control. At the age of sixteen, Anwell develops a fancy for a girl, which his Finnigan self views as a threat: "You do belong to me . . . and I don't share" (169). The Gabriel self needs to protect the girl from Finnigan. However, Finnigan's power proves too great.

The now of the story thus appears to be a short time, merely one day, just before Anwell dies, while the then is his whole life made up of disparate pieces, not even told chronologically, all of which focus on parental abuse and humiliation. In his dialogue with Finnigan, Anwell seems to justify himself. Partly, he has transferred his extreme violence onto his imaginary companion; partly he blames his surroundings for hostility and negligence. Each time Finnigan strikes, the "Gabriel" narrator states that the victim deserved it. And Finnigan confirms it and gives Anwell absolution. Yet the final crime is not committed by Finnigan.

The ambivalent meaning of the title refers not merely to the protagonist's final capitulation, but also to the name of his dog, which his father forces him to kill. The double existence of the dog amplifies the duality of Finnigan: at any given time, it is unclear whether the dog is dead or alive or, like Finnigan, has never existed at all. The dog is merely a further extension of Finnigan's superiority and evil. Together with Finnigan, Surrender becomes the protagonist's scourge; yet by the time Anwell opens his memory to the day he murdered his parents, he is unable to distinguish between his many selves, between then and now, between dark and light. The novel ends with the first-person narrator's death, an option only fiction allows. Needless to say, identification with the character is out of the question.

The Amalgamated Self

In Bart Moeyaert's *Bare Hands* (1995), a strong narrative filter is employed, that is, a discrepancy between the character/narrator's and the reader's point of view, which affects the subject position. Few texts are successful in breaching the gap between the adult implied author and a simultaneous young child narrator; *Bare Hands* is a rare exception, where the narrative voice never sounds false. The description of external events alternates with the character's mental discourse in a perfect blend. The novel starts *in medias res*, without giving us any background to the characters or any description of the setting or situation. The time of action is New Year's Eve, a magical day in myth and folklore, the day when anything can happen. The story takes just a few hours; in fact, it takes perhaps as long time as it takes to tell it. Such utter concentration of time is characteristic of contemporary children's literature, unlike the iterative of the eternal childhood in some classics, or the traditional biographical plot stretched into several years in others. Instead, the novel depicts a single poignant moment, a bifurcation point after which the child is no longer a child. Through the personal narration, the text conveys an extremely intense experience, a mixture of fear, shame and hate. The most minute details, such as the hissing of a stove, emphasizes the character's focused perception. It would seem that such persistent point of view enhances identification, but it fact it works the other way round.

On the surface, and up until a certain point in the novel, it reads like a conventional naughty-boy story. Like Tom Sawyer and Huck Finn, Ward the narrator and his friend Bernie venture into an enemy's territory. We can view them as fairy-tale heroes breaking into an ogre's house to steal a magical object. Ward and Bernie are, however, not fairy-tale characters, and what starts like an innocent prank develops into something more serious. The ogre, the neighbor Mr Betjeman, a monster with a plastic hand, kills Ward's dog. He is presented through the narrator's eyes as an evil and dangerous man. Yet suddenly, almost halfway through the novel, a flash of memory reveals to the reader that only six days ago, on Christmas, Mr Betjeman was sitting at the dinner table in Ward's home. Apparently, the narrator is not telling us the whole story, most likely because his present state of mind makes him suppress the memories. What is *not* said becomes more significant than what *is* said. The narrator's omission of the decisive part of the events immediately shifts the reader's subject position from him, even though our empathy may still be there. On the one hand, we are in complot with Ward, as he is after all the hero struggling against evil; on the other hand, with such an unreliable narrator we feel abandoned and perhaps even cheated. Slowly, sentence by sentence with many pages between, we learn the background for Ward's hatred for the monster, and, for an informed reader, the Hamlet intertext appears, a drama of a fatherless boy, his mother and the mother's new boyfriend, just about to invade the boy's secure home. Even without the intertext, the implication of the story is obvious, and the tension between the boy and the man, their mutual aversion is conveyed most effectively. The complexity of the story, the precision of its narrative structure, and the absence of resolution are the most conspicuous devices in subverting identification. In fact, Ward's intolerance may even make the reader dislike him, which however, by no means implies that the novel cannot be enjoyed.

Mark Haddon's *The Curious Incident of the Dog in the Night-Time* (2003) takes the narrator/protagonist's unreliability and subsequently alienation still one step further. The fifteen-year-old Christopher has Asperger's syndrome, which is unfortunately revealed on the back cover, while the narrator never mentions the fact. He is aware of being different, but he does not emphasize this since for him it is perfectly natural:

> My name is Christopher John Francis Boone. I know all the countries in the world and their capital cities and every prime number up to 7,507. (2)

Asperger-people are usually extremely talented, but insecure in their social networking and have problems with verbal expression. The latter makes the text's mission almost impossible: how can one convey the experience of an Asperger-afflicted young man when language is the only means to do this? The text reflects this dilemma through nonverbal expressive devices:

> Eight years ago, when I first met Siobhan, she showed me this picture
>
> ☹
>
> and I knew that it meant "sad", which is what I felt when I found the dead dog.
> Then she showed me this picture
>
> ☺
>
> and I knew that it meant "happy," like when I'm reading about the Apollo space missions . . . (2)

In this simple manner Chistopher learns to read other people's faces as well as express his own feelings for which he lacks words. On the other hand, he is extremely observant and notices details in his surroundings that other people do not, since for him every piece of information is just as significant as any other. For instance, seeing signs at a railway station he perceived them all at once, without sorting the information and selecting the important and relevant bits.

People with Asperger syndrome need order and strict routines to cope with the everyday. When something unexpected happens in Christopher's life, he gets confused and helpless, for instance, when he finds Wellington, the neighbor's dog dead in front of his house and tries to comprehend how this can have happened and why. The dog foreshadows significantly greater turbulence as Christopher discovers that his mother who everyone has told him was dead is in fact alive and has abandoned him. He decides to find her and undertakes a journey involving new and strange endeavors, such as finding the railway station, taking out money from a cash machine, buying a ticket, finding the right train, a chain of tasks that we normally perform without thinking. Christopher solves each problem through planning it carefully step by step. He pretends that he is playing a computer game called "A train to London". As he is exceptionally good at computer games, he manages the steps, and he conveys his experience with minute details:

> And the man said: "Single or return?"
> And I said: "What does *single or return* mean?
> And he said: "Do you want to go one way, or do you want to go and come back?"
> And I said: "I want to stay there when I get there."
> And he said: "For how long?"
> And I said: "Until I go to university."
> And he said: "Single then." and he said "That'll be £17." (189)

This is how the text expresses an Asperger-consciousness, which creates alienation, but invites empathy. In the end, Christopher has against all odds passed an advanced course in mathematics, and he concludes:

> And then I will get a First Class Honours Degree and I will become a scientist.
> And I know I can do this because I went to London on my own, and because I solved the mystery of Who Killed Wellington? And I found my mother and I was brave and I wrote a book and that means I can do anything. (268)

The implied author has completely disappeared in this narrative, and a young person's immediate and complex experience has come forward. There is no need for the text to exercise power; the protagonist is empowered precisely through his inferior position of which he is not aware.

Incidentally, in the three novels above, a dog that has been killed is employed as a powerful metaphor.

Narrator Dissolved

In Gérard Genette's theory, no difference is made between personal and impersonal narration: impersonal narrators focalize a character, while personal narrators focalize themselves. Instead, Genette stresses the importance of mood, including the narrator's presence in the narrative, the narrator's distance to the narrative and focalization patterns (Genette 1980). Strong internal focalization in many ways works similarly to personal narration, and just as readers need to stand free of the personal narrator they also need to liberate themselves from the focalizing character.

In Mirjam Pressler's *Let Sleeping Dogs Lie* (2003), Johanna, the eighteen-year-old granddaughter of the wealthiest and most respected man in a little German town in mid-1990s, suddenly discovers that her family has skeletons in the closet. The perspective lies totally with the protagonist, and the temporal structure of the narrative is extremely complex, alternating abruptly between the time right after the grandfather's unexpected suicide and Johanna's visit to Israel for a school project several months before. While Johanna is trying to complete a jigsaw puzzle from loose bits of information she hears from different people, the reader has both advantages and disadvantages as compared to the character. In the beginning of the novel, Johanna possesses the knowledge that the reader lacks: what happened when she was in Israel, what she heard from Meta Levin, the old Jewish woman that she is writing her school essay about, and not least what occurred between her and Mrs. Levin's grandson, Doron. The clues are planted carefully within the text to alert the reader, in the way a crime novel allows readers to be one step ahead of the investigator. For instance, the name Doron appears several times before we learn who he is, and even then the circumstances of Johanna's encounter with him are not clear; it is, for instance, referred to as "the thing with Doron." We may, however, suspect that something happened between them, since Johanna has bad feelings toward her boyfriend. Johanna is suppressing her memories because they are traumatic, and the reader is left to guess exactly what she is trying to deny for herself and why. Toward the end of the novel, it is revealed that Doron forced himself on Johanna, and that she mentally accepted it as his belated revenge upon her family. This reflection is left without any further comment, and the readers must take their own standpoint.

The name Mrs. Levin also appears early in the novel. When Johanna writes mental letters to Mrs. Levin informing her of grandfather's death, the readers have no intelligence of the premises. It is apparent that Mrs. Levin has some reasons for disliking, even hating Johanna's grandfather. It becomes clear that she once lived in Johanna's town. With some basic knowledge of history, it is not hard to figure out that, being Jewish, she was forced to leave Germany and has probably gone through the ordeals of concentration camps. Finally, we are given an essential piece of information, that it, what Mrs. Levin told Johanna in Jerusalem. By that time, a keen reader will have certainly understood more than the focalizer is prepared to admit. An efficient device to divert the readers' attention is to let Johanna's memories and perceptions glide away, expanding into a page-long descriptions of landscapes, views from her room, impressions from tourist sights in Israel, reflections on her classmates, fashion or music, as if she herself were trying to throw a veil over the painful reminiscences.

On the other hand, it is obvious that Johanna is blinded by her total loyalty to her own family. She has been told that her grandfather built up his fortune from scratch, by hard work. She has always been proud of him, but she lacks the insight about her own idyllic, protected life as a spoilt child of a rich family, heiress to unfathomable wealth. She attends a privileged school, drives an expensive car, has a huge bank account and gets whatever she points at. Thus she is poorly equipped to par the coming blows. The first discovery is that the family business once belonged to a Jewish family forced to flee when the Nazi came to power. Her parents explain that the grandfather honestly bought the business from the former owners and thereby helped them to escape. A well-versed reader would probably know how the expulsion of Jews in Nazi Germany actually happened; but even a less informed one is expected to wonder whether anything is not as simple as it sounds. It turns out that the grandfather was an active an enthusiastic member of the Nazi party, a fact that the family has tried to erase, literally erasing swastikas from old photographs. It further turns out that Meta Levin's family never received any money for their property, that Johanna's grandfather used his position to profit from the misfortunes of the Jews. If it comes as a shock to Johanna, the reader is supposed to be prepared. Johanna has grown up in a lie. Realizing that the family's well-being is based on her grandfather's highly dubious behavior turns her world upside down; yet the readers are not necessarily encouraged to sympathize. Not only Johanna's parents, but she herself has conveniently preferred not to know. The juxtaposition "didn't know"—"didn't want to know" reverberates throughout the text. Her father promptly responds to all her careful inquiries by "I don't want to hear about it," thus revealing that he does know. He simply does not want to wake the sleeping dogs. In her defense, Johanna thinks in terms of "didn't know," "wasn't told." It seems that even Johanna's classmates and her boyfriend know more than she does. It is up to the reader to judge her as naïve or arrogant.

Even after her visit to Israel, she does not have the courage to ask her parents, and it is only the grandfather's death that starts the process of penance: *"Now it's happened, now I can't act like nothing's wrong anymore"* (13; emphasis in the original). Yet she is not prepared to discuss the matter during or after the funeral—her father has also chosen to conceal the fact of suicide, thus adding to the many layers of deceit and dishonesty. It is on the very last pages that she is ready to admit that "she's just found out what was actually clear for her, anyway, even if she didn't allow herself to realize it" (176) .

Johanna has unveiled the uncomfortable truth by mere chance; otherwise she would have continued to live in happy ignorance. Naturally, the whole issue of Germany's national guilt is raised here, yet through strong focalization it is discussed on a personal and less abstract level. The sensitive topic is not presented through an authoritative voice (even though a teacher assists Johanna in the final verbalization of her insights), but through a multitude of views and opinions. After all, grandfather has been nice to Johanna; he was a good employer and a respected citizen. How many generations are responsible for their ancestors' guilt? Can Johanna in any way make it up for the old woman in a nursing home in Israel? Can she reconcile with her father, a cold despot, totally focused on continuing his father's life work? Is it her responsibility to share her insight with her little brother? Or shall she, to protect him, let the sleeping dogs lie? Is Johanna's self-imposed atonement, to go and work in Israel for a year instead of entering a prestigious university, justifiable, or is it just another escape, another illusion? The readers' engagement with Johanna's dilemma, the necessity to go on, the wish for atonement, does not prevent a distancing, but on the contrary requires it.

All the examples in this chapter point at the discrepancy between the desire to evoke empathy and the need to subvert the subject position tied to a fictive character. The notorious didacticism of early children's literature implies, among other things, fixed subjectivity, in which the characters are either models or cautionary examples. In both cases, the reader is seemingly encouraged to adopt the narrator's position, that is, admiration or contempt. The reader's freedom of independent subjectivity would appear to be limited, yet paradoxically, repulsion and perfection equally subvert identification.

In contemporary children's literature, the tendency is to make protagonists more like ordinary people, which implies that subjectivity of the text shifts from the narrator to the character. It is natural that authors want the reader to be engaged in their characters' trials and quests; otherwise the reader will simply put the book aside. However, if the subject position inflicted by the text is too strong and there are no narrative devices that displace subjectivity, the readers are likely to be trapped. The various strategies outlined above can support a mature subject position.

It can be argued that young readers can enjoy books even though they share the protagonist's subjectivity. I would certainly agree that they can, just as they can enjoy reading for the plot exclusively, ignoring characterization, psychological implications, ideology and style. However, character-tied position endorses solipsism, an immature child's conviction that the world rotates around himself. As mediators of literature, we want children to be able to place themselves in other people's life situations, to develop understanding and compassion, to be self-reflective, and not least, to be able to assess ideology. As suggested earlier, independent subjectivity is one of the major constituents of reading competence. If we want to foster children as mature readers, the first and most important step is to make them aware of identification fallacy.

Conclusion
The Adult's Self-Denial

Aetonormative theory, presented and developed in this study, attempts at complementing a number of earlier concepts and definitions concerning children's literature. Aetonormativity does not operate in a vacuum, but is intertwined with other heterological structures, including gender, ethnicity and class. By taking these into consideration, we can reveal how power hierarchies amplify or obscure each other. Adult norms can in a literary text be blurred because other alterities are more prominent.

Adults can never fully interrogate their own power position, and the overwhelming majority of children's books do not even attempt at such interrogation, either by ignoring the issue altogether or by unconditionally affirming adult norms. The affirmation, as well as subversion of aetonormativity, involves a number of strategies, deliberate or unconscious, some of which have been examined in this study.

The three elements featured in the title, power, voice and subjectivity, are tightly connected with these strategies. In terms of social conditions, in real as well as in fictive world, adults are and will always be superior to children. Here, power hierarchy is non-negotiable, unlike other heterological situations (gender, class, sexual preference), and power is inevitably self-reproducing. Growing up as the central theme of children's and young adult fiction emphasizes the traumatic experience of constant power negotiations. In some cases, symbolic or real death seems to be the only possible solution, reflecting the adult author's capitulation to the demands of adult norms. Even when a child is occasionally allowed to triumph, it occurs with at least one adult's support. Further, solutions on individual level do not obliterate the existing norms and do not necessarily illuminate them.

The only way to circumvent adult normativity completely is through non-mimetic modes, similarly to the deconstruction of gender in adult fantasy and science fiction. However, most of the texts analysed in this study do not embrace this opportunity, but resort to the circular movement of carnival to

203

create a temporary state of empowerment. This involves the various genres and modes discussed, such as fairy tale, fantasy, dystopia or adventure, as well as particular themes and devices, including cross-dressing, metamorphosis, and animal disguise. In regard to recent fantasy fiction, Philip Pullman has approximated child normativity in *His Dark Materials*; yet the child is at the end of the trilogy already on the verge of adulthood.

In terms of narrative perspective, adult voice has—and will always—have more authority than a child's voice. Linguistic oppression against the child character as well as the young reader is a distinctive feature of children's literature, even when—or perhaps especially when—it is employed for educational purposes. Although the didactic, omniscient adult voice may seem to belong to the past, there is always an adult narrative agency behind a child focalizer or a personal child narrator. The use of other alterities, such as setting or gender, effectively blurs aetonormativity.

Picturebooks provide a wider margin for power negotiations because of their multimodal nature, where the visual can be more radical than the verbal (occasionally the other way round). On the other hand, covert ideology is more ambivalent in the images than in the words. Here, the adult can hide behind the visual narrative while pretending, in the verbal, to be on the child's side. The phenomenon of "postmodern" picturebooks that frequently flirt with the adult co-reader over the young reader's head is revealing.

Subjectivity is an essential component of power. By imposing a particular subject position on the reader, whether tied to the character or the narrator, the implied author exercises power over the reader. Whenever an independent subject position emerges in a text, aetonormativity is subjected to scrutiny. For instance, a strong female voice creates a strong subject position that, although not directly subverting aetonormativity, interrogates other norms and by extension, adult norms. By subverting identification compulsion, texts create autonomous subject positions that substantially empower the implied young readers against implied adult authors. This is perhaps the furthest adult authors can venture in their self-denial.

As shown throughout this study, children's writers can empower their child characters and disempower them in various ways, but the principle is essentially the same: empowerment is allowed on certain conditions, and is almost without exceptions limited in time. What is then the point of portraying a fictional child with unlimited power? Wouldn't it involve lying to young readers—and lying in a less innocent way than it is common, according to Pippi Longstocking, in Belgian Congo? Here "the impossibility of children's literature" once again puts barriers for our pursuits, and here we can again resort to the main premise of heterology. As adults—writers as well as promoters of children's literature—we cannot unconditionally abolish adult normativity, since we would then be subverting our own existence. Yet we can, through the carnival of children's literature, make young readers aware of the fact that adult norms and rules are not absolute. At best, they will not force their children to eat the hateful cereal.

Bibliography

Primary Sources

Aldrich, Thomas Bailey. *The Story of a Bad Boy.* New York: Echo Lobraray, 2006.

Alexander, Lloyd. *Time Cat.* New York: Dell, 1963.

———. *The Town Cats and Other Stories.* New York: Dell, 1977.

———. *The First Two Lives of Lukas-Kasha.* New York: Dutton, 1978.

———. *The Remarkable Journey of Prince Jen.* New York: Dutton, 1991.

Alcott, Louisa May. *Little Women* [1868]. Harmondsworth: Penguin, 1994.

Andersen, Hans Christian. *The Complete Fairy Tales and Stories.* New York: Doubleday, 1974.

Anderson, M. T. *Feed.* Cambridge, MA: Candlewick, 2002.

Anstey, F. *The Brass Bottle.* New York: Appleton, 1900.

Avi. *The True Confessions of Charlotte Doyle* [1990]. New York: Avon, 1992.

———. *Nothing but the Truth* [1991]. New York: Avon, 1992.

Asimov, Isaac. *The End of Eternity* [1955]. London: HarperCollins, 2000.

Babbitt, Natalie. *Tuck Everlasting.* New York: Farrar, 1975.

Baum, L. Frank. *The Wonderful Wizard of Oz* [1900]. New York: HarperCollins, 2000.

Blackman, Malorie. *Noughts and Crosses.* London: Doubleday, 2001.

Bojunga, Lygia. *A bolsa amarela* (The Yellow Bag). Rio de Janeiro: AGIR, 1976.

———. *A casa da madrinha* (Granny's House). Rio de Janeiro: AGIR, 1978.

———. *Corda bamba* (Loose Rope). Rio de Janeiro: Civilização Brasileira, l979.

———. *O sofá estampado* (Flowery Sofa). Rio de Janeiro: Civilização Brasileira, 1980.

———. *My Friend the Painter.* Trans. Giovanni Pontiero. San Diego: Harcourt Brace Jovanovich, 1991 (*O meu amigo pintor*, 1987).

———. *Seis vezes Lucas* (Six Times Lucas). Rio de Janeiro: AGIR, 1995.

Burgess, Melvin. *Junk.* London: Andersen, 1996 (published in the USA as *Smack*).

———. *Lady: My Life as a Bitch.* London: Andersen, 2001.

Burnett, Frances Hodgson. *Little Lord Fauntleroy* [1886]. London: Penguin, 1995.

Burningham, John. *Hey, Get Off Our Train!* New York: Crown, 1989

Carroll, Lewis. *Alice's Adventures in Wonderland* [1865]. In *The Penguin Complete Lewis Carroll.* Harmonsworth: Penguin, 1982.

———. *Through the Looking Glass* [1872]. In *The Penguin Complete Lewis Carroll.* Harmonsworth: Penguin, 1982.

Chambers, Aidan. *Dance on My Grave* [1982]. London: Random House, 1995.

———. *This is All. The Pillow Book of Cordelia Kenn.* London: Bodley Head, 2005.

Cleary, Beverly. *Dear Mr Henshaw.* New York: Morrow, 1983.

Collodi, Carlo. *The Adventures of Pinocchio.* Trans. Anne Lawson Lucas. Oxford: Oxford University Press, 1996 (*Le avventure di Pinocchio*, 1881).

Coolidge, Susan. *What Katy Did* [1897]. London: Penguin, 1997.

Cooper, Susan. *The Dark Is Rising.* London: Chatto & Windus, 1973.

Dahle, Gro, and Svein Nyhus. *Bak Mumme bor Moni* (Behind Mumme Lives Moni). Oslo: Cappelen, 2000.

De Brunhoff, Jean. *Bonjour, Babar!* New York: Random House, 2000.

Druon, Maurice. *Tistou of the Green Thumbs.* Trans. Humphrey Hare. New York: Scribner, 1958. (*Tistou les pouces verdes*, 1957).

Duvoisin, Roger. *Veronica.* New York: Knopf, 1961.

Ekman, Fam. *Hva skal vi gjøre med lille Jill?* (What shall we do with little Jill?) Oslo: Cappelen, 1976.
Ende, Michael. *Momo.* New York: Doubleday, 1985. (*Momo*, 1973).
Gaiman, Neil. *Coraline.* New York: HarperCollins, 2002.
Gandolfi, Silvana. *Aldabra, or the Tortoise Who Loved Shakespeare.* London: Arthur A. Levine, 2004. (*Aldabra. La tartaryga che amava Shakespeare*, 2001).
George, Jean Graighead. *My Side of the Mountain.* London: Harper, 1960.
———. *Julie of the Wolves.* London: HarperCollins, 1972.
———. *The Talking Earth.* London: HarperCollins, 1983.
———. *Julie's Wolf Pack.* London: HarperCollins, 1997.
Gubarev, Vitaly. *Troye na ostrove.* Available at: http://www.lib.ru/TALES/GUBAREW/gubarev.txt.
Haddon, Mark. *The Curious Incident of the Dog in the Night-time* [2003]. London: Vintage, 2004.
Haller, Bent, and Dorte Karrebæk. *Ispigen* (Ice Girl). Copenhagen: Høst & Søn, 2001.
Hamberg, Emma. *Linas kvällsbok* (Lina's Noctuzy). Stockholm: Bonnier, 2003.
Hartnett, Sonya. *Thursday's Child.* Sydney: Penguin, 2000.
———. *Forest. Journey From the Wild.* Sydney: Penguin, 2001.
———. *Surrender.* Sydney: Penguin, 2005.
———. *The Ghost's Child.* Sydney: Penguin, 2007.
Hinton, S. E. *The Outsiders* [1967]. Harmondsworth: Penguin, 1997.
———. *That Was Then, This Is Now* [1971]. Harmondsworth: Penguin, 1998.
Hoffman, E.T.A. *The Life and Opinions of Tomcat Murr* [1820]. London, Penguin, 1999.
———. *Das fremde Kind* (The Alien Child) [1818]. Berlin: Rohrwall, 2001.
———. *Tales of Hoffmann.* Penguin, 2004.
———. *The Nutcracker and Mouse King* [1816]. London: Penguin 2007.
Hoffmann, Heinrich. *Struwwelpeter* [1845]. New York: Dover, 1995.
Hofmeyr, Dianne. *Boikie You Better Believe It.* Cape Town: Tafelberg, 1994.
Hunter, Erin W. *Into the Wild.* London: HarperCollins, 2003.
Jones, Diana Wynne. *The Homeward Bounders.* London: Macmillan, 1981.
———. *The Lives of Christopher Chant.* London: Methuen, 1988.
———. *Castle in the Air.* London: Methuen, 1990.
———. *A Tale of Time City* [1987]. London: HarperCollins, 2000.
Joyce, James. *The Cat and the Devil* [1957]. London: Moonlight, 1980.
Kadefors, Sara. *Sandor slash Ida.* Stockholm: BonnierCarlsen, 2001.
Karlsson, Ylva. *Dit man längtar* (Whither You Long). Stockholm: Alfabeta, 2001.
Karrebæk, Dorte. *Pigen der var go' til mange ting*(The Girl Who Was Good at Many Things). Copenhagen: Forum, 1996.
———. *Lille frøken Buks og de små sejre* (Little Miss Pants and Small Victories). Copenhagen: Gyldendal, 2004.
Katayev, Valentin. *Tsvetik-semitsvetik.* Available at: http://www.2lib.ru/getbook/5081.html.
Kemp, Gene. *The Turbulent Term of Tyke Tiler* (1977). Harmondsworth: Penguin, 1979.
Kieri, Katarina. *Ingen grekisk gud, précis* (Not a Greek God Exactly). Stockholm: Rabén & Sjögren, 2002.
———. *Dansar Elias? Nej!* (Does Elias Dance? No!) Stockholm: Rabén & Sjögren, 2004.
Kingsley, Charles. *The Water Babies* [1863]. London: Wordfsworth, 1994.
Kipling, Rudyard. *The Complete Just So Stories.* Available at: http://www.gutenberg.org/dirs/etext01/jusss10.txt.
Korczak, Janusz. *King Matt the First.* Trans. Richard Lourie. Introduction Bruno Bettelheim. New York: Farrar, Straus and Giroux, 1986. (*Krol Macius Pierwszy* 1923).
Kuijer, Guus. *The Book of Everything* [2005]. Trans. John Nieuwenjuizen. London: Arthur A. Levine, 2006.
Lagin, Lazar. *Starik Hottabych.* Available at: http://www.lib.ru/LAGIN/hottab.txt.
Le Guin, Ursula. *A Wizard of Earthsea.* New York: Parnassus, 1968—The first book in the Earth-sea suite.
Lewis, C. S. *The Lion, the Witch and the Wardrobe.* London: The Bodley Head, 1950.
———. *The Horse and His Boy.* London: The Bodley Head, 1954.
———. *The Magician's Nephew.* London: The Bodley Head, 1955.
Lindenbaum, Pija. *Bridget and the Gray Wolves.* Stockholm: R & S Books, 2001. (*Gittan och grå-vargarna*, 2000).
———. *När Åkes mamma glömde bort* (When Ake's Mom Forgot). Stockholm: Rabén & Sjögren, 2005.

Lindgren, Astrid. *Pippi Longstocking.* Trans. Tiina Nunneli. Oxford: Oxford University Press, 2007 (*Pippi Långstrump* 1945).
———. *Pippi in the South Seas.* Trans. Gerry Bothmer. Harmondsworth: Penguin, 1997. (*Pippi Långstrump i Söderhavet* 1948).
———. *Karlsson on the Roof.* Trans. Sarah Death. Oxford: Oxford University Press, 2008. (*Karlsson på taket* 1955).
Lowry, Lois. *The Giver.* New York: Doubleday, 1993.
MacDonald, George. *The Princess and the Goblin* [1872]. London: Penguin, 1964.
———. *The Princess and Curdie* [1882]. London: Penguin, 1966.
———. *At the Back of the North Wind* [1871]. London: Penguin, 1984.
———. *The Complete Fairy Tales.* London: Penguin, 1999.
———. *Lilith* [1895]. Grand Rapids, MI: Eerdman, 2000.
———. *Phantastes* [1858]. Grand Rapids, MI: Eerdman, 2000.
Machado, Ana Maria. *História meio ao contrário* (The Upside-Down Story). São Paulo: Ática, 1978.
———. *O menino Pedro e seu boi voador* (Pedro and His Flying Bull). São Paulo: Ática, 1979.
———. *De olho nas penas* (Eyes on feathers). Rio de Janeiro: Salamandra, 1981.
———. *Bisa Bia Bisa Bel* (Grandmother Bisa, Grandmother Bel). Rio de Janeiro: Salamandra, 1982.
———. *Beijos mágicos* (Magic Kisses). São Paulo: FTD, 1992.
———. *Palavras, palavrinhas, palavrões* (Big Words, Little Words, Four-letter Words). São Paulo: Quinteto, 1998.
Malot, Hector. *The Foundling.* New York: Harmony, 1986. (*Sans famille*, 1878).
Marsden, John. *Letters from the Inside.* Sydney: Macmillan, 1991.
Major, Kevin. *Dear Bruce Springsteen.* Toronto: Doubleday, 1987.
———. *Diana: My Autobiography.* Toronto: Doubleday, 1993.
Marshall, James. *George and Martha.* New York: Houghton Mifflin, 1972.
McCaughrean, Geraldine. *The Kite Rider.* Oxford: Oxford University Press, 2001.
Milne, A. A. *Winnie-the-Pooh* [1926]. London: Methuen, 1965a.
———. *The House At Pooh Corner* [1928]. London: Methuen, 1965 (b).
Moeyeart, Bart. *Bare Hands.* Trans. David Colmer. Asherville, NC: Front Street, 2005 (*Blote handen*, 1996).
Molesworth, Mary. *The Cuckoo Clock* [1877]. London: Jane Nissen, 2002.
Morpurgo, Michael. *Kensuke's Kingdom.* London: Heinemann, 1999.
Nesbit, Edith. *The Story of the Amulet* [1906]. London: BiblioBazaar, 2007.
———. *The House of Arden* [1908]. London: Penguin, 1986.
———. *The Phoenix and the Carpet* [1904]. London: Wordsworth, 1995.
———. *The Railway Children* [1906]. London: Penguin, 1995.
———. *The Enchanted Castle* [1907]. London: Penguin, 1999.
———. *Five Children and It* [1901]. London: Penguin, 2004
Nöstlinger, Christine. *Konrad.* New York: Avon, 1982. (*Konrad oder das Kind aus der Konservenbüchse* 1975).
O'Dell, Scott. *Island of the Blue Dolphins.* Boston: Houghton Mifflin, 1960.
Park, Linda Sue. *A Single Shard.* Oxford: Oxford University Press, 2001.
Paterson, Katherine. *The Sign of the Chrysanthemum.* New York: HarperCollins, 1973.
———. *Of Nightingales That Weep.* New York: HarperCollins, 1974.
———. *The Master Puppeteer.* New York: HarperCollins, 1975.
———. *Rebels of the Heavenly Kingdom.* New York: Dutton, 1983.
———. *Jacob Have I Loved* [1980]. New York: HarperCollins, 1990.
———. *Preacher's Boy.* New York: HarperCollins, 1999.
Pearce, Philippa. *Tom's Midnight Garden* [1958]. Oxford: Oxford University Press, 2008.
Perrault, Charles. "Puss in Boots." Available at: http://www.surlalunefairytales.com/puss-boots/index.html.
Potter, Beatrix. *The Tale of Peter Rabbit.* London: Warne, 1902.
Pressler, Mirjam. *Let Sleeping Dogs Lie.* Trans. by Erik J. Macki. Asheville, NC: Front Street, 2007. (*Die Zeit der schafenden Hunde*, 2003).
Pullman, Philip. *The Firework Maker's Daughter.* London: Doubleday, 1995.
———. *Northern Lights.* London: Scholastic, 1995.
———. *The Subtle Knife.* London: Scholastic, 1997.
———. *The Amber Spyglass.* London: Scholastic, 2000.
Rey, H. A. *Curious George.* Boston: Houghton Mifflin, 1941.

———. *Curious George*. Boston: Houghton Mifflin, 1969.
Robson, Jenny. *The Denials of Kow-Ten*. Cape Town: Tafelberg, 1998.
Rowling, J. K. *Harry Potter and the Philosopher's Stone*. London: Bloomsbury, 1997.
———. *Harry Potter and the Chamber of Secrets*. London: Bloomsbury, 1998.
———. *Harry Potter and the Prisoner of Azkaban*. London: Bloomsbury, 1999.
———. *Harry Potter and the Goblet of Fire*. London: Bloomsbury, 2000.
———. *Harry Potter and the Order of the Phoenix*. London: Bloomsbury, 2003.
———. *Harry Potter Potter and the Half-Blood Prince*. London: Bloomsbury, 2005.
———. *Harry Potter and the Deathly Hallows*. London: Bloomsbury, 2007.
Sachar, Louis. *Holes*. New York: Dell, 1998.
Said, S. F. *Varjak Paw*. London: David Fickling, 2003.
Saint-Exupéry, Antoine. *The Little Prince*. London: Wordsworth 1995. (*Le petit prince*, 1943).
Salinger, Jerome D. *The Catcher in the Rye* [1951]. Philadelphia: Chelsea House, 2000.
Sendak, Maurice. *Where the Wild Things Are*. New York: Harper, 1963.
———. *Outside Over There*. New York: Harper & Row, 1981.
Seton, Ernest Thompson. *Animals Heroes* [1905]. Available at: http://www.gutenberg.org/etext/2284.
Seuss, Dr. *The Cat in the Hat*. New York: Random House, 1957.
Sigsgaard, Jens and Arne Ungermann. *Paul Alone in the World*. St Louis: McGraw-Hill, 1964. (*Palle alene i verden* 1942).
Spyri, Johanna. *Heidi* [1880]. London: Wordsworth, 1993.
"The Story of Dick Wittington." Available at: http://www.archive.org/stream/historyofdickwhi00cruiiala/historyofdickwhi00cruiiala_djvu.txt.
Stretton, Hesba. *Jessica's First Prayer* [1867]. London: Kessinger, 2004.
Taylor, G. P. *Shadowmancer*. London: Faber, 2004.
Taylor, Mildred D. *Roll of Thunder, Hear My Cry*. New York: Dial, 1976.
———. *Mississippi Bridge*. New York: Dial, 1990.
Thydell, Johanna. *I taket lyser stjärnorna* (The Stars Are Shining on the Ceiling). Stockholm: Natur och kultur, 2003.
Tolkien, J. R. R. *The Hobbit* [1937]. Boston: Houghton Mifflin, 1997.
———. *Lord of the Rings* [1954–55]. Philadelphia: Chelsea House, 1999.
Tomin, Yuri. *Shol po gorodu volshebnik*. Available at: http://www.lib.ru/TALES/TOMIN/.
Townsend, Sue. *The Secret Diary of Adrian Mole, Aged 13 3/4*. London: Mandarin, 1982.
Travers, Pamela. *Mary Poppins* [1934]. London: HarperCollins, 2008.
Trivizas, Eugene. *The Last Black Cat* [2001]. Trans. Sandy Zervas. London: Egmont, 2005.
Twain, Mark. *The Adventures of Tom Sawyer* [1876]. Harmondsworth, Penguin, 1985.
———. *The Adventures of Huckleberry Finn* [1884]. New York, Penguin, 1995.
Wahl, Mats. *Anna-Carolinas krig* (Anna-Carolins's War). Stockholm: Bonniers Junior, 1986.
———. *Vinterviken* (Winter Bay). Stockholm: Bonniers Junior, 1993.
———. *Lilla Marie* (Little Marie). Stockholm: BonnierCarlsen, 1995.
Webster, Jean. *Daddy-Long-Legs* [1912]. London: Penguin, 1995.

Secondary Sources

Auerbach, Erich. *Mimesis. The Representation of Reality in Western Literature*. 4th ed. Princeton, NJ: Princeton University Press, 1974.
Bakhtin, Michail. *Rabelais and His World*. Cambridge, MA: MIT Press, 1968.
———. "Epic and Novel" in *The Dialogic Imagination*. Austin: University of Texas Press, 1981(a), pp 3–40.
———. "From the Prehistory of Novelistic Discourse" in *The Dialogic Imagination*. Austin: University of Texas Press, 1981(b), pp. 41–83.
———. "Forms of Time and Chronotope in the novel" in *The Dialogic Imagination*. Austin: University of Texas Press, 1981(c), pp. 84–258.
———. "Discourse in the Novel" in *The Dialogic Imagination*. Austin: University of Texas Press, 1981(d), pp. 259–422.
———. *Problems of Dostoevsky's Poetics*, Manchester: Manchester University Press, 1984.
———. "The Bildungsroman and Its Significance in the History of Realism (Toward a Historical Typology of the Novel)" in *Speech Genres and Other Late Essays*. Austin: University of Texas Press, 1986, pp. 10–59.

———. "Author and Hero in Aesthetic Activity" in *Art and Answerability: Early Philosophical Essays*. Austin: University of Texas Press, 1990, pp. 4–256.

Beckett, Sandra. *Crossover Fiction: Global and Historical Perspectives*. London: Routledge, 2008.

Briggs, Katharine M. *Nine Lives. Cats in Folklore*. London: Routledge & Kegan Paul, 1980.

Butler, Judith. *Gender Trouble. Feminism and the Subversion of Identity*. 2nd ed. New York: Routledge, 1999.

Certeau, Michel de. *Heterologies. Discourse on the Other*. Minneapolis : University of Minnesota Press, 1986

Clark, Beverly Lyon. *Kiddie Lit. The Cultural Construction of Children's Literature in America*. Baltimore: The Johns Hopkins University Press, 2003.

Coats, Karen. *Looking Glasses and Neverlands*. Iowa City: University of Iowa Press, 2004.

———. "Keepin' It Plural: Children's Studies in the Academy" in *Children's Literature: Critical Concepts in Literary and Cultural Studies* edited by Peter Hunt. London, Routledge, 2006, vol. 2, pp. 181–199.

Eliade, Mircea. *The Sacred and the Profane*. New York: Harper & Row, 1961.

Flanagan, Victoria. *Into the Closet: Cross-dressing and the Gendered Body in Children's Literature and Film*. New York: Routledge, 2007.

Forster, E. M.: *Aspects of the Novel*. San Diego, CA: Harcourt, Brace, 1985.

Foucault, Michel. *Power: Essential Works of Michel Foucault 1954–1984 Volume 3*. London: Penguin, 2002.

Frye, Northrop. *Anatomy of Criticism. Four Essays*. Princeton, NJ: Princeton University Press, 1957.

Galbraight, Mary. "'Goodnight Nobody' Revisited: Using an Attachment Perspective to Study Picture Books about Bedtime." *Children's Literature Association Quarterly* 23 (1998–99) 4: 172–180.

Genette, Gérard. *Narrative Discourse. An Essay in Method*. Ithaca, NY: Cornell University Press, 1980.

Gilbert, Sandra M. and Susan Gubar. *The Madwoman in the Attic. The Woman Writer and the Nineteenth-Century Literary Imagination*. New Haven: Yale University Press, 1977.

Gray, William N. "George MacDonald, Julia Kristeva and the Black Sun". *Studies in English Literature: 1500–1900*. 36 (1996) 4: 877–93.

Hintz, Carrie and Elaine Ostry, eds. *Utopian and Dystopian Writing for Children and Young Adults*. New York: Routledge, 2003.

Holmgren, Virginia C. *Cats in Fact and Folklore*. New York: Howell, 1996.

Hourihan, Margery. *Deconstructing the Hero. Literary Theory and Children's Literature*. London: Routledge, 1997.

Hunt, Peter. "Narrative Theory and Children's Literature." *Children's Literature Association Quarterly* 9 (1984) 4: 191–194.

———. "Necessary Misreadings: Directions in Narrative Theory for Children's Literature." *Studies in the Literary Imagination* 18 (1985) 2: 107–121.

———. *Criticism, Theory and Children's Literature*. London: Blackwell, 1991.

———. "Dragons in the Department and Academic Emperors: Why Universities are Afraid of Children's Literature." *Compar(a)ison* (1995) 2: 19–31.

——— "Children's Literature Studies." *Canadian Children's Literature* 32 (2006a) 1: 112–115.

———. ed. "Childist Criticism: The Subculture of the Child, the Book and the Critic." In *Children's Literature: Critical Concepts in Literary and Cultural Studies*. London: Routledge, 2006b, vol. 2, pp. 263–279.

Inglis, Fred. *The Promise of Happiness. The Value and Meaning in Children's Fiction*. Cambridge: Cambridge University Press, 1981.

Jackson, Rosemary. *Fantasy: The Literature of Subversion*. New York: Methuen, 1981.

Jameson, Fredric. *Archaeologies of the Future. The Desire Called Utopia and Other Science Fictions*. London: Verso, 2005.

Jenkins, Ruth Y. "'I am Spinning This for You, My Child': Voice and Identity Formation in George MacDonald's Princess Books". *The Lion and the Unicorn* 28 (2004) 3: 325–344.

Kristeva, Julia. *Powers of Horror: An Essay on Abjection*. New York: Columbia University Press, 1982.

———. *Revolution in Poetic Language*. New York: Columbia University Press, 1984.

Lacan, Jacques. *Ecrits: A Selection*. New York: Norton, 1977.

Lanser, Susan Sniader. *The Narrative Act: Point of View in Prose Fiction*, Princeton, NJ: Princeton University Press, 1981.

———. *Fictions of Authority. Women Writers and Narrative Voice*. Ithaca, NY: Cornell University Press, 1992.

————. "Toward a Feminist Narratology." *Style* (1986) 3: 341–363.

Lassén-Seger, Maria. *Adventures into Otherness. Child Metamorphs in Late Twentieth-Century Children's Literature*. Åbo: Åbo Akademi University Press, 2006.

Lurie, Alison. *Don't Tell the Grownups. Subversive Children's Literature*. Boston: Little, Brown, 1990.

Lyotard, Jean-Francois. *The Postmodern Condition: A Report on Knowledge*. Minneapolis: Minnesota University Press, 1984.

MacDonald, George. "The Fantastic Imagination" in *Fantasists on Fantasy* edited by R. H. Boyer and K. J. Zahorski. New York: Avon, 1984.

May, Jill P. *Children's Literature and Critical Theory*. New York: Oxford University Press, 1995.

McCallum, Robyn. *Ideologies of Identity in Adolescent Fiction: The Dialogic Construction of Subjectivity*. New York: Garland, 1999.

McGavran, James Holt, ed. *Literature and the Child. Romantic Continuations, Postmodern Contestations*. Iowa City: University of Iowa Press, 1999.

McGillis, Roderick, ed. *For the Childlike. George MacDonald's Fantasies for Children*. Metuchen, NJ: Scarecrow, 1992.

————. *The Nimble Reader. Literary Theory and Children's Literature*. New York: Twayne, 1996.

————. "Postcolonialism, Children, and Their Literature." *Ariel* 28 (1997) 1:7–15.

———— ed. *Voices of the Other: Children's Literature and the Postcolonial Context*. New York: Garland, 2000.

————. "A Fairytale is Just a Fairytale: George MacDonald and the Queering of Fairy." *Marvels & Tales* 17 (2003) 1: 86–99.

————. "The Delights of Impossibility: No Children, No Books, Only Theory" in *Children's Literature: Critical Concepts in Literary and Cultural Studies* edited by Peter Hunt. London: Routledge, 2006 (a), vol. 2, pp. 323–335.

————. "One Way, No Return: Let's See Where is Here." *Canadian Children's Literature* 32.1 (2006b): 77–86.

Mezei, Kathy, ed. *Ambiguous Discourse. Feminist Narratology and British Women Writers*. Charlotte, NC.: The University of North Carolina Press, 1996.

Natov, Roni. *The Poetics of Childhood*. New York: Routledge, 2003.

Nikolajeva, Maria. *Children's Literature Comes of Age: Towards a New Aesthetic*. New York: Garland, 1996.

————. *From Mythic to Linear: Time in Children's Literature*. Lanham, MD: Scarecrow, 2000.

————. *The Rhetoric of Character in Children's Literature*. Lanham, MD.: Scarecrow, 2002.

————. *The Aesthetic Approaches to Children's Literature: An Introduction*. Lanham, Md.: Scarecrow, 2005

Nodelman, Perry. "Children's Literature as Women's Writing." *Children's Literature Association Quarterly* 13 (1988) 1: 31–34.

————. "The Other: Orientalism, Colonialism, and Children's Literature." *Children's Literature Association Quarterly* 17 (1992) 1: 29–35.

————. "Fear of Children's Literature: What's Left (or Right) After Theory?" in *Reflections of Change* edited by Sandra Beckett. Westport, CT: Greenwood, 1997, pp. 3–14.

————. "What Are We After? Children's Literature Studies and Literary Theory Now." *Canadian Children's Literature* 31 (2005) 1: 1–19.

————. "Interpretation and the Apparent Sameness of Children's Literature" in *Children's Literature: Critical Concepts in Literary and Cultural Studies* edited by Peter Hunt. London: Routledge, 2006, vol. 1, pp. 88–113.

————. *The Hidden Adult. Defining Children's Literature*. Baltimore: The Johns Hopkins University Press, 2008.

Paul, Lissa. "Enigma Variations. What Feminist Criticism Knows about Children's Literature" in *Children's Literature: Critical Concepts in Literary and Cultural Studies* edited by Peter Hunt. London: Routledge, 2006, vol. 3, pp. 208–223.

Perrot, Jean. "Shall We Burn Our Goddess 'Theory'?" *Canadian Children's Literature* 32 (2006) 1: 97–111.

Pratt, Annis, et al. *Archetypal Patterns in Women's Fiction*. Bloomington: Indiana University Press, 1981.

Prickett, Stephen. *Victorian Fantasy*. Hassocks: Harvester Press, 1979.

Reynolds, Kimberley. *Radical Children's Literature: Future Visions and Aesthetic Transformations in Juvenile Fiction*. Basingstoke: Palgrave Macmillan, 2007.

Rose, Jacqueline. *The Case of Peter Pan, or The Impossibility of Children's Fiction*. London: Macmillan, 1984.

Rudd, David. "Theorizing and Theories: The Conditions of Possibility of Children's Literature" in *Children's Literature: Critical Concepts in Literary and Cultural Studies* edited by Peter Hunt. London, Routledge, 2006, vol. 2, pp. 356–374.

Said, Edward W. *Orientalism*. New York: Pantheon, 1978.

Salminen, Jenniliisa. *Fantastic in Form, Ambiguous in Content: Secondary Worlds in Soviet Children's Fantasy Literature*. Turku: Turku University Press, 2009.

Schwarcz, Joseph and Chava Schwarz. *The Picture Book Comes of Age*. Chicago: American Library Association, 1991.

Scott, Carole. "Clothed in Nature or Nature Clothed: Dress as Metaphor in the Illustrations of Beatrix Potter and C. M. Barker." *Children's Literature* 22 (1994): 70–89.

Shavit, Zohar. "The Ambivalent Status of Texts. The Case of Children's Literature." *Poetics Today* 173 (1980): 75–86.

Showalter, Elaine. *Speaking of Gender*. New York: Routledge, 1989.

Spender, Dale. *Man Made Language*. London: Pandora, 1998.

Stephens, John. *Language and Ideology in Children's Fiction*. London: Longman, 1992.

———. "Gender, Genre and Children's Literature." *Signal* 79 (1996): 17–30.

Stephens, John, ed. *Ways of Being Male: Representing Masculinities in Children's Literature and Film*. New York: Routledge, 2002.

Thacker, Debora Cogan, and Jean Webb. *Introducing Children's Literature. From Romanticism to Poststructuralism*. London: Routledge: 2002.

Todorov, Tzvetan. *The Fantastic: A Structural Approach to a Literary Genre*. Cleveland: The Press of Case Western Reserve University, 1973.

Trites, Roberta Selinger. *Waking Sleeping Beauty. Feminist Voices in Children's Novels*. Iowa City: University of Iowa Press, 1997.

———. *Disturbing the Universe. Power and Repression in Adolescent Literature*. Iowa City: University of Iowa Press, 2000.

———. "The Harry Potter Novels as Test Case for Adolescent Literature." *Style* 35 (2001) 3: 472–485.

Usrey, Malcolm. "Johanna Spyri's *Heidi*: The Conversion of a Byronic Hero" in *Touchstones: Reflections on the Best in Children's Literature* edited by Perry Nodelman. West Lafayette, IN: Children's Literature Association, 1985, vol. 3, pp. 232–242.

Veglahn, Nancy. "Images of Evil: Male and Female Monsters in Heroic Fantasy." *Children's Literature* 15 (1987): 106–119.

von Franz, Marie-Louise. *The Cat: A Tale of Feminine Redemption*. Toronto, Unversity of Toronto Press, 1999.

Wall, Barbara. *The Narrator's Voice. The Dilemma of Children's Fiction*. London: Macmillan, 1991.

Watson, Victor. *Reading Series Fiction: From Arthur Ransome to Gene Kemp*. New York: Routledge, 2000.

Weinreich, Torben. *Children's Literature: Art or Pedagogy?* Roskilde, Denmark: Roskilde University Press, 2000.

Westwater, Martha. *Giant Despair Meets Hopeful. Kristevian Readings in Adolescent Fiction*. Alberta: University of Alberta Press, 2000.

Wilkie-Stibbs, Christine. *The Feminine Subject in Children's Literature*. New York: Routledge, 2002.

Wimsatt, William K., and Monroe C. Beardsley. *The Verbal Icon. Studies in the Meaning of Poetry*. London: Methuen, 1954.

Zipes, Jack. *Fairy Tales and the Art of Subversion*. New York: Wildman, 1983.

———. *Sticks and Stones. The Troublesome Success of Children's Literature from Slovenly Peter to Harry Potter*. New York: Routledge, 2001.

Zornado, John. *Inventing the Child. Culture, Ideology, and the Rise of Childhood*. New York: Garland, 2000.

Index

The central and recurring concepts of the present study are not included in the index, apart from the initial introduction, such as alterity, carnival, estrangement, heterology, normativity, othering, power, and subjectivity.

POWER, VOICE AND SUBJECTIVITY IN LITERATURE FOR YOUNG READERS

Children's Literature and Culture
Jack Zipes, *Series Editor*

Ideologies of Identity in
Adolescent Fiction
by Robyn McCallum

Recycling Red Riding Hood
by Sandra Beckett

The Poetics of Childhood
by Roni Natov

Voices of the Other
*Children's Literature and the
Postcolonial Context*
edited by Roderick McGillis

Narrating Africa
George Henty and the Fiction of Empire
by Mawuena Kossi Logan

Reimagining Shakespeare for Children
and Young Adults
edited by Naomi J. Miller

Representing the Holocaust in
Youth Literature
by Lydia Kokkola

Translating for Children
by Riitta Oittinen

Beatrix Potter
Writing in Code
by M. Daphne Kutzer

Children's Films
History, Ideology, Pedagogy, Theory
by Ian Wojcik-Andrews

Utopian and Dystopian Writing for
Children and Young Adults
edited by Carrie Hintz and Elaine Ostry

Transcending Boundaries
*Writing for a Dual Audience of
Children and Adults*
edited by Sandra L. Beckett

The Making of the Modern Child
*Children's Literature and Childhood in the
Late Eighteenth Century*
by Andrew O'Malley

How Picturebooks Work
by Maria Nikolajeva and Carole Scott

Brown Gold
*Milestones of African American Children's
Picture Books, 1845-2002*
by Michelle H. Martin

Russell Hoban/Forty Years
Essays on His Writing for Children
by Alida Allison

Apartheid and Racism in South African
Children's Literature
by Donnarae MacCann and
Amadu Maddy

Empire's Children
*Empire and Imperialism in Classic British
Children's Books*
by M. Daphne Kutzer

Constructing the Canon of
Children's Literature
Beyond Library Walls and Ivory Towers
by Anne Lundin

Youth of Darkest England
*Working Class Children at the Heart of
Victorian Empire*
by Troy Boone

Ursula K. Leguin Beyond Genre
Literature for Children and Adults
by Mike Cadden

Twice-Told Children's Tales
edited by Betty Greenway

Diana Wynne Jones
*The Fantastic Tradition and Children's
Literature*
by Farah Mendlesohn

Childhood and Children's Books in
Early Modern Europe, 1550-1800
edited by Andrea Immel and
Michael Witmore

Voracious Children
Who Eats Whom in Children's Literature
by Carolyn Daniel

National Character in South African
Children's Literature
by Elwyn Jenkins

Myth, Symbol, and Meaning in
Mary Poppins
The Governess as Provocateur
by Georgia Grilli